Suzuki GS 750 and GS 550 Owners Workshop Manual

by Mansur Darlington
with an additional Chapter on 1980 through 1982 models by Rik Paul

Models covered:

GS550 1977 to 1982	GS750 1976 to 1979
GS550E	GS750D
GS550L	GS750E
GS550T	GS750L
GS550M	

ISBN 978 0 85696 946 1

(363-11V9)

Haynes Group Limited
Haynes North America, Inc

www.haynes.com

Acknowledgements

Our thanks are due to P R Taylor and Sons of Chippenham who loaned the GS 750DB featured in the photographs throughout this manual. Our thanks are also due to Heron Suzuki GB Limited for permission to reproduce their drawings, and to Nick Barnes, Service Manager of that company, who gave much valuable advice and checked the content of this manual, suggesting ways in which the text could be improved.

Brian Horsfall supervised and assisted with the dismantling of the machine and also the rebuilding sequences, and devised various ingenious methods for overcoming the lack of service tools. Leon Martindale (Member of the Master Photographers Association) arranged and took the photographs and Jeff Clew edited the text.

We should also like to thank the Avon Rubber Company who kindly supplied us with information and advice about tyre fitting, and NGK Spark Plugs (UK) Ltd for information and photographs relating to spark plug conditions.

About this manual

The author of this manual is convinced that the only way meaningful and easy to follow text can be written, is to do the work himself, under conditions that exist in the ordinary household. As a result, the hands seen in the photographs are those of the author. The machine is not new, having covered a few thousand miles. Therefore the conditions encountered are the same as those found by the average owner/rider who through following the text can save himself costly repair bills. Suzuki service tools have not been used. We have proved that there are ways of removing or slackening vital components when special tools are not available, providing this is done carefully and a reasonable amount of time is allowed. Risk of damage must be avoided at all costs.

Each of the 6 Chapters is divided into numbered Sections. Within the Sections are numbered paragraphs. In consequence cross reference throughout the manual is both straightfoward and logical. When a reference is made "See Section 2.8" it means Section 2, paragraph 8 in the same Chapter. If another Chapter were meant the text would read "See Chapter 6, Section 2.8".

All photographs are captioned with a Section/paragraph number to which they refer and are always relevant to the Chapter text adjacent. Figure numbers (usually line drawings) appear in numerical order, within a given Chapter. Fig. 1.1 therefore refers to the first figure in Chapter 1. Left-hand and right-hand descriptions of the parts of the machines apply when the rider is seated on the machine in the normal riding position.

Motorcycle manufacturers continually make changes to specifications and recommendations, and these, when notified, are incorporated into our manuals at the earliest opportunity.

Whilst every care is taken to ensure that the information in this manual is correct, no liability can be accepted by the authors or publishers for loss, damage or injury, caused by any errors in or omissions from the information given.

We take great pride in the accuracy of information given in this manual, but motorcycle manufacturers make alterations and design changes during the production run of a particular motorcycle of which they do not inform us. No liability can be accepted by the authors or publishers for loss, damage or injury caused by any errors in, or omissions from, the information given.

Introduction to the Suzuki GS750 and GS550 models

The GS750 and GS550, introduced in 1976 and 1977, respectively, were at the forefront of Suzuki's move into the four-stroke motorcycle market. Both models are very similar, each powered by an overhead-cam, in-line four-cylinder engine, which was becoming increasingly popular at that time.

Upon its initial introduction, the GS750 became an immediate success, having the necessary performance and styling to compete with the proven models available from other manufacturers. The GS550 followed quickly on the heels of the 750 to fill out the GS line in the mid-size category. The few major differences in the GS550 were its displacement, a six-speed gearbox to contend with the narrower power band and a drum rear brake in place of the single disc used on the 750cc machine.

In later years, new versions of these basic machines were brought out to appeal to various specialized segments of the market, such as the 'customized' L and T models and the sportier E and M models. These are described in more detail in Chapter 7.

Moreover, each new model year is also designated by a letter; i.e. B (1977), C (1978), N (1979), T (1980), X (1981), and Z (1982). Therefore, a GS550E model released in 1979, for example, is called the GS550EN. For the purpose of simplification, the model year is used in place of the letter code in most instances throughout this book.

In 1980 the GS750 received a thorough redesign, including a new engine. Due to space limitations, the 1980 GS750 and later model years are not included in this manual.

Maintenance and repair procedures are the same for both the GS750 and the GS550, unless otherwise noted.

Contents

Suzuki GS 750 DB 1977 model

Suzuki GS 750 DB 1977 model

Safety first!

Professional motor mechanics are trained in safe working procedures. However enthusiastic you may be about getting on with the job in hand, do take the time to ensure that your safety is not put at risk. A moment's lack of attention can result in an accident, as can failure to observe certain elementary precautions.

There will always be new ways of having accidents, and the following points do not pretend to be a comprehensive list of all dangers; they are intended rather to make you aware of the risks and to encourage a safety-conscious approach to all work you carry out on your vehicle.

Essential DOs and DON'Ts

DON'T start the engine without first ascertaining that the transmission is in neutral.

DON'T suddenly remove the filler cap from a hot cooling system – cover it with a cloth and release the pressure gradually first, or you may get scalded by escaping coolant.

DON'T attempt to drain oil until you are sure it has cooled sufficiently to avoid scalding you.

DON'T grasp any part of the engine, exhaust or silencer without first ascertaining that it is sufficiently cool to avoid burning you.

DON'T allow brake fluid or antifreeze to contact the machine's paintwork or plastic components.

DON'T syphon toxic liquids such as fuel, brake fluid or antifreeze by mouth, or allow them to remain on your skin.

DON'T inhale dust – it may be injurious to health (see *Asbestos* heading).

DON'T allow any spilt oil or grease to remain on the floor – wipe it up straight away, before someone slips on it.

DON'T use ill-fitting spanners or other tools which may slip and cause injury.

DON'T attempt to lift a heavy component which may be beyond your capability – get assistance.

DON'T rush to finish a job, or take unverified short cuts.

DON'T allow children or animals in or around an unattended vehicle.

DON'T inflate a tyre to a pressure above the recommended maximum. Apart from overstressing the carcase and wheel rim, in extreme cases the tyre may blow off forcibly.

DO ensure that the machine is supported securely at all times. This is especially important when the machine is blocked up to aid wheel or fork removal.

DO take care when attempting to slacken a stubborn nut or bolt. It is generally better to pull on a spanner, rather than push, so that if slippage occurs you fall away from the machine rather than on to it.

DO wear eye protection when using power tools such as drill, sander, bench grinder etc.

DO use a barrier cream on your hands prior to undertaking dirty jobs – it will protect your skin from infection as well as making the dirt easier to remove afterwards; but make sure your hands aren't left slippery. Note that long-term contact with used engine oil can be a health hazard.

DO keep loose clothing (cuffs, tie etc) and long hair well out of the way of moving mechanical parts.

DO remove rings, wristwatch etc, before working on the vehicle – especially the electrical system.

DO keep your work area tidy – it is only too easy to fall over articles left lying around.

DO exercise caution when compressing springs for removal or installation. Ensure that the tension is applied and released in a controlled manner, using suitable tools which preclude the possibility of the spring escaping violently.

DO ensure that any lifting tackle used has a safe working load rating adequate for the job.

DO get someone to check periodically that all is well, when working alone on the vehicle.

DO carry out work in a logical sequence and check that everything is correctly assembled and tightened afterwards.

DO remember that your vehicle's safety affects that of yourself and others. If in doubt on any point, get specialist advice.

IF, in spite of following these precautions, you are unfortunate enough to injure yourself, seek medical attention as soon as possible.

Asbestos

Certain friction, insulating, sealing, and other products – such as brake linings, clutch linings, gaskets, etc – contain asbestos. *Extreme care must be taken to avoid inhalation of dust from such products since it is hazardous to health.* If in doubt, assume that they *do* contain asbestos.

Fire

Remember at all times that petrol (gasoline) is highly flammable. Never smoke, or have any kind of naked flame around, when working on the vehicle. But the risk does not end there – a spark caused by an electrical short-circuit, by two metal surfaces contacting each other, by careless use of tools, or even by static electricity built up in your body under certain conditions, can ignite petrol vapour, which in a confined space is highly explosive.

Always disconnect the battery earth (ground) terminal before working on any part of the fuel or electrical system, and never risk spilling fuel on to a hot engine or exhaust.

It is recommended that a fire extinguisher of a type suitable for fuel and electrical fires is kept handy in the garage or workplace at all times. Never try to extinguish a fuel or electrical fire with water.

Note: *Any reference to a 'torch' appearing in this manual should always be taken to mean a hand-held battery-operated electric lamp or flashlight. It does **not** mean a welding/gas torch or blowlamp.*

Fumes

Certain fumes are highly toxic and can quickly cause unconsciousness and even death if inhaled to any extent. Petrol (gasoline) vapour comes into this category, as do the vapours from certain solvents such as trichloroethylene. Any draining or pouring of such volatile fluids should be done in a well ventilated area.

When using cleaning fluids and solvents, read the instructions carefully. Never use materials from unmarked containers – they may give off poisonous vapours.

Never run the engine of a motor vehicle in an enclosed space such as a garage. Exhaust fumes contain carbon monoxide which is extremely poisonous; if you need to run the engine, always do so in the open air or at least have the rear of the vehicle outside the workplace.

The battery

Never cause a spark, or allow a naked light, near the vehicle's battery. It will normally be giving off a certain amount of hydrogen gas, which is highly explosive.

Always disconnect the battery earth (ground) terminal before working on the fuel or electrical systems.

If possible, loosen the filler plugs or cover when charging the battery from an external source. Do not charge at an excessive rate or the battery may burst.

Take care when topping up and when carrying the battery. The acid electrolyte, even when diluted, is very corrosive and should not be allowed to contact the eyes or skin.

If you ever need to prepare electrolyte yourself, always add the acid slowly to the water, and never the other way round. Protect against splashes by wearing rubber gloves and goggles.

Mains electricity and electrical equipment

When using an electric power tool, inspection light etc, always ensure that the appliance is correctly connected to its plug and that, where necessary, it is properly earthed (grounded). Do not use such appliances in damp conditions and, again, beware of creating a spark or applying excessive heat in the vicinity of fuel or fuel vapour. Also ensure that the appliances meet the relevant national safety standards.

Ignition HT voltage

A severe electric shock can result from touching certain parts of the ignition system, such as the HT leads, when the engine is running or being cranked, particularly if components are damp or the insulation is defective. Where an electronic ignition system is fitted, the HT voltage is much higher and could prove fatal.

Ordering spare parts

When ordering spare parts for any Suzuki, it is advisable to deal direct with an official Suzuki agent who should be able to supply most of the parts ex stock. Parts cannot be obtained from Suzuki direct and all orders must be routed via an approved agent even if the parts required are not held in stock. Always, quote the engine and frame numbers in full, especially if parts are required for earlier models.

The frame and engine numbers are stamped on a Manufacturer's Plate rivetted to the steering head on the left hand side. The frame number is also stamped on the frame itself on the right-hand side of the steering head. The engine number is stamped on the upper crankcase.

Use only genuine Suzuki spares. Some pattern parts are available that are made in Japan and may be packed in similar looking packages. They should only be used if genuine parts are hard to obtain or in an emergency, for they do not normally last as long as genuine parts, even although there may be a price advantage.

Some of the more expendable parts such as spark plugs, bulbs, tyres, oils and greases etc., can be obtained from accessory shops and motor factors, who have convenient opening hours, and can often be found not far from home. It is also possible to obtain parts on a Mail Order basis from a number of specialists who advertise regularly in the motor cycle magazines.

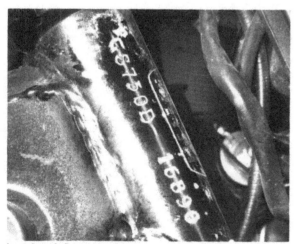

Location of : Frame number

Location of: Engine number

Routine maintenance

For additional information relating to 1978 and 1979 GS750 models and 1978 through 1982 GS550 models, refer to Chapter 7.

Periodic routine maintenance is a continuous process that commences immediately the machine is used and continues until the machine is no longer fit for service. It must be carried out at specified mileage recordings or on a calendar basis if the machine is not used regularly, whichever is the sooner. Maintenance should be regarded as an insurance policy, to help keep the machine in the peak of condition and to ensure long, trouble-free service. It has the additional benefit of giving early warning of any faults that may develop and will act as a safety check, to the obvious advantage of both rider and machine alike.

The various maintenance tasks are described under their respective mileage and calendar headings. Accompanying photos or diagrams are provided, where necessary. It should be remembered that the interval between the various maintenance tasks serves only as a guide. As the machine gets older, is driven hard, or is used under particularly adverse conditions, it is advisable to reduce the period between each check.

For ease of reference each service operation is described in detail under the relevant heading. However, if further general information is required it can be found within the manual in the relevant Chapter.

Although no special tools are required for routine maintenance, a good selection of general workshop tools are essential. Included in the tools must be a range of metric ring or combination spanners, a selection of crosshead screwdrivers, and two pairs of circlip pliers, one external opening and the other internal opening. Additionally, owing to the extreme tightness of most casing screws on Japanese machines, an impact screwdriver, together with a choice of large or small cross-head screw bits, is absolutely indispensable. This is particularly so if the engine has not been dismantled since leaving the factory.

Weekly or every 200 miles

Tyre pressures

1   Check the tyre pressures with a pressure gauge that is known to be accurate. Always check the pressures when the tyres are cold. If the tyres are checked after the machine has travelled a number of miles, the tyres will have become hot and consequently the pressure will have increased, possibly as much as 8 psi. A false reading will therefore always result.

		Solo	Pillion
Tyre pressures:	Front tyre	25 psi (1.75 kg/cm²)	25 psi (1.75 kg/cm²)
	Rear tyre	28 psi (2.0 kg/cm²)	32 psi (2.25 kg/cm²)

At continuous high speeds the pressure in both tyres should be increased by 3 psi (0.25 kg/cm²).

Engine oil level

2   Place the machine on the centre stand and by viewing the sight-glass in the primary drive casing, check that the engine/transmission oil level is between the two level marks. The machine must be upright because even a slight lean will give a false reading. If necessary, replenish the engine with the correct quantity of SAE 20W/50 engine oil. The filler cap is situated in the top of the primary drive cover.

Check engine/transmission oil level in sight-glass

Replenish through aperture in casing

Safety check

3   Give the machine a close visual inspection, checking for loose nuts and fittings, frayed control cables etc.

Legal check

4   Ensure that the lights, horn and traffic indicators function correctly, also the speedometer.

Monthly or every 500 miles

Complete the tasks listed under the weekly/200 mile heading and then carry out the following checks:

Tyre damage

1   Rotate each wheel and check for damage to the tyres, especially splitting on the sidewalls. Remove any stones or other objects caught between the treads. This is particularly important on the front tyre, where rapid tyre deflation due to penetration of the inner tube will almost certainly cause total loss of control of the machine.

Spoke tension

2   Check the spokes for tension, by gently tapping each one with a metal object. A loose spoke is identifiable by the low pitch noise emitted when struck. If any one spoke needs considerable tightening, it will be necessary to remove the tyre and inner tube in order to file down the protruding spoke end. This will prevent it from chafing through the rim band and piercing the inner tube.

Hydraulic fluid level

3   Check the level of the hydraulic fluid in the master cylinder reservoir mounted on the handlebars. The level can be seen through the transparent reservoir and should be between the upper and lower level marks. Ensure that the handlebars are in the central position when a level reading is taken and also when the cap and diaphragm are removed. Replenish the reservoir with an hydraulic fluid of the following specifications:

DOT 3 or DOT 4 (USA)
SAE J1703a, b or c
SAE 70R3 may also be used   *(UK)*

Care should be taken that a specified fluid is used. An incorrect fluid may perish the piston seals and cause brake failure.

On GS 750 models the rear brake master cylinder should be checked in a similar manner. The cylinder/reservoir unit is located on the right-hand side of the machine, below the frame side cover.

Rear brake adjustment

4   When the rear brake is in correct adjustment the total brake pedal travel measured at the toe tread should be within the range 20 – 30 mm (0.8 – 1.2 in). If the travel is greater or less than this, carry out the necessary adjustment by means of the shouldered nut at the brake arm end of the cable.

Final drive chain lubrication

5   In order that final drive chain life be extended as much as possible, regular lubrication and adjustment is essential. This is particularly so when the chain is not enclosed or is fitted to a machine transmitting high power to the rear wheel. The chain may be lubricated whilst it is in situ on the machine by the application of a heavy oil or grease. Ordinary engine oil can be used, though owing to the speed with which it is flung off the rotating chain, its effective life is limited. Do not use aerosol chain lubricant as this may damage the sealing 'O' rings causing early chain failure.

It is strongly recommended that the chain is cleaned using paraffin before the application of the lubricant. This will remove any road grit which would otherwise become sealed in and accelerate wear of the rollers and sprocket teeth. The use of petrol or other solvents is not recommended as these too may damage the 'O' rings.

Final drive chain adjustment

6   Check the slack in the final drive chain. The correct up and down movement, as measured at the mid-point of the chain lower run, should be 15 – 20 mm (0.6 – 0.8 in). Adjustment should be carried out as follows: Place the machine on the centre stand so that the rear wheel is clear of the ground and free to rotate. Remove the split pin from the wheel spindle and slacken the wheel nut a few turns. Loosen the locknuts on the two chain adjuster bolts, and slacken off the brake torque rod nuts.

Rotation of the adjuster bolts in a clockwise direction will tighten the chain. Tighten each bolt a similar number of turns so that wheel alignment is maintained. This can be verified by checking that the mark on the outer face of each chain adjuster is aligned with the same aligning mark on each fork end. With the adjustment correct, tighten the wheel nut and fit a new split pin. Finally, retighten the adjuster bolt locknuts, and tighten the torque rod nuts, securing them by means of the split pins.

Check hydraulic fluid level in brake reservoir

Remove cap, seal and diaphragm to replenish

Battery electrolyte level

7 On GS 750 models release the seat catch and hinge the dualseat up so that access to the battery may be gained. Detach the battery retaining strap and the breather pipe and lift the battery sufficiently that the level may be checked.

Access to the battery on GS 550 models may be made after removal of the frame left-hand side cover.

The electrolyte solution should be between the upper and lower level lines. If the electrolyte solution is low it should be replenished, using distilled water.

Three monthly or every 1500 miles

Complete the checks listed under weekly/200 mile and monthly/500 mile headings and then carry out the following tasks:

Engine oil change

1 Drain the engine oil by removing the drain plug from the underside of the sump and the filler cap from the top of the primary drive cover. Unscrew also the oil filter chamber drain plug (where fitted) to allow the small amount of lubricant within to escape. It is preferable to complete this task when the engine has reached normal running temperature. The oil will be thinner and so flow more easily. Ensure that a container of sufficient size is placed below the engine to catch the oil. When all the oil has drained off, refit and tighten the drain plugs, after checking that their sealing washers are in good condition. Replenish the engine with approximately the following quantity of SAE 20W/50 motor oil.

GS 750   3.4 lit (3.6 US qt/6.0 Imp pint)
GS 550   2.4 lit (2.5 US qt/4.2 Imp pint)

Allow the oil to settle and then check the level by means of the sight-glass. Add more lubricant, if necessary.

Six monthly or every 3000 miles

Carry out the tasks described in the weekly, monthly and three monthly sections and then carry out the following:

Oil filter renewal

1 The oil filter element should be renewed at every second oil change. After draining the engine oil remove the three domed nuts from the oil filter chamber cover. The cover is under tension from the filter locating spring and so may fly off if care is not taken. Lift out the spring and oil filter element. No attempt should be made to clean the old filter; it must be discarded and a new component fitted. Clean the filter chamber before inserting the new element which should be fitted with the rubber seal

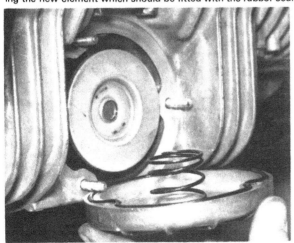

Remove cover plate for access to filter element

end facing inwards. Check the condition of the chamber cover sealing ring before replacing the cover. Refill the engine with an increased amount of the recommended oil whenever the filter is renewed:

GS 750   3.6 lit (3.8 US qt/6.3 Imp pint)
GS 550   2.6 lit (2.8 US qt/4.6 Imp pint)

Control cable lubrication

2 Use motor oil or an all purpose oil to lubricate the control cables. A good method for lubricating the cables is shown in the accompanying illustration, using a plasticine funnel. This method has a disadvantage in that the cables usually need removing from the machine. An hydraulic cable oiler which pressurises the lubricant overcomes this problem. Nylon lined cables should not be lubricated; in some cases the oil will cause the lining to swell leading to seizure.

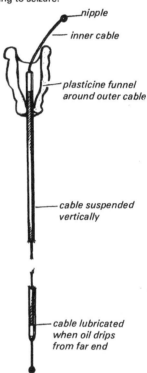

— nipple

— inner cable

— plasticine funnel around outer cable

— cable suspended vertically

— cable lubricated when oil drips from far end

Oiling control cable

Valve clearance checking and adjustment

3 To gain access to the camshafts and cam followers the petrol tank must be removed as described in Chapter 2, Section 2, and the camshaft cover detached. After removal of the cover bolts, the seal between the cover and the gasket may be broken by the judicious use of a rawhide mallet. Strike only those parts of the cover which are well supported by lugs.

Unscrew the spark plugs and remove the contact breaker cover from the right-hand side of the engine. The clearance between each cam and cam follower must be checked and if necessary adjusted by removal of the existing adjuster pad and replacement of a pad of suitable thickness. Make the clearance check and adjustment of each valve in sequence and then continue with the next valve. As shown in the accompanying diagram, both operations should be carried out with the cam lobe in question placed in one of two alternative positions. Rotate the engine in a forward direction by means of the engine turning hexagon on the contact breaker cam end. Use only the 19 mm hexagon for this purpose.

Using a feeler gauge, determine and record the clearance at the first valve. If the clearance is incorrect, not being within the range of 0.03 – 0.08 mm (0.001 – 0.003 in), the adjuster pad must be removed and replaced by one of suitable thickness. A special tool is available (Suzuki part No. 09916 – 64510) which may be pushed between the camshaft adjacent to the cam lobe and the raised edge of the cam follower, to allow removal of the shim. If the special tool is not available, a simple substitute may be fabricated from a portion of steel plate.

The final form of the tool which has a handle about 6 inches long, can be seen in the accompanying photograph.

The Suzuki tool may be pushed into position, depressing the cam follower and securing it in a depressed position, in one operation. Where a home-made tool is used, the cam follower may be depressed using a suitable lever placed between the adjuster pad and the cam lobe. The tool may then be inserted to secure the cam follower whilst the adjuster pad is removed. Before installing either type of tool, rotate the cam follower so that the slot in the raised edge is not obscured by the camshaft. Insert a small screwdriver through the slot to displace the adjuster shim.

Adjustment pads are available in 20 sizes ranging from 2.15 mm to 3.10 mm, in increments of 0.05 mm. Each pad is identified by a three digit number etched on the reverse face. The number (eg. 235) indicates that the pad thickness is 2.35 mm thick. To select the correct pad subtract 0.03 mm from the measured clearance and add the resultant figure to that of the existing pad. Select the largest available pad whose thickness is slightly smaller than the final figure. Refer to the accompanying table for the selection of available pads.

Although the adjuster pads are available as a complete set their price is prohibitive. It is suggested that pads are purchased individially, after an accurate assessment of requirement has been made. It is possible that some Suzuki service agents will be prepared to exchange needed pads for others of the correct size, providing that the original pads are not worn.

Before installing a replacement pad, lubricate both sides thoroughly with engine oil. Always fit the pad with the identification number downwards, so that it does not become obliterated by the action of the cam. After fitting new adjuster pads, rotate the engine forwards a number of times and then recheck the clearances to verify that no errors have occurred.

Before refitting the cam cover, together with a new gasket, lubricate the camshafts with copious quantities of clean engine oil.

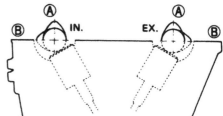

Alternative cam position when checking valve clearances

Valve clearance adjuster pad table

No.	Thickness (mm)	Part No.	No.	Thickness (mm)	Part No.
1	2.15	12892–45000	11	2.65	12892–45010
2	2.20	12892–45001	12	2.70	12892–45011
3	2.25	12892–45002	13	2.75	12892–45012
4	2.30	12892–45003	14	2.80	12892–45013
5	2.35	12892–45004	15	2.85	12892–45014
6	2.40	12892–45005	16	2.90	12892–45015
7	2.45	12892–45006	17	2.95	12892–45016
8	2.50	12892–45007	18	3.00	12892–45017
9	2.55	12892–45008	19	3.05	12892–45018
10	2.60	12892–45009	20	3.10	12892–45019

Check valve clearance using a feeler gauge

Use special tool to permit pad removal

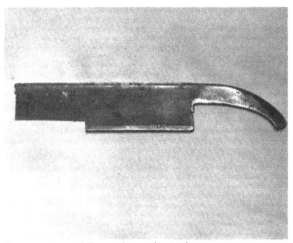

Home made camfollower depression tool

Adjuster pads are identified by etched number

Contact breaker adjustment

4   To gain access to the contact breaker assembly it is necessary to remove the engine right-hand cover which is retained by three screws.

Before adjusting the points, examine each set for burning or pitting. Clean or renew the points as necessary. See Section 5 of Chapter 2. The points are marked '1.4' and '2.3' adjacent to the relevant contact set, indicating the pair of cylinders they serve.

Set the gap of points marked 1.4 first. Turn the crankshaft using a spanner on the large hexagonal washer securing the cam, until these points are fully open. Measure the gap with a feeler gauge, and adjust if necessary. Standard gap: 0.3 – 0.4 mm (0.012 – 0.016 inch).

If the gap requires adjustment, slacken slightly the slotted screw which secures the fixed contact. A screwdriver should be engaged between the slot in the fixed contact, and the two pins on the contact breaker back plate; by turning the screwdriver the gap may be opened or closed. Tighten the screw and re-check the gap.

Turn the crankshaft so that the points marked 2.3 are fully open, and repeat the procedure above. Do not slacken the two screws which secure the 2.3 contact set base plate to the main base plate; this will upset the timing. It is important that both points should be set to the same gap, as the gap determines the moment when the contacts open, and thus the ignition timing.

Check points gap in Fully Open Position

Ignition timing

5   Whenever the contact breaker unit receives attention, the ignition timing should be checked as a matter of course and adjusted, if necessary.

Apply a spanner to the engine turning hexagon and turn the engine in a forward direction, whilst viewing the automatic timing unit through the inspection aperture in the contact breaker stator plate. It will be seen that there is a set of three scribed lines on each side of the ATU.

Commence ignition timing on the left-hand contact breaker set, which controls cylinders No. 1 and 4. To determine the point at which the points open, connect a 12 volt bulb between the moving point and a suitable earth point on the engine. With the ignition turned on, the bulb will illuminate when the points are open. Rotate the engine until the 'FI-4' mark on the ATU is in **exact** alignment with the index pointer mark on the plate fitted to the rear of the stator plate. If the ignition is correct, the points should be on the verge of opening when this position is reached. This will be indicated by the flickering of the bulb. To adjust the ignition timing on No. 1 and 4 cylinders, slacken the three screws which pass through the elongated holes in the stator plate periphery. Rotate the plate until the light flickers and then tighten the screw. Turn the engine backwards 90° and then forwards again to check the setting.

Loosen centre screw to adjust points gap

Check the ignition timing on No.2 and 3 cylinders in a similar manner, by connecting the bulb to the right-hand contact breaker set and referring to the F2-3 mark on the ATU. If the timing is incorrect, slacken the two screws which hold the right-hand contact breaker assembly mounting plate to the main stator plate. Move the plate to the correct position and tighten the screw. Recheck the timing on No. 2 and 3 cylinder.

The ignition timing may also be checked by the use of a stroboscope when the engine is running.

Check and adjust the 1 – 4 contact breaker first and then the 2 – 3 contact breaker. At 1500 rpm and below, the F mark should align with the index mark. Full advance should be reached at 2500 rpm, when the unmarked advance line to the right of the F mark should be in line with the index mark. Adjustment should be made in the same manner as described for manual ignition timing.

Before replacing the contact breaker cover, apply a small quantity of light oil or grease to the cam lubricating wick. Do not overlubricate, as excess oil may find its way onto the points, causing ignition failure.

Apply lubricant to cam felt wick

Carburettor synchronisation

6   In order that the engine maintains the best possible performance at all times, the carburettors must always remain correctly adjusted and synchronised. This check is essential and should be carried out at the specified intervals.

Synchronisation and adjustment of the carburettors requires the use of a set of four vacuum gauges or indicators, together with the appropriate adaptors which screw into the inlet tracts and to which are attached the vacuum take-off pipes. The adjustment of the carburettors is critical if smooth running and optimum fuel economy is to be expected and if damage to the engine due to incorrect mixture is to be avoided. Because of this and the prohibitive cost of the gauges required,it is recommended that the machine be returned to a Suzuki Service Agent, who will be able to carry out the work. If the vacuum gauges are available and some previous experience has been gained in their use, refer to Chapter 2 Section 6 for the prescribed adjustment procedure.

Cleaning and checking spark plugs

7   Remove the spark plugs and clean them, using a wire brush. Clean the electrodes using fine emery paper or cloth and then reset the gaps to 0.6 - 0.7 mm (0.024 - 0.028 in), using a feeler gauge. Before replacing the plugs, smear the threads with a small amount of graphite grease to aid future removal.

Air filter cleaning

8   Access to the air filter element differs between the two models. On GS 550 models raise the dualseat and remove the air filter box lid, which is secured by two screws. The air filter element and carrier can be lifted out, after removal of the single carrier screw. The air filter box on GS 750 models is fitted with a cover at each end, both of which are retained by two screws. Detach both covers and remove the single retaining screw from the left-hand side. The carrier and element may be pushed out. Detach the element from the carrier after removing the two remaining screws. The element is of the oil impregnated polyurethane sponge type, and should be washed thoroughly in petrol to remove all the oil and dust. After cleaning, squeeze out the sponge to remove the petrol and then allow a short time for the remaining petrol to evaporate. **Do not** wring out the sponge, as this may damage the fabric and lead to the need for early renewal.

Reimpregnate the sponge with engine oil and gently squeeze out the excess.

Reinstall the element and carrier by reversing the removal process.

The air filter element should be renewed if it becomes badly clogged or if the sponge hardens or perishes with age.

Nine monthly or 6000 miles

Perform all the maintenance tasks listed under the preceding time/mileage headings and then carry out the following:

Spark plug renewal

1   Remove and discard the existing spark plugs regardless of their condition. Although the plugs may give acceptable performance after they have reached this mileage, it is unlikely that they are still working at peak efficiency.

The correct spark plugs are NGK B8ES or Nippon Denso W24ES. Before fitting the new plugs, adjust the gap of each to 0.6 - 0.7 mm (0.024 - 0.028 in).

Front fork oil change

2   Place the machine on the centre stand so that it rests securely in a level position. The fork legs should be drained and refilled one at a time, so that the fork leg not being attended to will support the weight of the machine.

Remove the clamps holding the handlebars to the top fork yoke so that access may be made to the fork stanchion end bolts. Place a container below fork leg drain bolt which is situated above and to the rear of the wheel spindle clamp. Remove the end bolt and the drain plug.

Allow the damping fluid to drain and then pump the forks up and down to drain any residual oil. Replace and tighten the drain plug after checking that the sealing washer is in good condition. Replenish the fork leg with the following amount of fluid:

GS550 model   165 cc   (5.58/5.81 US/Imp fl oz)
GS750 model   170 cc   (5.75/5.98 US/Imp fl oz)

Suzuki recommend that the damping fluid be a 50/50 mixture of fork oil or ATF (automatic transmission fluid) and 10W/30 engine oil. After filling, refit the cap bolt and attend to the second fork leg in a similar way.

Oil filter gauze cleaning

3   When renewing the oil at this service interval, the sump should be removed and the oil pick-up strainer screen detached for cleaning. The screen is secured to the pick-up chamber by three screws. Wash the screen in clean petrol, using a soft brush.

Yearly or every 10000 miles

Again complete the checks listed under the previous routine maintenance interval headings. The following additional tasks are now necessary:
1   Dismantle and clean the carburettors (see Chapter 3, Sections 4 – 6).
2   Check the condition of the contact breaker assemblies and renew if necessary. (See Chapter 3, Section 5).
3   Remove the rear wheel and check the condition of the brake shoes. (See Chapter 5, Section 15). (GS 550 model only).
4   Remove and clean the wheel bearings. Renew worn bearings. Replace bearings and repack with grease. (See Chapter 5, Sections 8 and 17).

General adjustments and examination

Clutch adjustment
1   The intervals at which the clutch should be adjusted will depend on the style of riding and the conditions under which the machine is used.
     Adjust the clutch in two stages to ensure smooth operation, as follows:
     Remove the clutch adjustment cover which is retained by three cross-head screws, loosen the locknut on the cable adjuster, where it enters the cover, and screw the adjuster inwards approximately 6 turns, to give plenty of slack in the cable.
     Loosen the locknut on the lifting mechanism adjuster screw and screw the adjuster inwards until a resistance can be felt. To give the necessary running clearance, unscrew the adjuster $\frac{1}{4}$ – $\frac{1}{2}$ a turn and then tighten the locknut. The cable should be adjusted so that there is 4 mm (1/16 in) play measured between the stock and handlebar lever, before the clutch commences lifting. Finally tighten the locknut on the clutch cable and replace the adjustment cover and gasket.

Checking front brake pad wear
2   Brake pad wear depends largely on the conditions in which the machine is ridden and at what speed. It is difficult therefore to give precise inspection intervals, but it follows that pad wear should be checked more frequently on a hard ridden machine.
     The condition of each pad can be checked easily whilst still in situ on the machine. The pads have a red groove around their outer periphery which can be seen from the front of the caliper unit (front brakes), or from the top of the caliper after the inspection cap has been prised off (rear brake, GS 750 model only). Removal and replacement of the brake pads in both the front and rear calipers may be accomplished without removing the respective wheel.
     If wear has reduced either or both pads in one caliper down to the red line, the pads should be renewed as a pair. In practice, where a double front disc set-up is used, if one set of pads requires renewal, it will be necessary to renew the other pair, too.
     To gain access to the front brake pads for renewal, each caliper unit must be detached from the fork leg, although separation of the caliper from the hydraulic hose is not required. Remove the two bolts which pass through the fork leg into the caliper support bracket and lift the complete caliper unit upwards, off the disc. Remove the single screw and the convolute backing plate from the inner side of the caliper body.
     The inner pad is now free and may be displaced towards the centre of the caliper, and lifted out. The outer pad, which abuts against the caliper piston, is not retained positively and may be lifted out. Refit the new pads after coating lightly the periphery of each pad with disc brake assembly grease (silicon grease). Use the grease sparingly, ensuring that it **does not** come in contact with the friction surface of the pad. If necessary, push the piston inwards to increase the clearance between the pads and allow the pads to fit over the disc. To remove the brake pads from the rear brake caliper, pull out the stop pin which passes through the outer end of each pad mounting pin. Displace one mounting pin and remove the two hair springs. Push out the final pin and lift each pad out individually, removing the outer pad first.
     Install new pads by reversing the dismantling procedure. The shim fitted to the piston side of each pad must be positioned with the punched arrowmark pointing in the direction of normal wheel travel. If required, push back each piston to give the necessary clearance between each piston and the disc face into which the pad can be inserted.

Working conditions and tools

When a major overhaul is contemplated, it is important that a clean, well-lit working space is available, equipped with a workbench and vice, and with space for laying out or storing the dismantled assemblies in an orderly manner where they are unlikely to be disturbed. The use of a good workshop will give the satisfaction of work done in comfort and without haste, where there is little chance of the machine being dismantled and reassembled in anything other than clean surroundings. Unfortunately, these ideal working conditions are not always practicable and under these latter circumstances when improvisation is called for, extra care and time will be needed.

The other essential requirement is a comprehensive set of good quality tools. Quality is of prime importance since cheap tools will prove expensive in the long run if they slip or break when in use, causing personal injury or expensive damage to the component being worked on. A good quality tool will last a long time, and more than justify the cost.

For practically all tools, a tool factor is the best source since he will have a very comprehensive range compared with the average garage or accessory shop. Having said that, accessory shops often offer excellent quality tools at discount prices, so it pays to shop around. There are plenty of tools around at reasonable prices, but always aim to purchase items which meet the relevant national safety standards. If in doubt, seek the advice of the shop proprietor or manager before making a purchase.

The basis of any tool kit is a set of open-ended spanners, which can be used on almost any part of the machine to which there is reasonable access. A set of ring spanners makes a useful addition, since they can be used on nuts that are very tight or where access is restricted. Where the cost has to be kept within reasonable bounds, a compromise can be effected with a set of combination spanners – open-ended at one end and having a ring of the same size on the other end. Socket spanners may also be considered a good investment, a basic $3/8$ in or $1/2$ in drive kit comprising a ratchet handle and a small number of socket heads, if money is limited. Additional sockets can be purchased, as and when they are required. Provided they are slim in profile, sockets will reach nuts or bolts that are deeply recessed. When purchasing spanners of any kind, make sure the correct size standard is purchased. Almost all machines manufactured outside the UK and the USA have metric nuts and bolts, whilst those produced in Britain have BSF or BSW sizes. The standard used in USA is AF, which is also found on some of the later British machines. Others tools that should be included in the kit are a range of crosshead screwdrivers, a pair of pliers and a hammer.

When considering the purchase of tools, it should be remembered that by carrying out the work oneself, a large proportion of the normal repair cost, made up by labour charges, will be saved. The economy made on even a minor overhaul will go a long way towards the improvement of a toolkit.

In addition to the basic tool kit, certain additional tools can prove invaluable when they are close to hand, to help speed up a multitude of repetitive jobs. For example, an impact screwdriver will ease the removal of screws that have been tightened by a similar tool, during assembly, without a risk of damaging the screw heads. And, of course, it can be used again to retighten the screws, to ensure an oil or airtight seal results. Circlip pliers have their uses too, since gear pinions, shafts and similar components are frequently retained by circlips that are not too easily displaced by a screwdriver. There are two types of circlip pliers, one for internal and one for external circlips. They may also have straight or right-angled jaws.

One of the most useful of all tools is the torque wrench, a form of spanner that can be adjusted to slip when a measured amount of force is applied to any bolt or nut. Torque wrench settings are given in almost every modern workshop or service manual, where the extent to which a complex component, such as a cylinder head, can be tightened without fear of distortion or leakage. The tightening of bearing caps is yet another example. Overtightening will stretch or even break bolts, necessitating extra work to extract the broken portions.

As may be expected, the more sophisticated the machine, the greater is the number of tools likely to be required if it is to be kept in first class condition by the home mechanic. Unfortunately there are certain jobs which cannot be accomplished successfully without the correct equipment and although there is invariably a specialist who will undertake the work for a fee, the home mechanic will have to dig more deeply in his pocket for the purchase of similar equipment if he does not wish to employ the services of others. Here a word of caution is necessary, since some of these jobs are best left to the expert. Although an electrical multimeter of the AVO type will prove helpful in tracing electrical faults, in inexperienced hands it may irrevocably damage some of the electrical components if a test current is passed through them in the wrong direction. This can apply to the synchronisation of twin or multiple carburettors too, where a certain amount of expertise is needed when setting them up with vacuum gauges. These are, however, exceptions. Some instruments, such as a strobe lamp, are virtually essential when checking the timing of a machine powered by CDI ignition system. In short, do not purchase any of these special items unless you have the experience to use them correctly.

Although this manual shows how components can be removed and replaced without the use of special service tools (unless absolutely essential), it is worthwhile giving consideration to the purchase of the more commonly used tools if the machine is regarded as a long term purchase Whilst the alternative methods suggested will remove and replace parts without risk of damage, the use of the special tools recommended and sold by the manufacturer will invariably save time.

Summary of routine

maintenance adjustments and capacities

For additional information relating to 1978 and 1979 GS750 models and 1978 through 1982 GS550 models, refer to Chapter 7.

Spark plugs . . . . NGK B8ES or Nippon Denso W24ES
Spark plugs gap . . . . 0.6 – 0.7 mm (0.024 – 0.028 in)
Contact breaker gap . . . . 0.35 mm (0.014 in)

Tyre pressures
Solo   **Pillion**
   Front 25 psi (1.75 kg–cm^2) . . . . 25 (1.75 kg – cm^2)
   Rear 28 psi (2.0 kg – cm^2) . . . . 32 (2.25 kg – cm^2)

Increase pressure in both tyres by 3 psi (0.25 kg – cm^2) for continuous high speed cruising

Valve clearance (cold) . . . . 0.03 – 0.08 mm (0.001 – 0.003 in)

Recommended lubricants

For additional information relating to 1978 and 1979 GS750 models and 1978 through 1982 GS550 models, refer to Chapter 7.

Components	Viscosity/Product	Quantity
Engine and transmission		
GS 750:		
At oil change	20W/50 engine oil	3.4 lit (3.6 US qt/6.0 Imp pint)
At oil and filter change	20W/50 engine oil	3.6 lit (3.8 US qt/6.3 Imp pint)
GS 550:		
At oil change	20W/50 engine oil	2.4 lit (2.5 US qt/4.2 Imp pint)
At oil and filter change	20W/50 engine oil	2.6 lit (2.8 US qt/4.6 Imp pint)
Front forks		
GS 750	50/50 mixture of ATF and 10W/30 engine oil	170 cc (5.75/5.98 US/Imp fl oz)
GS 550	50/50 mixture of ATF and 10W/30 engine oil	165 cc (5.58/5.81 US/Imp fl oz)
Disc brakes	Brake fluid conforming to DOT 3 (US) or SAE J1703 (UK) Specifications	As required
Grease points	High melting point grease	As required

Dimensions and weights

For additional information relating to 1978 and 1979 GS750 models and 1978 through 1982 GS550 models, refer to Chapter 7.

Dimensions	GS 750	GS 550
Overall length	2225 mm (87.6 in)	2175 mm (85.6 in)
Overall width	870 mm (34.3 in)	850 mm (33.5 in)
Overall height	1170 mm (46.1 in)	1155 mm (45.5 in)
Wheelbase	1490 mm (58.7 in)	1435 mm (56.5 in)
Weight (dry)	223 kg (492 lbs)	196 kg (432 lbs)

Chapter 1 Engine, clutch and gearbox

For additional information relating to 1978 and 1979 GS750 models and 1978 through 1982 GS550 models, refer to Chapter 7.

Contents

Specifications

GS 750 model
Engine

Type	Four cylinder, double overhead camshaft, air-cooled, four-stroke
Bore	65.0 mm (2.56 in)
Stroke	56.4 mm (2.22 in)
Capacity	748 cc (45.6 cu in)
Compression ratio	8.7 : 1
bhp	68 @ 8,500 rpm

Cylinder head

Max. cylinder head warpage .... 0.25 mm (0.0098 in)
Valve stem diameter:
    Inlet .... 6.965 – 6.980 mm (0.2742 – 0.2748 in)
    Service limit .... 6.90 mm (0.2717 in)
    Exhaust .... 6.955 – 6.970 mm (0.2738 – 0.2744 in)
    Service limit .... 6.805 mm (0.2679 in)
Valve stem/guide clearance:
    Inlet .... 0.02 – 0.05 mm (0.0008 – 0.0020 in)
    Service limit .... 0.09 mm (0.0035 in)
    Exhaust .... 0.03 – 0.06 mm (0.0012 – 0.0024 in)
    Service limit .... 0.10 mm (0.0039 in)
Valve spring minimum free length
    Inner .... 33.8 mm (1.331 in)
    Outer .... 41.5 mm (1.634 in)

Camshafts

Cam height
    Inlet .... 36.265 – 36.295 mm (1.4278 – 1.4289 in)
    Service limit .... 36.150 mm (1.4232 in)
    Exhaust .... 35.735 – 35.765 mm (1.4069 – 1.4081 in)
    Service limit .... 35.600 mm (1.4016 in)
Camshaft/bearing clearance (max) .... 0.150 mm (0.0059 in)
Camshaft bearing ID .... 21.959 – 21.980 mm (0.8645 – 0.8654 in)
Camshaft run-out (max) .... 0.10 mm (0.04 in)

Cylinder bores

Bore diameter (standard) .... 65.000 – 65.015 mm (2.5591 – 2.5595 in)
Service limit .... 65.100 mm (2.5630 in)
Cylinder/piston clearance .... 0.050 – 0.060 mm (0.0020 – 0.0024 in)

Pistons and rings

Piston diameter (standard) .... 64.945 – 64.960 mm (2.5569 – 2.5575 in)
Service limit .... 64.800 mm (2.5512 in)
Gudgeon pin diameter .... 15.995 – 16.000 mm (0.6297 – 0.6299 in)
    Service limit .... 15.96 mm (0.6283 in)
Piston ring side clearance (maximum)
    1st and 2nd ring .... 0.18 mm (0.0071 in)
    Oil control ring .... 0.15 mm (0.0059 in)
Ring end gap (max)
    1st and 2nd ring .... 0.6 mm (0.024 in)
Ring free end gap (max)
    1st and 2nd ring .... 6.0 mm (0.24 in)

Crankshaft and connecting rods

Crankshaft run-out (max) .... 0.06 mm (0.0024 in)
Main bearing radial clearance
    Standard .... 0.015 – 0.040 mm (0.0006 – 0.0016 in)
    Service limit .... 0.08 mm (0.0031 in)
Connecting rod side to side deflection
    Maximum .... 3.0 mm (0.12 in)
Connecting rod axial float
    Standard .... 0.65 – 0.10 mm (0.026 – 0.004 in)
    Wear limit .... 1.0 mm (0.04 in)
Small end/gudgeon pin clearance
    Standard .... 0.0110 – 0.014 mm (0.0004 – 0.0008 in)
    Wear limit .... 0.090 mm (0.0035 in)

Clutch

Type .... Wet, multi-plate
No of plates
    Plain 6
    Friction 7
Friction plate thickness
    Standard .... 2.9 – 3.1 mm (0.114 – 0.122 in)
    Service limit .... 2.7 mm (0.106 in)
No of springs 6
Spring free length
    Standard .... 40.4 mm (1.59 in)
    Wear limit .... 39.0 mm (1.54 in)

Gearbox

Type	....	5-speed constant mesh
Ratios		
1st gear	....	2.571 : 1
2nd gear	....	1.777 : 1
3rd gear	....	1.380 : 1
4th gear	....	1.125 : 1
5th gear	....	0.961 : 1

GS 550 model

Engine/gearbox dimensional specifications are as given for GS 750 models, except for the following:

Engine

Type	....	Four cylinder, double overhead camshaft, air cooled, four stroke
Bore	....	56.0 mm (2.205 in)
Stroke	....	55.8 mm (2.197 in)
Capacity	....	549 cc (33.5 cu in)
Compression ratio	....	8.6 : 1
bhp	....	48 @ 9000 rpm

Camshafts .... Refer to Chapter 7 Specifications

Cylinder bores

Bore diameter	....	56.000 – 56.015 mm (2.2047 – 2.2053 in)
Service limit	....	56.100 mm (2.2087 in)

Pistons and rings

Piston diameter	....	55.945 – 55.960 mm (2.2026 – 2.2031 in)
Service limit	....	55.800 mm (2.1969 in)
Piston ring free end gap (max)	....	5 mm (0.20 in)

Clutch

Spring free length		
Standard	....	37.7 – 39.1 mm (1.48 – 1.54 in)
Service limit	....	37.0 mm (1.46 in)

Gearbox

Ratios		
1st gear	....	2.666 : 1
2nd gear	....	1.777 : 1
3rd gear	....	1.380 : 1
4th gear	....	1.173 : 1
5th gear	....	1.045 : 1
6th gear	....	0.956 : 1

1 General description

The engine unit fitted to the Suzuki GS 750 and GS 550 models are of notably similar design throughout, both being of the four-cylinder in-line type, fitted transversely across the frame. The valves are operated by double overhead camshafts driven off the crankshaft by a centre chain. The two camshafts are located in the cylinder head casting, and the camshaft chain drive operates through a cast-in tunnel between the four cylinders. Adjustment of the chain is effected by a chain tensioner, fitted to the rear of the cylinder block. The chain tensioner is of an unusual type in that it maintains automatic tensioning of the chain, compensating for chain wear, after initial assembly and adjustment.

The engine/gear unit is of aluminium alloy construction, with the crankcase divided horizontally.

The GS series have a wet sump, pressure fed lubrication system, which incorporates a gear driven oil pump, an oil filter, a safety by-pass valve, and an oil pressure switch.

Oil vapours created in the crankcase are vented through an oil breather to the air cleaner hose where they are recirculated into the crankcase, providing an oil tight system.

An Eaton trochoid oil pump is fitted, driven by a gear pinion to the rear of the clutch outer drum. Oil is picked up from the sump via a chamber integral with the upper crankcase half, the mouth of which is closed by a detachable wire mesh screen. The screen protects the oil pump from any larger impurities which may have contaminated the oil. The oil pump forces the oil, under pressure, through a full flow paper-element oil filter which is housed within a chamber at the front of the crankcase. In the event of the filter becoming blocked, a by-pass valve is included which prevents cessation of the oil flow by opening at a preset pressure.

After passing through the oil filter, the oil flow is separated into three branch systems. The main system feeds the crankshaft main bearings and the big end bearings, and the two remaining systems supply the camshafts and valve and the gearbox shafts and pinions. Returning oil from the engine and gearbox components falls under gravity to the sump, where it is picked up once more by the oil pump and the cycle is repeated.

2 Operations with the engine/gearbox unit in the frame

1 It is not necessary to remove the engine from the frame to carry out certain operations; in fact it can be an advantage. Tasks that can be carried out with the engine in situ are as follows;
a)   Removal of cylinder head, cylinder block and pistons.
b)   Removal of the clutch
c)   Removal of the alternator and starter motor.
d)   Removal of the carburettors.
e)   Removal of the gearchange external selector mechanism.
f)   Removal of the oil pump and oil filter.

2 When several tasks have to be undertaken simultaneously, it will probably be advantageous to remove the complete engine unit from the frame, an operation that should take about an hour and a half. This gives the advantage of much better access and more working space.

3 Operations with the engine/gearbox unit removed from the frame

a) Removal of the crankshaft assembly, complete with main bearings and connecting rod assemblies.
b) Removal of the gearbox components including the gearchange internal selection mechanism.
c) Removal of the kickstart shaft and engagement mechanism.

4 Method of engine/gearbox removal

As described previously, the engine and gearbox are a built in unit and it is necessary to remove the unit complete in order to gain access to either unit. Separation of the crankcase is achieved after the engine unit has been removed from the frame and refitting cannot take place until the engine/gear unit is assembled completely. Access to the gearbox is not available until the engine has been dismantled and vice-versa in the case of attention to the bottom end of the engine. Fortunately, the task is made easy by arranging the crankcase to separate horizontally.

5 Removing the engine/gearbox unit

1 Place the machine on the centre stand, so that it is standing firmly on level ground. Place a receptacle that will hold at least a gallon under the crankcase and remove the drain plug so that the oil will drain off. It is preferable to do this whilst the engine is warm, so that the oil will drain more readily.
2 Transfer the container so that it rests below the oil filter chamber at the front of the engine. Remove the three domed nuts and the washers and detach the cover. The cover is spring loaded by the filter element retainer spring and so should be released in a controlled manner. Lift out the spring and the element.
3 Raise the dualseat and disconnect both battery leads from the terminals. Isolating the electrical system in this way will prevent accidental shorting of wires which are subsequently disconnected. If it is expected that the machine is to be unused for a protracted length of time, the battery should be removed at this stage and given a refresher charge from an independent source at approximately monthly intervals. The battery may be lifted from the carrier after displacing the retainer strap and pulling the small breather hose from the union at the side of the battery.
4 Place the petrol tap lever to the On or Reserve position and disconnect from the tap unions the petrol feed pipe and the smaller vacuum pipe which controls the tap diaphragm. The feed pipe is secured by a spring clip, the ears of which should be squeezed together to release the grip on the pipe. Remove the single bolt which passes through the lug at the rear of the petrol tank and into the frame. The tank is supported at the front by two steel cups which locate with a rubber buffer each side of the frame top tube. Ease the tank rearwards until the cups clear the buffers and then lift it away. Drainage of the tank is not strictly necessary although to do so will reduce the overall weight and hence facilitate removal. A full tank will weigh in the region of 50 lbs.
5 Detach the left-hand and right-hand frame covers. Each is retained at the lower edge by a projection which is a push fit in

a rubber grommet or by a screw knob and at the upper edge on two rubber covered hook tabs projecting from the frame.
6 Pull off the engine breather hose from the breather cover union on top of the cam cover. The hose is secured by a spring clip. Disconnect both throttle cables from the operating pulley at the carburettors. Each may be detached in a similar manner. Loosen the upper and lower locknuts on the cable adjuster screw and displace the adjuster and outer cable from the abutment bracket. Rotate the pulley until the nipple can be pushed out.
7 Loosen the screw clips which secure the carburettors to the inlet stubs, and those securing the air filter hoses to the carburettor mouths. Remove the air filter mounting bolts and ease the air filter box rearwards, so the hoses leave the carburettors. On GS 750 models the air filter box can now be removed from the machine, towards the right-hand side. The air filter box on GS 550 models can be displaced after carburettor removal. Pull the carburettors from the inlet stubs and remove them as a complete unit.
8 Detach both forward footrests, each of which is retained by two bolts passing into the frame. From the left-hand side of the machine remove the clutch mechanism cover. The cover is located to the rear of the alternator cover and is secured by three screws. To disconnect the clutch cable at the operating mechanism arm a large amount of slack is required in the cable. Displace the rubber and plastic guards from the handlebar control lever and screw the adjuster screw inwards fully. Arrange the slots in the adjuster screw and knurled locking ring so that they align with the lever stock slot. Pull the rubber boot off the cable adjuster at the lower end of the cable and screw the adjuster in fully, after loosening the locknut. The clutch cable can now be freed from the handlebar lever. Bend down the security tab on the operating mechanism arm so that the cable nipple can be displaced from the arm.
9 Remove the gearchange lever from the splined operating shaft. The lever is retained by a pinch bolt which must be unscrewed fully before the lever can be displaced. Remove the screws which secure the final drive sprocket cover, and detach the cover. Because the final drive chain is of the endless type (ie. has no spring link) the chain and sprocket must be removed simultaneously from the gearbox output shaft. Bend down the tab washer which secures the sprocket nut and remove the nut. To prevent rotation of the shaft whilst loosening the nut apply the rear brake fully. The sprocket can now be eased off the splined shaft, meshed with the chain.
10 Slacken the bolts holding the four exhaust pipe silencer joint clamps. Slide each clamp back up the pipe to clear the joint. Note the fibre packing sleeve at each joint. Commencing with either outer exhaust pipe, the pipes may be removed individually. Slacken evenly and then remove the two bolts, securing each finned exhaust port flange. Slide the flange down the pipe and then ease the pipe simultaneously from the exhaust port and silencer. Removal of the silencers is not strictly necessary during engine removal. It may, however, be wise to detach the right-hand silencer to prevent damage when the engine is removed from that side. The silencer is retained by two bolts.
11 Remove the cover which encloses the starter motor, and is held by two screws. Detach the heavy cable from the terminal projecting from the starter motor body. Pull the lead from the top of the oil pressure warning switch. The lead is a push fit. Pull both leads from where they are routed and lodge them out of harm's way, towards the rear of the machine. Follow the leads from the alternator up to the rubber shroud to the rear of the battery carrier. Peel back the shroud and disconnect the alternator leads at their individual snap connectors. The two leads from the contact breakers are similarly protected by a rubber sleeve, forward of the left-hand rear down tube. Disconnect the black wire and white wire. Follow the lead from the neutral indicator switch located in the gearbox left-hand wall and disconnect the block connector and single lead. All wires leading from the engine should be arranged at the rear of the engine so that they do not become snagged on engine removal.

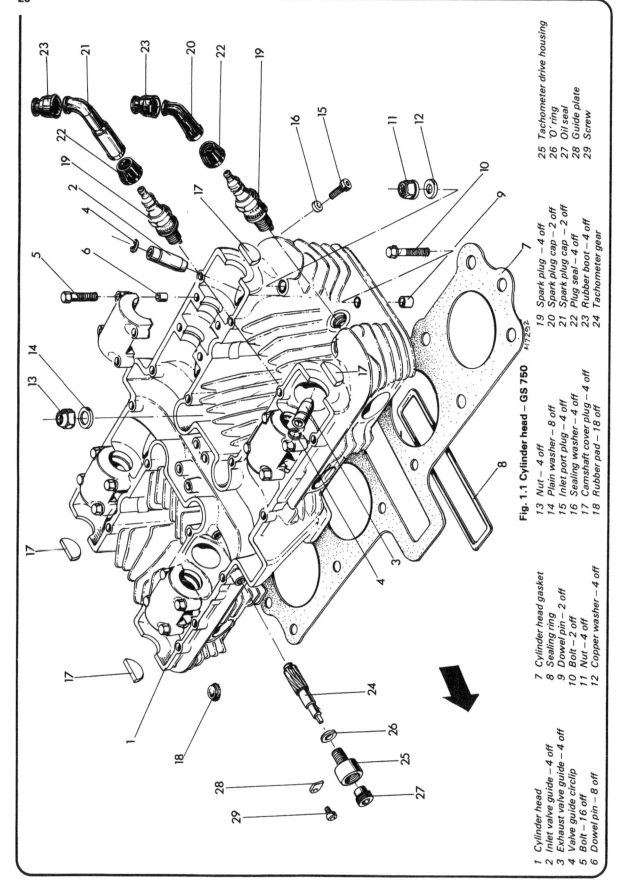

Fig. 1.1 Cylinder head – GS 750

1 Cylinder head
2 Inlet valve guide – 4 off
3 Exhaust valve guide – 4 off
4 Valve guide circlip
5 Bolt – 16 off
6 Dowel pin – 8 off

7 Cylinder head gasket
8 Sealing ring
9 Dowel pin – 2 off
10 Bolt – 2 off
11 Nut – 4 off
12 Copper washer – 4 off

13 Nut – 4 off
14 Plain washer – 8 off
15 Inlet port plug – 4 off
16 Sealing washer – 4 off
17 Camshaft cover plug – 4 off
18 Rubber pad – 18 off

19 Spark plug – 4 off
20 Spark plug cap – 2 off
21 Spark plug cap – 2 off
22 Plug seal – 4 off
23 Rubber boot – 4 off
24 Tachometer gear

25 Tachometer drive housing
26 'O' ring
27 Oil seal
28 Guide plate
29 Screw

Pull the plug caps from the spark plugs and secure the HT leads to the upper frame tubes. Each lead is numbered, to aid correct replacement.

12 Remove the rear brake pedal from the splined shaft, after unscrewing fully the pinch bolt. Prise the end of the pedal return spring from the anchor peg so that the spring comes away with the pedal.

13 To improve the clearance between the top of the engine and the upper frame tubes, and so aid engine removal, the breather cover should be detached from the cam cover. The breather cover is retained by four bolts. In addition, it may be necessary to rearrange the various cables and leads running below the upper frame tubes.   Disconnection of the main harness at the large block connector will aid this. Detach the tachometer cable from the front of the cylinder head.

14 The engine/gearbox unit is massive and cumbersome and although not particularly heavy for its size, it is recommended that at least three people are present when lifting the engine from place.Remove first the lower rear mounting bolt followed by the two short central bolts and then the front mounting bolt. Detach also the two small engine front mounting plates. Note that the centre bolts are fitted with threaded triangular plates, in place of normal nuts, which are restrained within recesses in the crankcase casting. On early models, which have a detachable central mounting bracket on the right-hand side, the plate

should be removed. After removal of the rear upper mounting bolt and the right-hand plate,the engine may be lifted up and out of the frame from the right-hand side.

6 Dismantling the engine and gearbox: general

1   Before commencing work on the engine unit, the external surfaces should be cleaned thoroughly. A motor cycle engine has very little protection from road grit and other foreign matter, which will find its way into the dismantled engine if this simple precaution is not taken. One of the proprietary cleaning compounds, such as Gunk or Jizer can be used to good effect, particularly if the compound is permitted to work into the film of oil and grease before it is washed away. Special care is necessary when washing down to prevent water from entering the now exposed parts of the engine unit.

2   Never use undue force to remove any stubborn part unless specific mention is made of this requirement. There is invariably good reason why a part is difficult to remove, often because the dismantling operation has been tackled in the wrong sequence. Dismantling will be made easier if a simple engine stand is constructed to correspond with the engine mounting points. This arrangement will permit the complete unit to be clamped rigidly to the workbench, leaving both hands free.

5.6a Disconnect breather hose, secured by spring clip

5.6b Displace the cable adjuster from bracket and ...

5.6c ... slide inner cable nipple from the pulley

5.7 Displace air filter box before carburettor removal (GS 750)

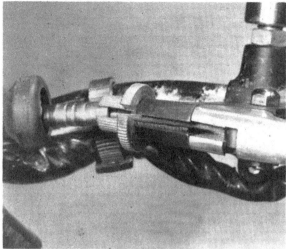

5.8a Prise off the boot and displace clutch cable to allow ...

5.8b ... removal of the cable from the operating lever

5.9a Bend down tab washer before loosening nut

5.9b Withdraw sprocket together with the chain

5.10a Slacken and pull back exhaust clamps to clear packing

5.10b Remove flange bolts and detach the exhaust pipes

5.10c Each silencer is retained by a bolt at forward end and ...

5.10d ... a second bolt at the rear

5.11a Detach heavy cable from motor terminal

5.11b Main alternator lead shrouded at rear of battery

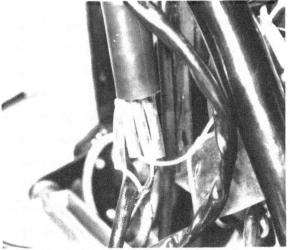

5.11c Contact breaker leads are similarly shrouded at connectors

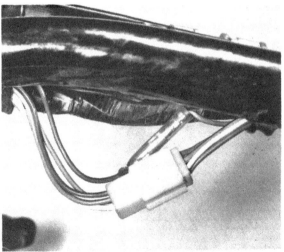

5.11d Separate gear indicator and neutral switch wires

5.12 Displace the return spring before removing the brake pedal

5.13a Remove the breather cover to increase engine clearance

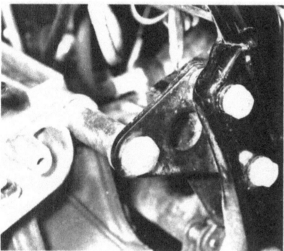

5.13b The engine is retained by upper and ...

5.13c ... lower bolts passing through lugs at rear ...

5.13d ... a single front bolt and ...

5.13e ... two central short bolts which ...

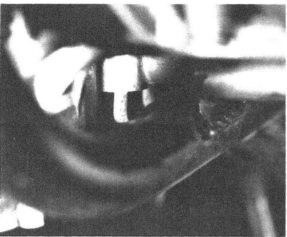

5.13f ... screw into plate nuts restrained by crankcase recesses

5.13g Lift engine out towards right-hand side

7   Dismantling the engine unit: removing the camshaft cover and the camshafts

1   Remove the four end caps from the camshaft cover, and unscrew the bolts holding the camshaft cover in position. If the cover is stuck firmly to the gasket, a rawhide mallet may be used to break the seal. Use the mallet judiciously, striking only those parts of the cover which are well strengthened by lugs.

2   Unscrew the spark plugs and remove the contact breaker cover from the engine right-hand casing. Using a spanner applied to the large hexagon fitted to the end of the contact breaker cam, rotate the engine forwards until the piston in the left-hand cylinder (No. 1 cylinder) is at top dead centre. TDC may be found by viewing the timing marks on the Automatic Timing Unit (ATU) through the inspection aperture in the contact breaker stator plate. Turn the engine until the T mark, which is to the left of the F1-4 mark, is in alignment with the index pointer in the casing.

3   Removal of the automatic cam chain tensioner must be carried out in a special sequence. Commence by loosening the locknut securing the grubscrew in the left-hand side of the tensioner body. Turn the screw inwards so that it tightens against the plunger within the body. The tensioner can now be removed without the spring loaded plunger being displaced.

4   Detach the jockey sprocket assembly (GS 750 only) from between the two camshaft sprockets by removing the four mounting bolts. Mark the sprocket carrier so that it may be refitted in the same position. GS 550 models are fitted with a rubber backed guide which slots into the cam tunnel between the sprockets. This guide will lift out.

5   Having removed the tensioner and jockey sprocket, the camshafts may be removed individually, without separating the cam chain. It will be noted that no matter in what position the engine is placed, at least one cam lobe will be depressing one valve and spring to some extent.To prevent uneven stress to the camshafts when removing the camshaft bearing caps, Suzuki recommend that a large self-grip wrench be used to hold the camshaft down. A G-clamp of suitable size will make a substitute if a wrench is not available. Fit the wrench as shown in the accompanying photograph, ensuring that it is so placed that slipping is not possible. Loosen evenly the four bolts holding each of the two cam bearing caps and then remove the bolts and caps. Note that each cap is marked A, B, C or D. The casing below each cap is marked similarly, to enable the caps to be refitted in their original locations and positions. Displace the clamping tool to free the camshaft.

6   If a suitable clamping tool is not available, it is acceptable to slacken the bearing cap bolts without restraining the camshafts, providing extreme caution is exercised. The bolts must be loosened evenly a little at a time, so that neither the camshaft nor the bearing caps are allowed to hit.

7   Lift the cam chain off the sprocket and remove the camshaft, complete with the sprocket. Repeat the procedure for the other camshaft. Removal of the sprockets is not required unless the components require renewal.

8   If a top-end overhaul only is anticipated, the cam chain should not be allowed to fall down into the chain tunnel, as retrieval can be very difficult. Insert a long bar through the chain so that it rests on the cylinder head or use a length of stout wire secured to an adjacent stud or bolt hole.

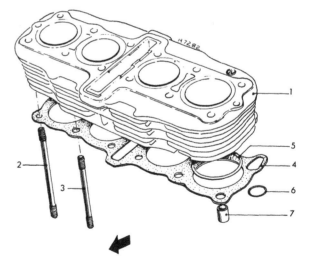

Fig. 1.2. Cylinder block

1 Cylinder block
2 Stud – 2 off
3 Stud – 8 off
4 Cylinder base gasket
5 'O' ring – 4 off
6 'O' ring – 2 off
7 Dowel pin – 2 off

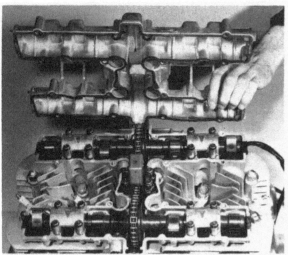

7.1 Exercise care when separating cam cover from cylinder head

7.2 Place pistons 1 and 4 at TDC by aligning T mark

7.3a Slacken locknut and tighten plunger locking screw before

7.3b ... removing the chain tensioner unit

7.4 Jockey sprocket (GS 750) is held by four bolts

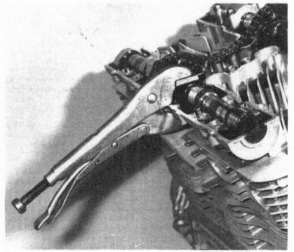

7.5a Suzuki recommend this method of camshaft retention

7.5b Lift camshafts out together with sprocket

connecting rod, complete with rings. Make sure the piston is supported during this operation, or there is risk of bending the connecting rod.

7 If the gudgeon pin is a tight fit, do not resort to force. Warm the piston by placing a rag soaked in hot water on the crown,so that the piston bosses will expand and release their grip on the pin.

8 Each piston is fitted with three piston rings; two compression and one oil scraper. To remove the rings, spread the ends sufficiently with the thumbs to allow each ring to be eased from its groove and lifted clear of the piston. This is a very delicate operation necessitating great care. Piston rings are very brittle and will break easily.

An alternative method of removing piston rings safely, especially when the rings are gummed up, is shown in the accompanying illustration. Use three narrow strips of tin cut from an old oil can, slipped between the rings and the piston.

9 Unscrew the single bolt which secures the cam chain rear guide blade and lift the blade from position.

8 Dismantling the engine unit: removing the cylinder head, cylinder block and pistons

1 Do not disturb the cam followers and adjusters at this juncture. These components should be left in place until the examination stage. The cylinder head is retained by twelve nuts and two bolts. Slacken off the bolts and then loosen the nuts in the reverse order of that given in Fig. No. 1.20 which accompanies Section 44. The nuts must be loosened evenly in this sequence, to avoid stressing the cylinder head casting.

2 Separate the cylinder head from the gasket, using a rawhide mallet. Strike only those portions of the casing which are adequately supported, taking special care not to damage the fins. Under no circumstances should levers be used between the mating surfaces of the cylinder head and cylinder block in an effort to facilitate separation. This action will lead to damage to the faces with subsequent risk of leakage. When lifting the cylinder head from position, the cam chain must be guided through the central tunnel and prevented from falling free. An extra pair of hands is beneficial at this stage.

3 Separate the cylinder block from the base gasket, using the technique described for the cylinder head. Once again, levers should not be used. Lift the cylinder block upwards along the holding down studs until the piston skirts are visible but the piston rings are still obscured by the cylinder bore spigots. If a top-end overhaul only is to be carried out, the crankcase mouths must be padded with clean rags to prevent pieces of broken piston ring from falling into the crankcase. The padding will also prevent the ingress of foreign matter during further dismantling or work. With the padding in place, lift the cylinder block off the pistons as squarely as possible to prevent the pistons from tying in the bore. Catch the pistons as they emerge from each bore, to prevent damage occurring.

4 Before removing the pistons, each should be marked using a metal scribe on the inside of the skirt. Number the pistons from 1 to 4, so that if they are to be re-used they may be fitted in their original locations. An arrow mark cast on each piston crown indicates the correct position in which the piston should be replaced.

5 Remove both circlips from each piston boss and discard them. Circlips should never be re-used if risk of displacement is to be obviated.

6 Using a drift of the correct diameter, tap each gudgeon pin out of the piston bosses until the piston can be lifted off the

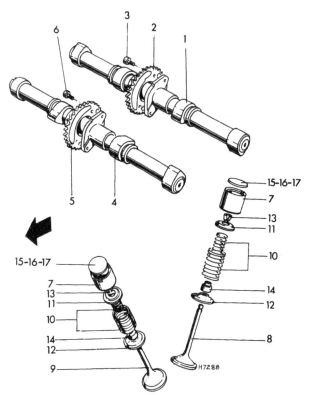

Fig. 1.3. Camshafts and valves

1 Inlet camshaft
2 Inlet cam sprocket
3 Socket bolt – 2 off
4 Exhaust camshaft
5 Exhaust cam sprocket
6 Sprocket bolt – 2 off
7 Camfollower – 8 off
8 Inlet valve – 4 off
9 Exhaust valve – 4 off
10 Valve spring set – 8 off
11 Spring collar – 8 off
12 Spring seat – 8 off
13 Collet – 16 off
14 Oil seal – 8 off
15 Adjuster pad – AR
16 Adjuster pad – AR
17 Adjuster pad – AR

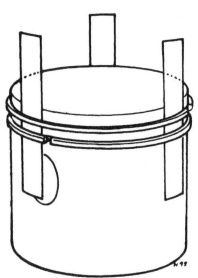

Fig. 1.4. Freeing gummed rings

8.1 Keep cylinder head square to studs when removing

8.3 Lift the cylinder block off the pistons

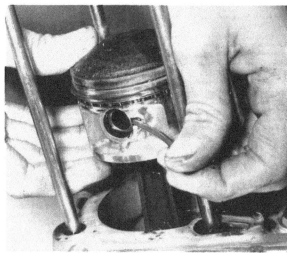

8.5 Prise out the piston circlips and ...

8.6. ... push out the gudgeon pin to free the piston

8.9 Unscrew the single bolt securing the chain tensioner blade

9 Dismantling the engine unit: removing the contact breaker and automatic timing unit (ATU)

1   Free the contact breaker wiring leads from the clips positioned on the underside of the engine and displace the grommet from the casing wall. Place a spanner on the engine turning hexagon and loosen the contact breaker cam centre bolt. Remove the bolt and also the hexagon.

2   Before removing the contact breaker main baseplate, mark the relative position of the plate to the main casing, using a centre punch. On reassembly, the marks can be realigned, simplifying the ignition timing checking and adjustment operation. Unscrew the three screws which pass through the elongated holes in the main base plate periphery. Detach the contact breaker assembly as a complete unit and remove the ignition timing index plate which is positoned behind the base plate. Lift the automatic advance unit (ATU) from position, noting the drive pin in the crankshaft end which locates with a recess in the rear of the ATU. Check the fit of the drive pin in the crankshaft, removing it if loose, to avoid accidental loss.

3   At this stage detach also the gear position indicator switch which is held by two screws. Do not lose the switch contact.

9.2a Punch mark contact breaker stator plate before ...

9.2b ... removal of complete contact breaker assembly

10 Dismantling the engine unit: removing the starter motor and intermediate gear

1   Remove the two screws which pass through the starter motor end cap flange into the crankcase. Ease the starter motor towards the right-hand side of the engine until the motor boss leaves the casing. Lift the starter motor up at the rear and out of the compartment. If the starter motor boss is tight in the casing, insert a wooden lever between the front of the motor and the casing wall. Use the lever to push the motor from place.

2   Free the alternator wiring lead from the guideway in the top of the crankcase. On removal of the alternator cover the lead must be fed through the casing wall because the leads are connected to the alternator stator. Loosen evenly and remove the alternator cover retaining screws. Lift the cover away and pull the lead through. Pass the connectors through the aperture individually.

3   Withdraw the intermediate gear spindle and lift the spindle and gear from position. Note the two shims, one of which is fitted to the spindle, either side of the gear.

10.2 Lift off alternator cover and feed wires through

10.3 Withdraw spindle and remove intermediate gear

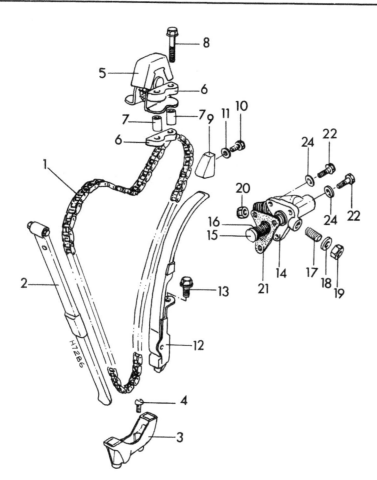

1   Cam chain
2   Cam chain guide blade
3   Cam chain guide holder
4   Screw – 2 off
5   Camshaft   idler   assembly
    (Jockey wheel)
6   Damper rubber – 4 off
7   Spacer – 4 off
8   Bolt – 2 off
9   Cam chain guide
10 Bolt – 2 off
11 Washer – 2 off
12 Cam chain tensioner blade
13 Bolt
14 Tensioner assembly
15 Plunger
16 Spring
17 Tensioner adjuster screw
18 Sealing washer
19 Nut
20 Nut
21 Gasket
22 Bolt – 2 off
23 Bolt
24 Plain washer – 3 off

Fig. 1.5. Camshaft chain tensionser – GS 750 model

11 Dismantling the engine unit: removing the alternator, rotor and starter motor clutch

1   Loosen and remove the alternator rotor centre bolt after applying a spanner to the two flats on the rotor centre boss to prevent rotation. The rotor is a very tight fit on the tapered crankshaft end and will require pulling from position. The rotor boss is threaded internally to take a slide hammer. This tool consists of a headed shaft upon which is placed a free sliding steel weight. After screwing the shaft into the centre boss the steel weight is slid forcibly along the shaft away from the rotor until it contacts the shaft head. The force imparted should release the taper. If the correct slide hammer is not readily available, an alternative tool of the same type may be constructed using the pivot shaft which supports the machine's rear swinging arm. The shaft should be pushed out, after removal of the nut, using a suitable substitute rod of approximately the correct diameter. A large socket spanner makes an ideal sliding weight, though in the absence of this an alternative must be found.
2   It may be found that the alternator rotor resists all attempts at removal. If this is the case, expert advice should be sought because the pressed up crankshaft and the rotor itself may suffer severe damage if excess force is employed. Provided that the rotor does not require attention and that the starter clutch and crankshaft oil seal are in good condition, these two components may be left on the crankshaft as their presence does not obstruct further dismantling. If work on the crankshaft and bearings is envisaged, the crankshaft will in any event require

returning to a Suzuki Service Agent who may be entrusted to remove the alternator at the same time.
3   To continue dismantling, pull the rotor off the shaft complete with the starter clutch to which it is attached. Slide the starter motor clutch gear off the shaft and remove the thrust washer.

11.1a Place spanner on alternator centre to loosen bolt

11.1b Improvised slide hammer made from swinging arm pivot and a large socket

12 Dismantling the engine unit: removing the kickstart return spring and the clutch

1 Remove the kickstart lever from the splined shaft after unscrewing fully the pinch bolt. Loosen evenly and remove the screws which secure the primary drive cover to the right-hand side of the engine. If necessary, use a rawhide mallet to release the cover from the gasket.

2 Remove the end washer and circlip (where utilised) from the kickstart shaft. Using a large pair of pliers, grasp the outer turned end of the kickstart return spring and pull it from the anchoring recess in the casing. Allow the spring to unwind in a controlled manner. Withdraw the spring guide and then free the spring by displacing the inner turned end from the radially drilled hole in the shaft. Pull the spring from position.

3 Unscrew the clutch pressure spring bolts evenly and remove them, together with the springs. Remove the clutch pressure plate and then withdraw the clutch plates one at a time, noting the alternating sequence. Pull the clutch operating thrust piece from the centre of the hollow shaft and then displace the pushrod, scroll end first. Note the thrust bearing and washer which fit on the thrust piece. These components are easily mislaid.

4 Bend down the ear of the tab washer which secures the clutch centre nut. The nut may be very tight, and in order to prevent the shaft rotating the following procedure should be adopted: Refit temporarily the final drive sprocket and the gear change lever. Select top gear and then hold the sprocket firmly by passing a suitable lever across one of the sprocket teeth so that it locates with any well supported lug on the crankcase. The lever should be held so that it will not slip or damage the casing. The nut can now be removed, followed by the tab washer.

5 Withdraw the clutch centre boss and remove the thrust washer from the shaft. The clutch outer drum revolves on a caged needle roller bearing, supported on a large central spacer. To enable the edge of the outer drum to clear the casing on removal, the spacer must be withdrawn. Use a clutch spring bolt screwed into one of the threaded holes in the spacer as a means of removal. Pull out the needle bearing and then lift the outer drum towards the rear and out of the primary drive case. The oil pump drive gear fitted to the rear of the clutch may now be removed together with the bearing, spacer and backing washer.

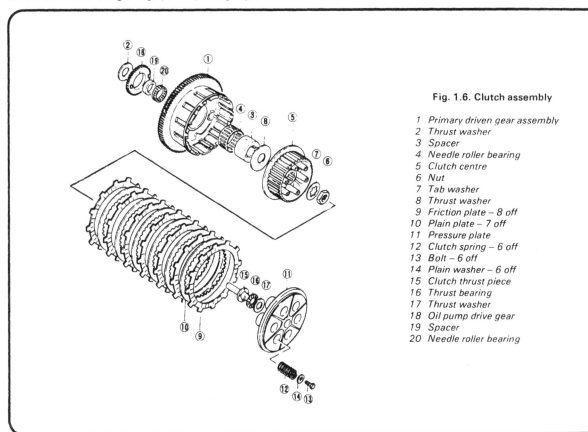

Fig. 1.6. Clutch assembly

1 Primary driven gear assembly
2 Thrust washer
3 Spacer
4 Needle roller bearing
5 Clutch centre
6 Nut
7 Tab washer
8 Thrust washer
9 Friction plate – 8 off
10 Plain plate – 7 off
11 Pressure plate
12 Clutch spring – 6 off
13 Bolt – 6 off
14 Plain washer – 6 off
15 Clutch thrust piece
16 Thrust bearing
17 Thrust washer
18 Oil pump drive gear
19 Spacer
20 Needle roller bearing

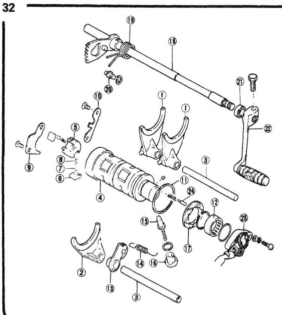

Fig. 1.7. Gearchange mechanism – GS 750 model

1 Layshaft selector fork – 2 off
2 Mainshaft selector fork
3 Selector fork rod – 2 off
4 Gearchange drum
5 Selector quadrant
6 Change pawl
7 Plunger – 2 off
8 Spring – 2 off
9 Change pawl lifter plate
10 Change drum guide
11 Thrust washer
12 Needle roller bearing
13 Stopper arm
14 Spring
15 Plunger
16 Bolt
17 Stopper plate
18 Gearchange selector arm/shaft
19 Centraliser spring
20 Selector arm stopper bolt
21 Oil seal
22 Gear lever
23 Digital display switch
24 Contact brush

12.3a Remove the clutch springs and bolts and ...

12.3b ... lift out pressure plate and clutch plates

12.3c Withdraw the clutch thrust piece

12.4 After centre nut removal pull boss off shaft

12.5a Use screw to displace bearing spacer to allow ...

12.5b ... removal of the clutch drum/primary driven gear

12.5c Oil pump drive gear, spacer and bearing

13 Dismantling the engine unit: removing the gear selector external components and oil pump

GS 750 models

1   Grasp the gearchange shaft at the quadrant end and withdraw it from the casing, complete with the centraliser spring. Detach the change drum guide plate and the pawl operating plate, both of which are retained by two countersunk screws. Pinch together the two spring loaded pawls which are fitted to the selector quadrant, and withdraw the quadrant, complete with pawls, from the end of the change drum. Store the pawls and springs safely to avoid loss. Removal of all these components can be carried out at this stage or later, after separation of the crankcase halves.

GS 550 models

2   Detach the change drum stopper arm by removing the pivot bolt which also secures the rear of the drum guide plate. Disconnect the return spring from the anchor to free the arm completely. Remove the guide plate after unscrewing the second bolt. From the left-hand end of the gearchange shaft, displace the spring clip. Pull the pawl arm downwards to clear the pins in the change drum end and pull the gearchange shaft, complete with pawl arm, from the casing.

All models

3   Remove the three screws which retain the oil pump in position and pull the oil pump from place. Note the two O rings which are fitted to the rear of the pump. Detach the mainshaft bearing retainer plate, which is retained by three countersunk screws, and on GS 750 models the layshaft lubrication end plate, which is also retained by four screws. On GS 750 models the remaining plate fitted to this casing, closes the gearshaft oilways. Removal of the plate is necessary only to aid cleaning. The countersunk screws which secure all the plates within the gear casing may be very tight. An impact screwdriver should be used to facilitate removal.

4   Detach also the retainer plate from the left-hand side of the gearbox adjacent to the final output (layshaft) shaft.

13.3 Oil pump is held to rear of casing by three screws

14 Dismantling the engine unit: removing the sump and oil strainer

1   Invert the engine so that sump is facing upwards and the crankcase lower half is resting on its rear edge and on the cylinder holding studs. Loosen evenly and remove the sump retaining screws. Lift the sump away after releasing it from the gasket, using a rawhide mallet if necessary.

2   The oil strainer is retained on the oil pick-up chamber by three screws. Remove the screws and lift the screen away.

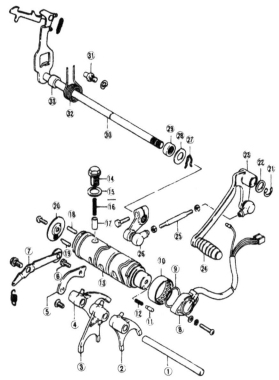

Fig. 1.8. Gear change mechanism – GS 550 model

1 Gear selector fork rod	18 Change pin – 5 off
2 Gear selector fork	19 Neutral pin
3 Gear selector fork	20 Change pin holder
4 Gear selector fork	21 Circlip
5 Drum guide plate	22 Washer
6 Bolt	23 Gearchange lever
7 Stopper arm	24 Rubber
8 Neutral and gear selector indicator switch	25 Link rod
9 O ring	26 Gearchange operating arm
10 Needle roller bearing	27 Spring clip
11 Contact brush	28 Washer
12 Spring	29 Oil seal
13 Gearchange drum	30 Gear selector shaft/arm
14 Plunger detent bolt	31 Selector arm stopper bolt
15 Sealing washer	32 Centralising spring
16 Spring	33 Spacer
17 Detent plunger	

15 Dismantling the engine unit: separating the crankcase halves

1   Slacken evenly and remove the crankcase upper half securing bolts, after moving the engine to gain access. Invert the engine again so that it is resting on the cylinder holding studs and the rear edge of the upper casing. Loosen evenly and remove the 6 mm and 8 mm securing bolts. Each 8 mm bolt is identified by a number stamped on an adjoining portion of the casing. To prevent stress in the casings, these bolts should be slackened in sequence, commencing with the highest number and continuing through to the lowest number. On GS 750 models, one of the forward mounting bolts is partially obstructed by the oil filter cover upper stud. To remove the stud, fit two 6 mm nuts to the threaded portion. Lock the nuts together and unscrew the stud.

2   On GS 550 models the engine may be left in this position so that on separation of the crankcase halves the lower half is lifted away, leaving the crankshaft, gearbox components and gear selector internal mechanism in the upper crankcase half. On GS 750 models the gear selector drum and forks are fitted to the lower casing and for this reason it is suggested that the engine be placed resting on the lower crankcase half. This will permit the upper half to be lifted away, leaving all the main components in the lower crankcase half.

3   Separation of the crankcase halves should be carried out with care, using a rawhide mallet initially, to release the two cases from the gasket compound which was used on original assembly. **DO NOT** use levers placed between the two mating surfaces in an effort to hasten separation. Treatment of this nature will almost certainly damage the machined surfaces, causing subsequent oil leakage.

4   After separation, study the internal components carefully before continuing with the dismantling operation. This will help prevent confusion when reassembly is being carried out. Note and remove the O ring which seats in a recess in the upper casing. Check the two location dowels for tightness. If loose, they should be removed, to avoid loss.

16 Dismantling the engine unit: removing the crankshaft and gear shafts

1   Grasp the crankshaft with both hands and lift it upwards, out of the casing, as a complete unit, together with the oil seals and the cam chain. If the crankshaft is firmly seated, use a rawhide mallet to free it from the casing. Note the main bearing outer race location pins in the upper crankcase half. If they are loose, remove them with a pair of pliers.

2   Lift out the two gearbox shafts individually, complete with pinions and seals. Note the positions of the bearing location half clips, which prevent axial movement, and prise them from position. The two shaft assemblies should be put to one side for further attention at a later stage.

15.1a Stud obstructs bolt removal; extract stud using locknuts (GS 750)

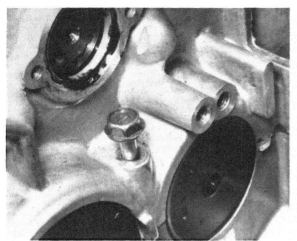

15.1b DO NOT forget to remove bolt in gearbox wall

15.2a Lift the upper casing away leaving main components

15.2b Main components in the lower casing (GS 750)

16.2a Lift out the mainshaft as a complete unit followed by ..

16.2b ... the layshaft

17 Dismantling the engine unit: removing the gear selector internal mechanism

1   Withdraw the selector fork rod(s) towards the primary drive side of the engine and displace the selector forks. The GS 550 is fitted with a single rod carrying three selector forks, and the GS 750 has two rods, of which the front carries two forks and the rear one fork.

2   On GS 750 models the cam stopper arm is contained within the gearbox casing, pivoting on the forward rod. The arm return spring is hooked over the rear rod.

3   Remove the neutral position drum detent housing bolt and displace the detent spring and plunger. The change drum can now be pulled out of the casing towards the primary drive side of the engine.

17.1a Pull out the gearchange shaft/arm assembly

17.1b Remove the drum guide plate and ...

17.1c ... plunger pawl lifter plate

17.2a Pull out fork rod to release stopper arm (GS 750) and ...

17.2b ... allow removal of selector forks

17.3 Withdraw the change drum from the casing

18 Examination and renovation: general

1 Before examining the component parts of the dismantled engine/gear unit for wear, it is essential that they should be cleaned thoroughly. Use a paraffin/petrol mix to remove all traces of oil and sludge which may have accumulated within the engine.

2 Examine the crankcase castings for cracks, or other signs of damage. If a crack is discovered, it will require professional attention, or in an extreme case, renewal of the casting.

3 Examine carefully each part to determine the extent of wear. If in doubt, check with the tolerance figures whenever they are quoted in the text. The following Sections will indicate what type of wear can be expected and in many cases, the acceptable limits.

4 Use clean, lint-free rags for cleaning and drying the various components, otherwise there is risk of small particles obstructing the internal oilways.

19 Crankshaft assembly: examination and renewal

1 The crankshaft assembly comprises four separate sets of flywheels with their respective big-ends, connecting rods and main bearings, pressed together to form a single unit.

2 Due to the complex construction of the crankshaft, exchange crankshafts are not available. In the event of multiple main bearing or big-end bearing failure a new crankshaft must be acquired. If a single item only fails, it may be possible to return a crankshaft to Suzuki through a Suzuki Service Agent, for the single item to be renewed.

3 Main bearing failure will immediately be obvious when the bearings are inspected after the old oil has been washed out. If any play is evident or if the bearings do not run freely, renewal is essential. The main bearings are of the caged roller type and as the outer races are not restrained axially they may be displaced to one side, to aid visual inspection. Warning of main bearing failure is usually given by a characteristic rumble that can be readily heard when the engine is running. Some vibration will also be felt, which is transmitted via the footrests.

4 Big-end failure is characterised by a pronounced knock that will be most noticeable when the engine is working hard. There should be no play whatsoever in any of the connecting rods, when they are pushed and pulled in a vertical direction. Check also the deflection of each connecting rod in line with the crankshaft, taking the measurement at the small end eye. Movement greater than 3 mm (0·118 inch) indicates a worn big-end bearing. Using a feeler gauge, check the axial side play at the big-ends. The total movement should be no greater than 1·00 mm (0·040 inch).

5 The oil seals at each end of the crankshaft are easy to renew when the engine is stripped; they are a push fit over each end of the crankshaft, one against and the other close to the outer main bearings. It is a wise precaution to renew these seals whenever the engine is stripped, irrespective of their condition.

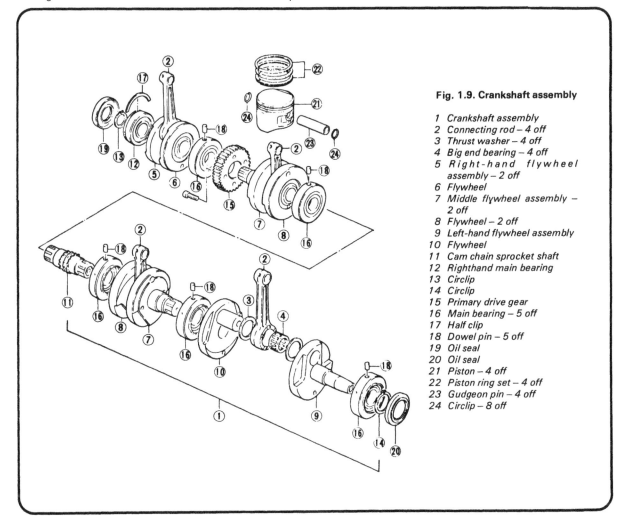

Fig. 1.9. Crankshaft assembly

1 Crankshaft assembly
2 Connecting rod – 4 off
3 Thrust washer – 4 off
4 Big end bearing – 4 off
5 Right-hand flywheel assembly – 2 off
6 Flywheel
7 Middle flywheel assembly – 2 off
8 Flywheel – 2 off
9 Left-hand flywheel assembly
10 Flywheel
11 Cam chain sprocket shaft
12 Righthand main bearing
13 Circlip
14 Circlip
15 Primary drive gear
16 Main bearing – 5 off
17 Half clip
18 Dowel pin – 5 off
19 Oil seal
20 Oil seal
21 Piston – 4 off
22 Piston ring set – 4 off
23 Gudgeon pin – 4 off
24 Circlip – 8 off

20 Connecting rods: examination and renovation

1   It is unlikely that any of the connecting rods will bend during normal usage, unless an unusual occurrence such as a dropped valve has caused the engine to lock. Carelessness when removing a tight gudgeon pin can also give rise to a similar problem. It is not advisable to straighten a bent connecting rod; renewal is the only satisfactory solution.

2   The small end eye of each connecting rod is unbushed and it will be necessary to renew the connecting rod if the gudgeon pin becomes a slack fit. Refer to the advice about crankshaft renewal given in Section 19. Check the clearance using the unworn end of a gudgeon pin, as the centre portion of a used pin will be slightly worn. The maximum clearance should not exceed 0·09 mm (0·0035 in). Always check that the oil hole in the small end eye is not blocked since if the oil supply is cut off, the bearing surfaces will wear very rapidly.

21 Cylinder block: examination and renovation

1   The usual indication of badly worn cylinder bores and pistons is excessive smoking from the exhausts and piston slap, a metallic rattle that occurs when there is little or no load on the engine. If the top of the bore of the cylinder block is examined carefully, it will be found that there is a ridge on the thrust side, the depth of which will vary according to the rate of wear that has taken place. This marks the limit of travel of the uppermost piston ring.

2   Measure the bore diameter just below the ridge. Take two measurements, at 90° to one another. Take two similar measurements half way down the bore and at a position just above the lower edge of the bore. If any measurement exceeds the maximum allowable, the cylinder should be rebored and fitted with an oversize piston. If the difference between the maximum and minimum measurement exceeds 0·085 mm (0·0035 in) a rebore is also required.

3   If an internal micrometer is not available, the amount of cylinder bore wear can be measured by inserting the piston without rings so that it is approximately $\frac{3}{4}$ inch from the top of the bore. If it is possible to insert a 0·060 mm (0·0024 in) feeler gauge between the piston and the cylinder wall on the thrust side of the piston, remedial action must be taken.

4   Oversize pistons are available in two sizes; + 0·5 mm (0·020 inch) and + 1·0 mm (0·040 in).

5   Check that the surface of the cylinder bores is free from score marks or other damage that may have resulted from an earlier engine seizure or a displaced gudgeon pin. A rebore will be necessary to remove any deep scores, irrespective of the amount of bore wear that has taken place, otherwise a compression leak will occur.

6   Make sure the external cooling fins of the cylinder block are not clogged with oil or road dirt, which will prevent the free flow of air and cause the engine to overheat.

22 Pistons and piston rings: examination and renovation

1   Attention to the pistons and piston rings can be overlooked if a rebore is necessary, since new components will be fitted.

2   If a rebore is not considered necessary, examine each piston closely. Reject pistons that are scored or badly discoloured as the result of exhaust gases by-passing the rings.

3   Remove all carbon from the piston crowns, using a blunt scraper, which will not damage the surface of the piston. Clean away all carbon deposits from the valve cutaways and finish off with metal polish so that a clean, shining surface is achieved. Carbon will not adhere so readily to a polished surface. Using an external micrometer or vernier gauge, measure the external diameter of each piston across the thrust faces (at 90° to the gudgeon pin line), at the bottom of the skirt. Take a second measurement approximately 15 mm (0·590 in) up from the lower edge of the skirt. If either measurement is less than that given for the service limit, the piston is in need of renewal.

4   Check that the gudgeon pin bosses are not worn or the circlip grooves damaged. Check that the piston ring grooves are not enlarged. Side float should not exceed 0·18 mm (0·007 in) for the top ring and second ring, and 0·15 mm (0·006 in) for the oil control ring.

5   Piston ring wear can be measured by inserting the rings in the bore from the top, pushing them down with the base of the piston so that they are square in the bore and about $1\frac{1}{2}$ inches down. If the end gap exceeds 0·6 mm (0·024 in) on any of the rings, renewal is necessary. A replacement set of rings is comparatively inexpensive and it is considered good practice to renew them as a matter of course whenever the engine is dismantled.

6   Check that there is no build up of carbon on the inside surface of the rings or in the grooves of the pistons. Any build-up should be removed by careful scraping.

7   The piston crowns will show whether the engine has been rebored on some previous occasion. All oversize pistons have the rebore size stamped on the crown. This information is essential when ordering replacement piston rings.

8   If new piston rings are fitted but a rebore has not taken place, the cylinder bores should be 'glaze busted'. This honing operation, as the name suggests, removes the highly polished glazed surface of the bore which has been caused by the countless up and down strokes of the piston and rings. If 'glaze busting' is not carried out, the time required to run-in the new rings will be greatly extended.

23 Examination and renovation: cylinder head and valves

1   Remove the cam followers and adjuster shims from the cylinder head, marking each follower so that it may be refitted in its original location. It is best to remove all carbon deposits from the combustion chambers before removing the valves for inspection and grinding-in. Use a blunt end chisel or scraper so that the surfaces are not damaged. Finish off with a metal polish to achieve a smooth, shining surface. If a mirror finish is required, a high speed felt mop and polishing soap may be used. A chuck attached to a flexible drive will facilitate the polishing operation.

2   A valve spring compression tool must be used to compress each set of valve springs in turn, thereby allowing the split collets to be removed from the valve cap and the valve springs and caps to be freed. Keep each set of parts separate and mark each valve so that it can be replaced in the correct combustion chamber. There is no danger of inadvertently replacing an inlet valve in an exhaust position, or vice-versa, as the valve heads are of different sizes. The normal method of marking valves for later identification is by centre punching them on the valve head. This method is not recommended on valves, or any other highly stressed components, as it will produce high stress points and may lead to early failure. Tie-on labels, suitably inscribed, are ideal for the purpose. After removing each valve the valve stem oil seal should be displaced and discarded. Some difficulty may be encountered when removing a seal from the top of the guide because the shoulder on the seal is a close fit in the locating groove in the guide. Use a stout pair of long-nose pliers and wriggle the seal from place. **Warning**: when removing seals take great care not to apply excessive side load to the guides. Each guide is located longitudinally by a circlip, and the thickness of the guide wall at the circlip groove is minimal. The guides are **very** easily sheared.

3   Before giving the valve and valve seats further attention, check the clearance between each valve stem and the guide in which it operates. Clearances are as follows:

Standard	*Service Limit*
Inlet valve/guide clearance	
0.02 - 0.05 mm	*0.09 mm*

(0.0008 - 0.0020 in)   *(0.0035 in)*
Exhaust valve/guide clearance
0.03 - 0.06 mm   *0.10 mm*
(0.0012 - 0.0024 in)   *(0.0039 in)*

Measure the valve stem at the point of greatest wear and then measure again at right-angles to the first measurement. If the valve stem is below the service limit it must be renewed.

Standard	*Service Limit*
Inlet valve stem	
6.965 - 6.980 mm	*6.90 mm*
(0.2742 - 0.2748 in)	*(0.2717 in)*
Exhaust valve stem	
6.955 - 6.970 mm	*6.805 mm*
(0.2738 - 0.2744 in)	*(0.2679 in)*

The valve stem/guide clearance can be measured with the use of a dial guage and a new valve. Place the new valve into the guide and measure the amount of shake with the dial guage tip resting against the top of the stem. If the amount of wear is greater than the wear limit, the guide must be renewed.

4   Removal of the old valve guides and refitting new items should not be attempted except by a Suzuki Service Agent. The guides are a high interference fit in the cylinder head, and require special, close fitting, pilots and drifts for successful removal and installation. In addition the bores in the cylinder head require reaming before new guides are fitted. Should valve guide renewal be necessary, return the cylinder head to a qualified agent.

5   Valve grinding is a simple task. Commence by smearing a trace of fine valve grinding compound (carborundum paste) on the valve seat and apply a suction tool to the head of the valve. Oil the valve stem and insert the valve in the guide so that the two surfaces to be ground in make contact with one another. With a semi-rotary motion, grind in the valve head to the seat, using a backward and forward action. Lift the valve occasionally so that the grinding compound is distributed evenly. Repeat the application until an unbroken ring of light grey matt finish is obtained on both valve and seat. This denotes the grinding operation is now complete. Before passing to the next valve, make sure that all traces of the valve grinding compound have been removed from both the valve and its seat and that none has entered the valve guide. If this precaution is not observed, rapid wear will take place due to the highly abrasive nature of the carborundum base.

6   If, after grinding, it is found that the width of the grey seating ring is greater than 1·5 mm (0·06 in) the valve seat must be recut using a special cutting tool. It will be seen from the accompanying illustration that angles of 75° and 15° must be cut in order to reduce the valve seat width, followed by a 45° cut in order to restore the correct seat angle and the correct

seat width to within the range 1·0 – 1·2 mm (0·04 – 0·05 in). Because of the expense of purchasing the three seat cutters and because of the accuracy with which cutting must be carried out, it is strongly recommended that the cylinder head be returned to a Suzuki Service Agent for attention.

It follows that when material is removed from the valve seat, the valve stem will protrude further from the upper side side of the cylinder head. In extreme cases it may be found that on adjustment of the cam clearances, the prescribed clearance cannot be arrived at even with the thinnest adjustment shim available. If this is found to be the case, removal of a small amount of metal from the valve stem end is permissible. Grinding should be carried out on a suitable machine so that the stem end remains square with the shank. Where grinding to attain the correct clearance reduces the distance between the top of the stem and the upper edge of the collet groove to less than 4·00 mm (0·1574 in) a new valve seat insert must be fitted. This operation is highly skilled requiring the use of very specialised equipment.

7   Where deep pitting of the seat and valve is encountered, the seat should be recut as previously described. The valve face may be ground back on a special grinding machine to an angle of 45°, provided that after grinding, the depth of the valve periphery has not been reduced to less than 0·5 mm (0·0197 in).

8   Examine the condition of the valve collets and the groove on the valve stem in which they seat. If there is any sign of damage, new parts should be fitted. Check that the valve spring collar is not cracked. If the collets work loose or the collar splits whilst the engine is running, a valve could drop into the cylinder and cause extensive damage.

9   Check the free length of each of the valve springs. The springs have reached their serviceable limit when they have compressed to the limit readings given in the Specifications Section of this Chapter.

10   Reassemble the valve and valve springs by reversing the dismantling procedure. Ensure that all the springs are fitted with the close coils downwards towards the cylinder head. Fit new oil seals to each valve guide and oil both the valve stem and valve guide, prior to reassembly. Take special care to ensure the valve guide oil seal is not damaged when the valve is inserted. As a final check after assembly, give the end of each valve stem a light tap with a hammer, to make sure the split collets have located correctly.

11   Check the cylinder head for straightness, especially if it has shown a tendency to leak oil at the cylinder head joint. If there is any evidence of warpage, provided it is not too great, the cylinder head must be either machined flat or a new head fitted. Most cases of cylinder head warpage can be traced to unequal tensioning of the cylinder head nuts and bolts by tightening them in incorrect sequence.

Fig. 1.10. Valve seat cutting angle profile.

23.10a Fit a new oil seal to the valve guide

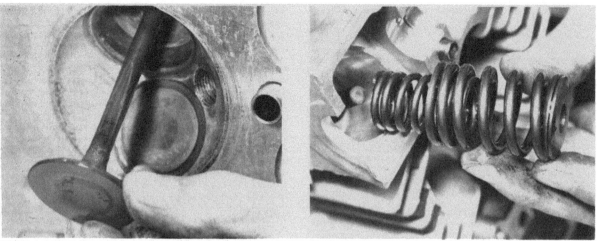

23.10b Lubricate the valve stem thoroughly before insertion

23.10c Replace the spring seat, springs and collar

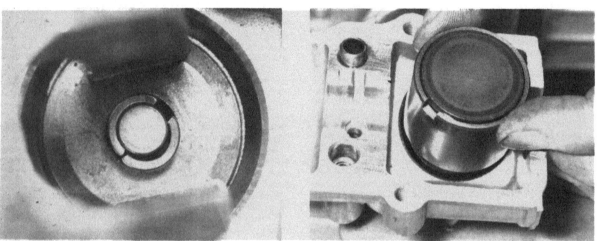

23.10d Compress the springs and refit the split collets

23.10e Cam followers must be inserted SQUARELY

24 Examination and renovation: camshafts, cam followers and camshaft drive sprockets

1   Inspect the cams for signs of wear such as scored lobes, scuffing, or indentation. The cams should have a smooth surface. The complete camshaft must be replaced if any lobes are worn or indented, through lubrication failure etc. In due course even normal wear of each cam lobe may progress to the stage where full valve lift is no longer possible. Measure each cam from the lobe to the base circle, comparing the overall height with these figures.

Minimum cam height
GS 750:
    Inlet   36.15 mm (1.4232 in)
    Exhaust   35.60 mm (1.4016 in)
GS 550:
    Inlet   35.19 mm (1.3854 in)
    Exhaust   34.99 mm (1.3776 in)

If any one cam on either camshaft is below the minimum figure, that camshaft should be renewed in order to restore performance.

2   Refit both camshafts in the cylinder head and fit the bearing caps and bolts. Tighten the bolts to a torque wrench setting of 0·8 – 1·2 kg m (6 – 8 ft lb). Check the clearance between the camshaft journals and the bearing surfaces. This is most easily accomplished by fitting a dial gauge to the cylinder head and moving the camshaft in a vertical or horizontal plane. If the clearances exceed those figures given in the specifications, remove the camshafts, refit the bearing caps and check the diameter of each bearing, to determine whether the camshaft or cam bearing is at fault.
3   If it is found that the camshaft bearings are worn or badly scored, the cylinder head and bearing caps must be renewed. There is no provision for renewing the bearings as the camshafts run directly in the cylinder head material.
4   Examine the camshaft chain sprockets for hooked, worn, or broken teeth. If any damage is found, the camshaft sprocket in question should be renewed. Each sprocket is retained on the camshaft flange by two socket screws. When refitting either sprocket note that each is marked IN or EX as are the camshafts. It is important that the sprockets are fitted on the correct camshaft and in the position shown in the accompanying illustration. Incorrect assembly will prevent accurate valve timing. Apply a small quantity of locking fluid to the securing

screws during reassembly.

5   The camshaft drive sprocket is an integral part of the crankshaft and therefore if damage is evident, the crankshaft must be renewed. Fortunately, this drastic course of action is rarely necessary since the parts concerned are fully enclosed and well lubricated, working under ideal conditions.

6   Inspect the external surfaces of the cam followers for signs of scoring or fracture. If damage is evident, the component must be renewed. If scoring has occurred it follows that similar damage may be found in the appropriate guide tunnel in the cylinder head. Damage to the tunnels cannot be rectified under normal circumstances and therefore a new cylinder head must be obtained. Insert each cam follower into the guide tunnel from which it was removed. Only the lightest pressure should be used to insert each follower. If a follower is inserted even at a slight angle, binding against the tunnel will result. Any effort made to tap the follower in will almost certainly jam the follower solidly. Removal is then very difficult!

Check the clearance between each cam follower and guide tunnel. Unfortunately no precise figures are available but the follower should be a good sliding fit, with no perceptible play from side to side. Excess play will allow the cam follower to tilt, causing noisy operation and accelerated wear of the cylinder head.

INLET   EXHAUST

Fig. 1.11. Cam sprocket position on camshaft

25 Examination and renovation: cam chain and chain tensioner mechanism

1   Inspect the cam chain for obvious signs of damage, such as broken or missing rollers or fractured links. Some indication of the amount of chain wear may be gained by checking the extent of adjustment remaining on the automatic tensioner assembly. If the plunger has moved towards the end of the stroke, it may be assumed that the chain is near the end of its useful life. Wear of the chain can be measured by washing it in petrol, then compressing it endwise so that the free play in both runs is taken up fully. Anchor one end, then pull on the chain so that it stretches as far as possible. If the extension measured exceeds $\frac{1}{4}$ inch per foot, the chain must be renewed. Although the cam chain works in almost ideal conditions, being fully lubricated and enclosed, wear will develop after an extended mileage. If there is any doubt as to the chain's condition, it should be renewed, as breakage will cause extensive engine damage.

2   Loosen the locking screw on the chain tensioner body to free the plunger pushrod. Rotate the adjuster knob anticlockwise so that the plunger may be pushed in fully, and check that the plunger moves in and out freely, without any tendency to bind. If plunger movement is not perfectly smooth, the complete unit should be renewed.

3   Inspect the surfaces of the two chain guide blades, and on GS 550 models the bridge guide. If the rubber has been badly scored by the chain or is coming away from the steel backing, the blade in question should be renewed.

4   On GS 750 models a jockey sprocket is fitted between the two camshafts. Clean the sprocket and carrier assembly thoroughly in petrol and check that the sprocket rotates freely. Inspect the sprocket teeth using criteria for renewal as given for the camshaft sprockets.

26 Examination and renovation: tachometer drive assembly

1   The worm drive to the tachometer is an integral part of the exhaust camshaft which meshes with a pinion attached to the cylinder head cover (GS 550) or cylinder head (GS 750). If the worm is damaged or badly worn, it will be necessary to renew the camshaft complete.

2   The driveshaft and pinion are a single part retained in a bush housing which is secured by a claw and screw. Renewal is therefore straightforward. It is unlikely that wear will develop on either the drive or driven pinion as both are well lubricated and lightly loaded.

27 Examination and renovation: gearbox components

1   It should not be necessary to dismantle either of the gear clusters unless damage has occurred to any of the pinions or if the caged needle roller bearings require attention.

2   The accompanying illustration shows how both clusters of the gearbox are assembled on their respective shafts. It is imperative that the gear clusters, including the thrust washers, are assembled in EXACTLY the correct sequence, otherwise constant gear selection problems will occur.

In order to eliminate the risk of misplacement, make rough sketches as the clusters are dismantled. Also strip and rebuild as soon as possible to reduce any confusion which might occur at a later date.

3   When dismantling the gear shafts, the journal ball bearings may be pulled from position, using a standard two or three-legged sprocket puller. On GS 750 models the layshaft right-hand bearing should be removed by placing the puller on the 1st gear pinion and drawing the two components off simultaneously. On both five-speed and six-speed gearboxes, a special locking washer is fitted to the layshaft between two adjacent gear pinions. The washer is placed between the 3rd gear and 5th gear pinions on GS 750 models and the 3rd gear and 4th gear pinions on GS 550 models. To free the washer, and release the next washer in the sequence, it must be turned slightly so that the internal serrations clear the shaft splines. The washer may then be pulled from place. Similarly, on reassembly, the washer should be turned so that it engages correctly.

3   The 2nd gear pinion on the GS 750 mainshaft is an interference fit and will require pulling from position. On refitting this pinion, it is essential that it is so placed that the distance between its outer face and that of the 1st gear pinion is 109·4 – 109·5 mm (4·307 – 4·311 in). This measurement is critical for correct rotational clearance and perfect alignment. Before refitting the pinion, treat the inner box with a high shear strength locking compound. Suzuki recommend the use of Thread Lock Super 103K.

After refitting the 2nd gear pinion, check that the 5th gear pinion is free to rotate and has not become locked by migrating locking fluid.

4   Give the gearbox components a close visual inspection for signs of wear or damage such as broken or chipped teeth, worn dogs, damaged or worn splines and bent selectors. Replace any parts found unserviceable because they cannot be reclaimed in a satisfactory manner.

5   The gearbox bearings must be free from play and show no signs of roughness when they are rotated. After thorough washing in petrol the bearings should be examined for roughness and play. Also check for pitting on the roller tracks.

6   It is advisable to renew the gearbox oil seals irrespective of their condition. Should a re-used oil seal fail at a later date, a considerable amount of work is involved to gain access to renew it.

7   Check the gear selector rods for straightness by rolling them on a sheet of plate glass. A bent rod will cause difficulty in selecting gears and will make the gear change particularly heavy.

8   The selector forks should be examined closely, to ensure that they are not bent or badly worn. The pegs which engage with the cam channels are integral with the forks therefore if they are worn the forks must be renewed. Under normal conditions, the gear selector mechanism is unlikely to wear quickly, unless the gearbox oil level has been allowed to become low.

9   The tracks in the selector drum, with which the selector forks engage, should not show any undue signs of wear unless neglect has led to under lubrication of the gearbox. Check the tension of the gearchange pawl (GS 550 model only), gearchange arm and drum stopper arm springs. Weakness in

the springs will lead to imprecise gear selection. Check the condition of the gear stopper arm roller and, on GS 550 models, the pins in the change drum end with which it engages. It is unlikely that wear will take place here except after considerable mileage.

10   Check the condition of the kickstart components. If slipping has been encountered a worn ratchet and pawl will invariably be traced as the cause. Any other damage or wear to the components will be self-evident. If either the ratchet or pawl is found to be faulty, both components must be replaced as a pair. Examine the kickstart return spring, which should be renewed if there is any doubt about its condition.

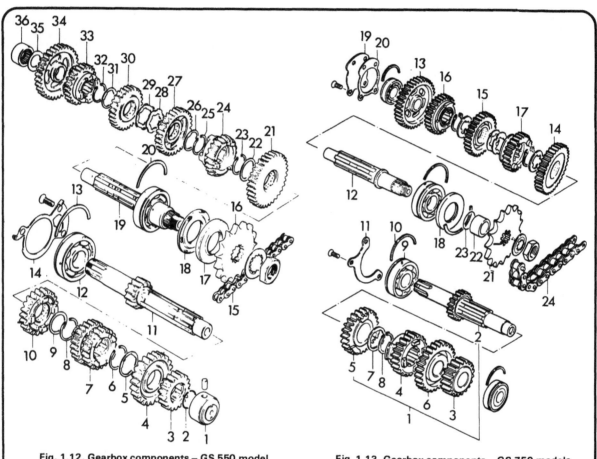

Fig. 1.12. Gearbox components – GS 550 model

1 Needle roller bearing	19 Layshaft
2 Circlip	20 Half clip
3 Mainshaft – 2nd gear pinion	21 Layshaft – 2nd gear pinion
4 Mainshaft – 6th gear pinion	22 Thrust washer
5 Splined thrust washer	23 Circlip
6 Circlip	24 Layshaft – 6th gear pinion
7 Mainshaft – 3rd gear pinion	25 Circlip
8 Circlip	26 Thrust washer
9 Thrust washer	27 Layshaft – 3rd gear pinion
10 Mainshaft – 5th gear pinion	28 Thrust washer
11 Mainshaft	29 Lockwasher
12 Journal ball bearing	30 Layshaft – 4th gear pinion
13 Half clip	31 Thrust washer
14 Bearing retainer plate	32 Circlip
15 Final drive chain	33 Layshaft – 5th gear pinion
16 Final drive sprocket	34 Layshaft – 1st gear pinion
17 Oil seal	35 Washer
18 Oil seal	36 Needle roller bearing

Fig. 1.13. Gearbox components – GS 750 models

1 Mainshaft assembly	13 Layshaft – 1st gear pinion
2 Mainshaft	14 Layshaft – 2nd gear pinion
3 Mainshaft – 2nd gear pinion	15 Layshaft – 3rd gear pinion
4 Mainshaft – 3rd gear pinion	16 Layshaft – 4th gear pinion
5 Mainshaft – 4th gear pinion	17 Layshaft – 5th gear pinion
6 Mainshaft – 5th gear pinion	18 Oil seal
7 Splined thrust washer	19 Blanking plate
8 Circlip	20 Gasket
9 Journal ball bearing	21 Final drive sprocket
10 Half clip	22 Sprocket spacer
11 Bearing retainer	23 O ring
12 Layshaft	24 Final drive chain

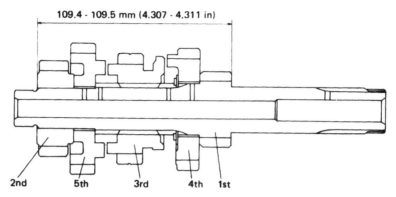

109.4 - 109.5 mm (4.307 - 4.311 in)

2nd 5th 3rd 4th 1st

Fig. 1.14. Installation distance when refitting 2nd gear mainshaft pinon – GS 750 models

28 Examination and renovation: clutch assembly

1 After an extended period of use the clutch linings will wear and promote clutch slip. The clutch plates should be measured with a vernier gauge or pair of calipers to ascertain the extent of wear. The measurement of the thickness for the inserted (friction) plates and the maximum wear limits are as follows:

Inserted plate width 2.9 – 3.1 mm (0.114 – 0.122 in)
Wear limit 2.7 mm (0.106 in)

If the plate width is less than the specified minimum, then the plate must be renewed.
2 The plain clutch plates should not show any evidence of overheating (blueing). If they do, check them for overall flatness by placing each plate on a flat surface. In the event of the plates being warped by more than 0.3 mm (0.012 in) they should be renewed.
3 Check the free length of each clutch spring. If the springs have shortened (set) to a length less than the specified minimum, they must be renewed, preferably as a set.

	GS 750	GS 550
Clutch spring length	40.4 mm	37.7 - 39.1 mm
	(1.59 in)	(1.48 - 1.54 in)
Wear limit	39.0 mm	37.0 mm
	(1.54 in)	(1.46 in)

4 Check the condition of the clutch centre spacer and the external caged needle roller bearing. If wear is evident in these components, they should be renewed. The bearing and spacer upon which the oil pump drive gear (fitted behind the clutch) is mounted should be checked similarly.
5 Check the condition of the slots in the outer surface of the clutch centre and the inner surfaces of the outer drum. In an extreme case, clutch chatter may have caused the tongues of the inserted plates to make indentations in the slots of the outer drum, or the tongues of the plain plates to indent the slots of the clutch centre. These indentations will trap the clutch plates as they are freed and impair clutch action. If the damage is only slight the indentations can be removed by careful work with a file and the burrs removed from the tongues of the clutch plates in similar fashion. More extensive damage will necessitate renewal of the parts concerned.
6 Check the clutch release thrust bearing in the pressure plate. If play is evident or the bearing rotates roughly, it should be renewed.
7 The clutch release mechanism in the clutch cover does not normally require attention, provided that it is greased from time to time. If the unit fails, it should be renewed as a complete assembly.

29 Crankcase covers: examination and renovation

1 The right-hand and left-hand crankcase covers and the inspection covers are unlikely to become damaged unless the machine is dropped or involved in an accident. Cracks in a casing can be repaired easily by special aluminium welding, providing the damage is not too extensive and care is taken to prevent distortion.
2 The covers are lightly polished and lacquered before leaving the factory. Badly scratched covers can be refurbished using a single cut file treated with chalk to prevent clogging, and finished off with fine emery paper and metal polish or aluminium cleaner. If required, the cases can be relacquered, using an aerosol paint spray.

30 Engine reassembly: general

1 Before reassembly of the engine/gear unit is commenced, the various component parts should be cleaned thoroughly and placed on a sheet of clean paper, close to the working area.
2 Make sure that all traces of old gaskets have been removed and that the mating surfaces are clean and undamaged. One of the best ways to remove old gasket cement is to apply a rag soaked in methylated spirit. This acts as a solvent and will ensure that the cement is removed without resort to scraping and the consequent risk of damage.
   If a gasket becomes bonded to the surface through the effects of heat and age, a new sharp scalpel blade should be used to effect removal. Old gasket compound can also be removed using a soft brass wire brush of the type used for cleaning suede shoes. A considerable amount of scrubbing can take place without fear of damaging the mating surfaces.
3 Gather together all the necessary tools and have available an oil can filled with clean engine oil. Make sure that all new gaskets and oil seals are to hand, also all replacement parts required. Nothing is more frustrating than having to stop in the middle of a reassembly sequence because a vital gasket or replacement part has been overlooked.
4 Make sure that the reassembly area is clean and that there is adequate working space. Refer to the torque and clearance settings wherever they are given. Many of the smaller bolts are easily sheared if overtightened. Always use the correct size screwdriver or bit for the crosshead screws never an ordinary screwdriver or punch. If the existing screws show evidence of maltreatment in the past, it is advisable to renew them as a complete set.

31 Engine reassembly: replacing the gear change drum and internal selector components

GS 550 models

1   Lubricate the gearchange drum needle roller bearing and then insert the change drum into the casing from the primary drive side of the upper casing. If, on examination, the change pins were found to be worn and the pins and retainer plate removed, do not refit them at this stage. The pins should be fitted in a special sequence, as described in Section 37 of this Chapter.

2   Insert the selector fork rod, locating it with each of the three selector forks as it is pushed home. The shortest of the forks is fitted in the centre of the rod, flanked on either side by the two long forks. Of the two longer forks, the one with the two strengthening webs is fitted to the right (primary drive side) of the centre fork. The guide pin on each fork must be pointing rearwards and engaged with the appropriate channel in the change drum.

3   After replacing the selector rod, fit and tighten the rod securing screw which is located in the primary drive chamber wall. Apply a locking fluid to the screw threads before installing. Invert the crankcase half and fit the change drum neutral detent plunger, spring and housing bolt. Do not omit the sealing washer fitted to the bolt. Rotate the change drum so that it is in the neutral position.

GS 750 models

4   If the change drum stopper plate was removed from the drum for inspection or renewal, it must be refitted at this stage. The plate must be positioned so that it locates correctly with the drive pin which is a push fit in the drum end boss. Secure the plate by means of the circlip. Assemble the gear selector quadrant together with the two selector pawls, the plungers and the springs. The pawls must be fitted so that the narrower edges adjacent to the plunger recesses face towards the rear of the selector quadrant. Depress the pawls against the spring pressure and insert the completed selector quadrant into the end of the change drum.

5   Lubricate the change drum needle roller bearing with engine oil, and slide the drum into place in the gearbox. Refit the neutral stopper plunger, detent spring and the bolt.

6   Slide the selector fork rods into position through the right-hand gearbox wall and refit the selector forks. The two rearmost selector forks, which share the same rod, are identical. Check that the forks are positioned the correct way round. Slide the change drum stopper arm onto the front selector rod. With the components correctly in place push both rods fully home and reconnect the stopper arm spring with the rear selector fork rod.

7   Coat the four countersunk screws which retain the change drum retainer plate, and the pawl plate, with locking fluid, and replace the two plates. Rotate the change drum until it is in the neutral position and the neutral stopper locates.

32 Engine reassembly: replacing the gear shaft assemblies and the kickstart shaft

1   Position the upper crankcase half so that it rests on the cylinder holding the studs and the rear of the casing. Before refitting, the gearshafts must be assembled as completed sub-assemblies, including the gear pinions bearings and oil seals. The oil seal lips should be lubricated before being installed to prevent damage. On GS 550 models note that the layshaft is fitted with two oil seals placed side by side. The inner seal which abuts against the drive side bearing must be positioned with the castellated projections facing outwards. The outer seal should be placed with the concave side facing inwards.

2   Install the bearing securing half clips in the casing grooves and lower the gear shafts into place, either individually or as a meshed pair. Three of the four bearings are fitted with a single

location pin each. Arrange each bearing so that the pin rests in the notch provided in the casing wall. The mainshaft needle roller bearing fitted to GS 550 models is located by a peg which is a push fit in the outer race and in the bearing housing.

3   On GS 750 models, replace the end plate and clutch pushrod oil seal at the blind end of the mainshaft. The end plate should be positioned with the raised dome against the bearing outer races so that there is a gap between the plate and bearing. The oil seal on the layshaft output end is supported by a crescent shaped plate, which locates with a groove in the upper casing.

4   If the kickstart shaft was dismantled for inspection, it must be reassembled before fitting into the crankcase. Refit the components into the kickstart shaft in the order shown in the accompanying illustration. Note that the ratchet pawl has a punch mark on the outer face which must be aligned with a similar mark on the shaft splines.

On GS 750 models ensure that the bearing locating dowels are fitted into the crankcase, and place the complete starter assembly into position. After assembly, the kickstart shaft unit on GS 550 models must be inserted through the gearbox wall in the crankcase lower casing. Once the kickstart shaft is in place, fit the pawl plate and the two countersunk screws. The screw threads must be treated with a locking fluid before insertion. Replace the circlip in the shaft groove adjacent to the shaft flanged bush.

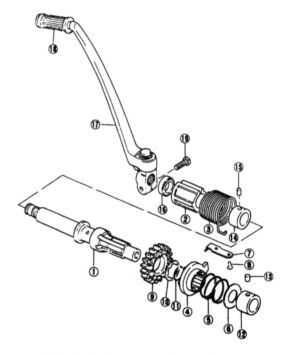

Fig. 1.15. Kickstart mechanism – GS 750 model

1 Kickstart shaft	11 Circlip
3 Spring guide	12 Bush
3 Kickstart return spring	13 Dowel pin
4 Starter pawl	14 Bush
5 Spring	15 Dowel pin
6 Thrust washer	16 Oil seal
7 Starter pawl guide	17 Kickstart lever
8 Screw – 2 off	18 Rubber
9 Kickstart drive pinion	19 Pinch bolt
10 Thrust washer	

31.4a Fit the stopper plate so that it locates with pin and ...

31.4b ... secure the plate by means of the circlip

31.4c Selector quadrant: component parts

31.4d Pawl must be fitted as shown

31.5a Insert the change drum into the casing and fit ...

31.5b ... the neutral detent plunger and ...

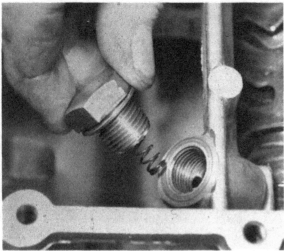

31.5c ... detent housing and spring

31.6a Fit the rear selector rod and two selectors

31.6b Install forward selector rod to secure the fork and arm

31.6c Stopper and spring anchors on the rear selector rod

31.7 Apply locking fluid to the four countersunk screws

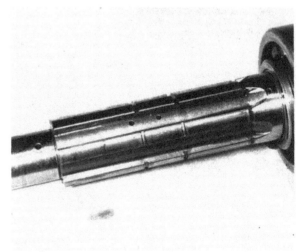

32.1a Ensure oil ways in gearshaft are free before reassembly

32.1b Locking plate and washer fitted to layshaft

32.1c Gear assemblies: general view (GS 750)

32.2a Install layshaft followed by the ...

32.2b ... completed mainshaft after ...

32.2c ... fitting the bearing locating half clips

32.2d Arrange bearing so that pin locates in recess

32.3 Fit oil seal and plate as shown (GS 750)

32.4a Align punch marks on kickstart shaft and pawl

32.4b Kickstart shaft assembly: general view (GS 750)

32.4c Install assembled kickstart shaft to engage with ...

32.4d ... the two dowel pins in the casing (GS 750)

33 Engine reassembly: replacing the crankshaft

1   Lubricate the main bearings thoroughly and also the crankshaft ends onto which are to be fitted the oil seals. The crankshaft right-hand seal should be fitted so that the cupped side is
facing outwards, with the projections facing inwards in contact
with the bearing. The left-hand seal is fitted with the spring
garter side facing inwards.
2   Insert the five main bearing locating pegs into the holes
provided in the casing. The right-hand main bearing is located
by a half clip in a manner similar to that of the gearbox ball
bearings. In addition a small dowel is fitted, which on installation of the crankshaft must be positioned in the recess adjacent
to the bearing housing.
3   Fit the cam drive chain over the crankshaft so that it
meshes with the drive sprocket. Grasp the crankshaft at both
ends and lower the completed assembly into position. Ensure
that the main bearing outer races engage correctly with the
locating dowels. A tiny punch mark is provided on each main
bearing outer race, diametrically opposed to the centre of the
dowel hole. Lining up all five marks in a perfectly straight line
will aid correct location of the bearings. It should be noted

however that on the machine featured in this manual, one punch mark had been made inaccurately. Even when the crankshaft was correctly positioned the dots did not align. A rawhide mallet may be used judiciously to seat each bearing firmly in its bearing housing. This should, of course, only be attempted after ensuring correct location of the pegs and the half clip.

34 Engine reassembly: joining the crankcase halves

1   Carefully clean the crankcase halves mating surfaces. Replace the two hollow locating dowels, tapping them into position carefully so as not to distort them. If the dowels have become slightly burred they should be cleaned up with a small file.

2   Smear the upper crankcase half mating face with a thin layer of jointing compound. Suzuki recommend that Suzuki Bond No. 4 be used to make the joint. A good quality non-hardening compound will make a suitable substitute. Fit the small O ring into the recess to the front of the mainshaft assembly.

3   Let the gasket compound set for at least 10 mins and then lower the upper casing down into place. No difficulty should be encountered in fitting the upper case but special care should be taken on GS 750 models that the three selector forks locate with their respective guide ways in the sliding pinions. To aid this operation, ensure that the change drum is in the neutral position and arrange the gears so that they too are in neutral. When the lower casing is lowered into position, the selector forks fall naturally into a vertical position and so engage easily with the pinions.

4   Fit the crankcase retaining bolts to the lower crankcase. Tighten the 8 mm bolts evenly a little at a time, following the numerical sequence stamped on the bolts, commencing with No. 1. Tighten the remaining bolts and then invert the crankcase and fit the upper bolts. All crankcase bolts should be tightened to the torque settings specified:

Crankcase bolts

8 mm	*2.0 kg m (14.5 ft lbs)*
6 mm	*1.0 kg m (7.2 ft lbs)*

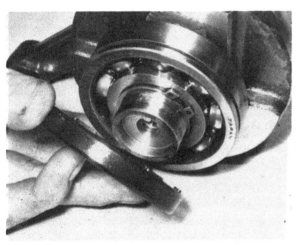

33.1 RH oil seal is fitted with castellated projections inwards

33.2a Install the five main bearing pegs and the ...

33.2b ... right-hand main bearing half clip

33.2c Pegs must locate with recesses on crankshaft installation

33.2d Fit the cam chain to the drive sprocket

33.3a Installed components: general view (GS 750)

33.3b .Dot on main bearing races aids alignment of peg holes

33.3c RH main bearing is located by pin lying in recess

34.2 DO NOT OMIT 'O' ring in crankcase

34.3a Lower crankcase lower half into position

34.3b Selector forks should self-align (GS 750)

34.4 Ensure layshaft oil seal crescent plate is correctly fitted (GS 750)

35 Engine reassembly: replacing the oil strainer screen, sump and oil filter

1   Place the oil strainer screen in position on the underside of the pick-up chamber and fit the retaining screws. A little locking fluid may be used on the screws, to ensure that they cannot become loose.
2   Fit a new sump gasket followed by the sump and retaining bolts. No gasket cement is required at this joint. Tighten the screws evenly, to avoid distortion. Fit and tighten the oil drain plug.
3   On GS 750 models, the oil filter chamber cover stud, which was unscrewed to allow removal of the adjacent crankcase bolt, must now be replaced. Use the same technique for refitting as was adopted for removal.
4   Place a new gasket over the oil filter chamber studs and insert the oil filter element with the O ring end facing inwards. Position the coil spring against the filter and then replace the cover. Fit and tighten the three domed retaining nuts.

36 Engine reassembly: replacing the gear selector external components

1   Refit the mainshaft bearing retainer plate in the primary chain case, and in addition, on GS 750 models, the layshaft blind end plate and the lubrication passage end plate. Apply locking fluid to the thread of all these screws, to ensure security.

GS 750 models
2   Grease the gear change shaft oil seal on the left-hand side of the gearbox. Insert the change shaft, complete with the main change arm, into position, taking care that the splines on the shaft end do not damage the oil seal. Mesh the teeth on the change arm with the teeth on the change drum, as shown in the accompanying photograph. The change arm centraliser spring must be fitted on the arm as shown. When in position the spring arms must lie either side of the anchor peg in the casing.

GS 550 models
3   Position the change drum guide plate in the casing and insert and screw in lightly the rearmost retaining bolt. Grease the splined end of the gearchange arm so that when it passes through the oil seal in the left-hand wall of the gearbox, the sealing lip will not be damaged. Insert the gearchange shaft,

complete with the pawl arm and return spring, into the primary drive chamber. Push the assembly fully home, simultaneously pulling back the pawl arm so that it clears the end of the change drum and engages with the change pins. If the change pins and retaining plate were removed for pin renewal, the replacement pins can now be fitted, using the correct positioning procedure.
4   Install the change drum stopper arm. The pivot bolt is of the shouldered type and serves also as the change drum guide plate front securing bolt. Tighten both bolts and check that the stopper arm is free to move and has not been trapped by the bolt shoulder. Reconnect the arm return spring with the anchor lug on the bearing retainer plate. Of the six change pins, one is of differing dimensions, having a relieved portion at one end. It is against this recess that the stopper arm roller abuts when the gearbox is in the neutral position. Check that the gearbox is still in the neutral position and then insert the neutral pin in the change drum pin hole nearest to the stopper arm roller. Push the roller hard up against the recess so that the two components self-align. Insert the five remaining pins in the holes provided. Position the pin retainer plate on the end of the change drum so that the punched depression engages with the neutral pin. Fit and tighten the central screw.
5   Fit the washer and spring clip to the left-hand end of the gearchange shaft, to secure if firmly in place.

37 Engine reassembly: replacing the oil pump and oil pump drive gear

1   The oil pump must be re-installed in the primary drive casing as a complete unit, either before or after the driven gear is fitted. The driven gear is retained by a circlip on the shaft end, and is located by a drive pin which passes through the shaft, engaging with a recess in the rear face of the pinion.
2   Place a new O ring in each of the casing recesses against the wall of which the pump is secured. Omission of the O rings will lead to lubrication failure. Position the oil pump and fit and tighten the three mounting screws.
3   The oil pump drive gear assembly can now be replaced. Fit the heavy backing washer onto the clutch shaft, followed by the drive gear bearing spacer and needle roller bearing. Lubricate the bearing thoroughly and then refit the drive pinion. The pinion must be fitted with the two projecting dogs facing outwards, as it is these that locate with the rear of the clutch drum and so provide the driving medium.

35.1 Apply locking fluid to oil strainer screws

35.2 Fit new gasket and sump

35.4 Refit filter cover stud after tightening bolts (GS 750)

36.1 Oil passage plate must be fitted with a gasket

36.2a Gear change arm centraliser spring must be fitted as shown

36.2b Install change arm to mesh with quadrant

37.1a Fit the two 'O' rings into the casing before ...

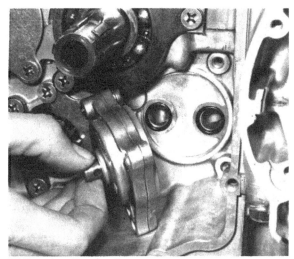

37.1b ... installing the oil pump

37.1c Oil pump gear is located by a drive pin and ...

37.1d ... secured by a small circlip

37.3a Fit oil pump drive pinion and bearing

37.3b On installation, pump gear must locate with drum recesses

38 Engine reassembly: replacing the clutch

1   Place the clutch outer drum over the clutch shaft (mainshaft) and into the casing. Centralise the drum and after lubrication, fit the spacer and needle bearing. The spacer should be fitted with the radially grooved face inwards. When fitting the outer drum, it is essential that the two projecting dogs on the oil pump drive gear engage with two recesses in the drum rear face. Insert a narrow shanked screwdriver through one of the two holes in the clutch spacer so that the drive pinion is prevented from rotating. Turn the clutch outer drum until it can be felt that the pinion and drum have engaged correctly.

2   Install the heavy thrust washer on the clutch shaft, with the milled channel facing inwards, and then refit the clutch centre boss onto the clutch shaft splines. Fit the tab washer and then fit and tighten the centre nut. Use the same procedure for tightening the nut as was used for loosening. Place the machine in top gear and temporarily refit the final drive sprocket onto the output shaft. Take care on GS 750 models that the gearchange shaft is not pushed towards the right-hand side of the engine or the main change arm will come out of engagement with the selector quadrant. Due to the obstructed view of the meshed components by the clutch drum, remeshing in the correct position can be difficult. After tightening the nut, do not omit to bend up the tab washer to secure the nut in place.

3   Replace the clutch plates one at a time, commencing with a friction (inserted) plate followed by a plain plate and so on, alternately. Grease the clutch operating pushrod and insert it into the hollow clutch shaft. The scrolled end can be placed only on the right-hand side of the engine. Lubricate the clutch thrust piece and fit it, together with the thrust bearing and shim. Refit the clutch pressure plate and the clutch springs, washers and bolts. Tighten the bolts fully.

39 Engine reassembly: replacing the kickstart return spring and refitting the primary drive cover

1   Place the kickstart return spring over the kickstart shaft, with the outer turned end facing towards the gearbox wall. Insert the inner turned end of the spring in the axial drilling in the shaft. Rotate the shaft clockwise as far as possible so that it comes up against the stop. Using a stout pair of pliers, grasp the outer end of the spring and tension the spring in a clockwise direction until the turned end can be located in the anchor recess in the casing. With the spring tensioned correctly, insert the spring guide. On GS 550 models the guide should be placed with the large diameter inwards.

2   Where utilised, fit the guide retaining circlip (GS 550 models) and also the thrust washer (some GS 750 models) to the shaft.

3   The primary drive cover can now be replaced. Lubricate the primary drive gears with engine oil and then fit a new gasket to the mating surface. Push the cover into position on the two hollow locating dowels and then fit the screws. The screws should be tightened evenly, in a diagonal sequence, to help prevent distortion.

40 Engine reassembly: replacing the starter motor clutch and intermediate gear and alternator

1   Place the starter clutch pinion bearing thrust washer onto the left-hand end of the crankshaft so that the face with the chamfered inner radius is towards the main bearing. Lubricate the double needle roller bearings and fit them, together with the clutch pinion.

2   Before fitting the combined alternator rotor/starter clutch unit, clean thoroughly the external taper on the crankshaft end and the internal taper in the alternator rotor. Position the rotor/clutch assembly on the shaft, turning it anti-clockwise so that the three clutch rollers slide easily onto the pinion boss. Insert and tighten the rotor centre bolt. The correct torque wrench setting is 6.0 - 7.0 kg m (43.0 – 50.6 lb ft).

3   Place the intermediate double gear on its stub shaft and fit one thrust washer either side of the gear. Position the assembly in the casing with the larger gear to the rear of the starter clutch pinion, and push the stub shaft fully home into the casing recess.

4   Fit a new gasket to the crankcase surface and place the alternator cover close to the engine so that the alternator leads may be threaded through the wall of the starter clutch chamber into the starter motor compartment. Pull the wires through whilst fitting the outer cover. Fit and tighten evenly the casing holding screws.

38.1a Lubricate and refit clutch bearing and spacer

38.1b Use pointed tool to engage oil pump drive dogs

38.2a Heavy washer must be fitted, plain face outwards

38.2b Fit clutch boss, lockwasher and centre nut

38.3a Replace plain and friction clutch plates, alternately, one at a time

38.3b Lubricate and insert the clutch pushrod and ...

38.3c ... the thrust piece, thrust bearing and washer

38.3d Replace the clutch pressure plate and ...

38.3e ... fit the clutch springs, washers and bolts

39.1a Tension the kickstart spring in a clockwise direction

39.1b Insert the spring guide

39.2 Fit thrust washer if utilised

40.2a Turn rotor anti-clockwise to clear roller faces

40.2b Fit and tighten the centre bolt

40.3 Fit thrust washer each side of intermediate gear

40.4 Feed alternator wires through the casing

41 Engine reassembly: replacing the neutral indicator switch

1   Before refitting the switch, replace the oil seal retainer plate which is fitted to the outside of the gearbox left-hand wall. On GS 750 models the tongue projecting from the plate must be fitted pointing upwards, as it serves as a routing clip for the neutral indicator switch lead.

2   Position the O ring in the switch recess and insert the contact spring in the hole in the change drum end. Replace the neutral indicator body and tighten down the two retaining bolts. The wire outlet must be positioned upwards on GS 550 models and downwards on GS 750 models. Route the wire through the guide channel provided and additionally, on GS 750 models, restrain the wire by means of the oil seal plate tongue.

42 Engine reassembly: replacing the ATU and contact breaker assembly

1   Position the ATU against the end of the crankshaft so that

the drive pin projecting from the shaft end engages with the recess in the rear of the unit. Fit the timing index pointer plate into the casing so that scribed mark is at the 12 o'clock position, and then install the complete contact breaker assembly stator plate. The stator plate should be fitted so that the wiring lead grommet can locate with the rebated hole in the casing wall.

2   If, on dismantling, a punch mark was made on the stator plate aligning with a similar mark on the casing, these marks should be realigned and the three retaining screws fitted. It is probable that the ignition timing will be correct but a check must be made as a precautionary measure. Where no alignment marks were made, ignition timing should be set as a matter of course, as described in Chapter 3, Section 7.

3   Before checking or setting the ignition timing, replace the ATU centre bolt and the hexagonal engine turning piece. To tighten the bolt, pass a close fitting bar through one small-end eye, bearing down on two wooden blocks placed across the crankcase mouth. Do not fit the contact breaker cover before fitting and timing the valves.

41.1 Replace the oil seal plate with the tongue upwards (GS750)

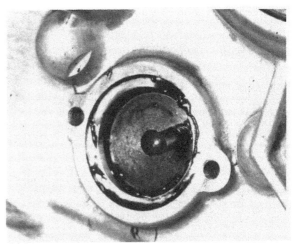

41.2a Fit the contact brush and spring

41.2b Do not omit the 'O' ring

42.1a Install ATU so that recess locates with drive pin

42.1b Fit index plate in position shown

42.3 Use bar through small end eye when tightening centre bolt

43 Engine reassembly: replacing the pistons and the cylinder block

1   Fit the piston rings to each piston, commencing with the three-piece oil control ring. The first of the three parts to be fitted should be the corrugated spacer band. Where the N type spacer is used, ensure that the band ends are not allowed to overlap when the spacer is in place in the ring groove. Fit the oil control ring side rails one at a time. When fitting the two compression rings, ensure that both are fitted with the T or N mark facing upwards. The two letter marks indicate the manufacturer of the ring. Do not mix rings of different makes in the same engine. The two compression rings are of differing type and cross-section. The upper ring has a chrome plated face which is slightly curved. The 2nd ring is not chrome plated and has a tapered face. Before replacing the pistons, pad the mouths of the crankcase with rag in order to prevent any displaced component from accidentally dropping into the crankcase.

2   Fit the pistons in their original order with the arrow on the piston crown pointing toward the front of the engine.
3   If the gudgeon pins are a tight fit, first warm the pistons to expand the metal. Oil the gudgeon pins and small end bearing surfaces, also the piston bosses, before fitting the pistons.
4   Always use new circlips **never** the originals. Always check that the circlips are located properly in their grooves in the piston boss. A displaced circlip will cause severe damage to the cylinder bore, and possibly an engine seizure.
5   Replace the chain tensioner rear guide blade, ensuring that the lower end locates correctly with the guide seat retained in the crankcase. Fit and tighten the single securing bolt. Install the two sealing rings in the recesses surrounding the outer rear cylinder studs and then fit a new cylinder base gasket over the studs. Check that the two hollow locating dowels are fitted to the outer front holding down studs. A new O ring should be placed on each of the four cylinder bore spigots. Push the O rings fully home, so that they seat correctly in the grooves provided.

6   Arrange the piston ring gaps as shown in the accompanying diagram, in order to maintain the best sealing characteristics. Using clean engine oil, lubricate thoroughly the cylinder bores. Lift the cylinder block up onto the studs and support it there whilst the camshaft chain is threaded through the tunnel between the bores. This task is best achieved by using a piece of stiff wire to hook the chain through, and pull up through the tunnel. The chain must engage with the crankshaft drive sprocket.

7   The cylinder bores have a generous lead in for the pistons at the bottom, and although it is an advantage on a large engine such as this to use the special Suzuki ring compressor, in the absence of this, it is possible to gently lead the pistons into the bores, working across from one side. Great care has to be taken NOT to put too much pressure on the fitted piston rings. When the pistons have finally engaged, remove the rag padding from the crankcase mouths and lower the cylinder block still further until it seats firmly on the base gasket.

8   Take care to anchor the camshaft chain throughout this operation to save the chain dropping down into the crankcase.

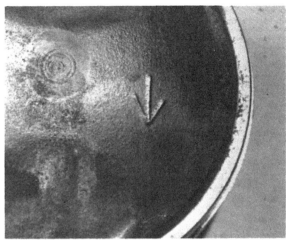

43.2 Piston must be fitted with arrow mark facing forward

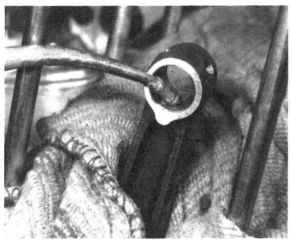

43.3 Lubricate the small end eye before ...

43.4a ... pushing in gudgeon pin to secure piston

43.4b Ensure that circlips are correctly fitted in groove

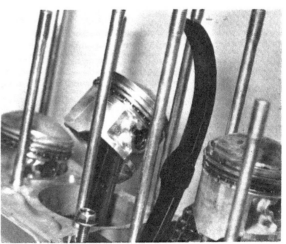

43.5a Refit the chain tensioner blade

43.5b Fit new 'O' rings to base of each cylinder and ...

43.5c install new base gasket and oil way seals

43.6 Guide cylinder block over cam chain

43.7 Fit pistons two at a time

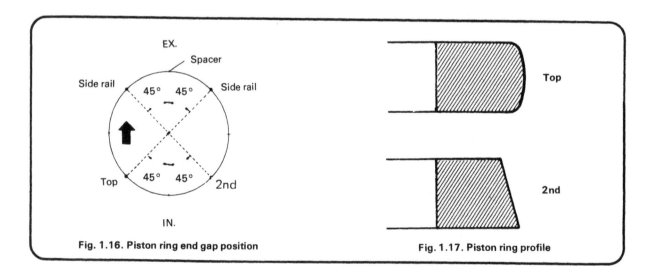

Fig. 1.16. Piston ring end gap position

Fig. 1.17. Piston ring profile

44 Engine reassembly: replacing the cylinder head

1   Place a new cylinder head gasket in position on the holding down studs. The gasket is marked TOP and should be fitted accordingly. Replace the cam tunnel rectangular seal.

2   Slide the cylinder head down the studs into position whilst guiding the cam chain through the tunnel. Secure the chain once again. Fit the cylinder head holding nuts, washers and bolts. It should be noted that the four outer studs are fitted with copper washers, to prevent oil seepage from the stud holes which serve also as oilways.

Tighten the cylinder head nuts evenly, in the sequence shown in the accompanying illustration, to the following setting.

GS 750   3.5 - 4.0 kg m (25.3 - 29.0 lb ft)
GS 550   2.3 - 2.7 kg m (14.5 - 16.6 lb ft)

Finally, tighten the two 6 mm bolts to 0.7 - 1.1 kg m (5.0 - 8.0 lb ft).

3   Insert the cam chain tensioner forward blade into the cylinder head central tunnel so that the lower end engages in the recess in the guide seat and the upper end locates with the recesses each side of the tunnel. Make a special check that the lower end of the blade is restrained; if it is allowed to float in operation the cam chain may become damaged.

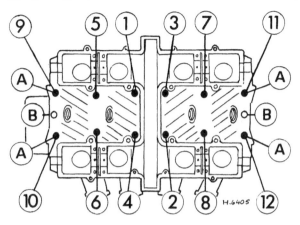

Fig. 1.18. Cylinder head nut torque sequence

A = *Domed nuts fitted with copper washers*
B = *Two 6 mm bolts.*

44.1a Replace cam chain tunnel seal and ...

44.1b ... fit cylinder head gasket according to mark

44.2a Guide cam chain as head is lowered into place

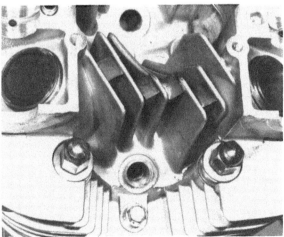

44.2b Ensure copper washer is fitted below each domed nut

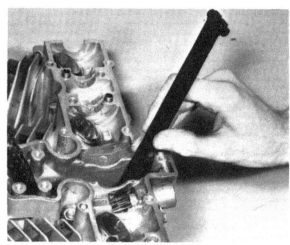

44.3 Insert forward chain guide carefully

45 Engine reassembly: replacing the camshafts and timing the valves

1   Lubricate thoroughly and insert the cam followers into their original guide tunnels in the cylinder head. Provided the followers are fitted squarely, very little pressure should be required to insert them in the tunnels. Do not attempt to tap (even lightly) a follower into place as it will probably jam solidly. Removal is then very difficult. Fit also the original adjuster shims.

2   Because the cam chain is endless, the camshaft replacement and valve timing operations must be made simultaneously. Fit a spanner to the engine turning hexagon and rotate the engine forwards until the T mark to the left of the

F1—4 mark on the ATU is in **exact** alignment with the index mark on the static plate. In this position Nos. 1 and 4 cylinders are at TDC. Whilst turning the engine, the cam chain will have to be hand fed so that it does not become snagged or bunched up.

3   Select the exhaust camshaft (marked EX) and feed it through the cam chain. Pull the forward run of the chain taut and mesh the cam sprocket to the chain so that when the camshaft is lying across the bearing housings, the 2 marked arrow is pointing vertically. Insert the inlet camshaft through the cam chain in a similar way. To mesh the sprocket in the correct place, count the chain roller pins from the exhaust camshaft to the inlet camshaft. Start with the pin directly above the 2 marked arrow on the exhaust sprocket and count to the 20th pin along the chain. Mesh the 3 marked arrow on the inlet sprocket with the 20th pin. Provided that the crankshaft has not moved during this procedure, the valve timing is now correct.

4   The two bearing caps holding each camshaft can now be refitted. Note that each cap is marked A, B, C or D and each should be fitted to the bearing housing similarly marked. The caps should be placed so that the letters are not inverted relative to one another. The same problem is now encountered as was found on dismantling, in that the upward pressure of the valve springs is preventing immediate seating of the camshafts.

The system of clamping the camshaft down, using a self-grip wrench or G-clamp, may be adopted. Alternatively the bearing caps and bolts may be fitted and tightened down evenly and diagonally a small amount at a time. The latter procedure should be used only if great care is exercised and neither the camshaft nor the caps are allowed to tilt.

Whichever procedure is chosen, the final tightening torque for the bearing cap bolts is 0.8 - 1.2 kg m (5.6 – 8.6 lb ft). After tightening the cap bolts, re-check the valve timing.

5   Fit the cam chain tensioner jockey sprocket (GS 750 models) or the bridge guide (GS 550 models). On GS 750 models ensure that the sprocket is fitted in its original position and tighten the holding bolts to 0.6 - 0.8 kg m (4.3 - 5.8 lb ft). The performance of the rubber damper blocks upon which is mounted the sprocket depends upon the bolts being tightened to the correct torque.

6   Insert the tachometer driveshaft and housing into the front of the cylinder head and fit the retaining plate and bolt.

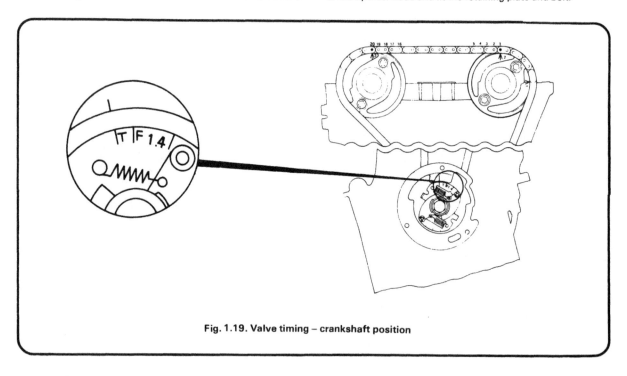

Fig. 1.19. Valve timing – crankshaft position

45.3a Each camshaft marked R (or L) to avoid confusion

45.3b Exhaust cam sprocket timing mark (2)

45.3c Inlet cam sprocket timing mark (3)

45.4 Fit cam bearing caps so that letters match

45.6a Insert tachometer drive gear and housing

45.6b Secure the housing with plate and screw

46 Engine reassembly: replacing and adjusting the cam chain tensioner

1   Hold the cam chain tensioner in one hand and whilst restraining the plunger rod, slacken the locking screw a few turns. Push the plunger inwards fully, simultaneously rotating the knurled adjuster wheel anti-clockwise. Continue turning until the plunger is fully retracted and the knurled adjuster has moved as far as possible. Tighten the lock screw to secure the pushrod.

2   Fit a new gasket to the tensioner body flange and install the completed unit to the rear of the cylinder block. Tighten the securing bolts evenly, to a torque setting of 1.0 kg m (7.2 lb ft).

3   With the tensioner fitted to the engine, unscrew the locking screw $\frac{1}{4} - \frac{1}{2}$ a turn so that the plunger is free to move forwards under tension from the spring. Without allowing further rotation of the locking screw, tighten the locknut to secure the screw.

4   The cam chain tensioner is now set for automatic adjustment in service. To check that the unit is functioning correctly, rotate the engine backwards to take up all the slack in the rear run of the chain. Whilst turning the engine backwards rotate the knurled adjuster wheel slowly anti-clockwise as far as possible. Now turn the engine in a forward direction, which will have the effect of slackening the chain on the rear run. The knurled adjuster wheel should be seen to rotate in a clockwise direction as the plunger moves out and automatically tensions the chain.

5   **WARNING.** After initial adjustment of the cam chain tensioner, the tensioner will continue to function automatically. **DO NOT** under any circumstances rotate the knurled adjuster wheel either clockwise or anticlockwise except when making this adjustment in the prescribed manner. Rotation of the wheel except at this stage will cause excessive chain tightness and will lead to tensioner damage and chain damage.

47 Engine reassembly: checking and adjusting the valve clearances

1   The clearance between each cam and cam follower must be checked and if necessary adjusted by removal of the existing adjuster pad and replacement of a pad of suitable thickness. Make the clearance check and adjustment of each valve in sequence and then go on to the next valve. As shown in the diagram in the Routine Maintenance section both operations should be carried out with the cam lobe in question placed in one of two alternative positions.

2   Using a feeler gauge, verify and record the clearance at the first valve. If the clearance is incorrect not being within the range 0.03 – 0.08 mm (0.001 – 0.003 inch), the adjuster pad must be removed and replaced by a shim of suitable thickness. A special tool is available (Suzuki part no. 09916-64510) which may be pushed between the camshaft adjacent to the cam lobe and the raised edge of the cam follower, to allow removal of the shim. If the special tool is not available, a simple substitute may be fabricated from steel plate. The final form of the tool which has a handle approximately 6 inches long is shown in the photograph accompanying the cam adjustment section in the Routine Maintenance Chapter. The Suzuki tool may be pushed into position, depressing and securing the cam follower in a depressed position in one operation. Where a home-made tool is used, the cam follower may be depressed by inserting a suitable lever between the adjuster pad and the cam lobe. The tool may then be inserted to secure the cam follower whilst the adjuster pad is removed. Before installing either type of tool, rotate the cam follower so that the slot in the follower raised edge is not obscured by the camshaft. Insert a screwdriver through the slot to displace the adjuster pad.

3   Adjustment pads are available in 20 sizes ranging from 2.15 mm to 3.10 mm, in increments of 0.05 mm. Each pad is identified by a three digit number etched on the reverse face. The number (eg. 235) indicates that the pad thickness is 2.35 mm thick. To select the correct pad subtract 0.03 mm from the measured clearance and add the resultant figure to that of the existing pad. Select the largest available pad whose thickness is slightly smaller than the final figure. Refer to the table accompany the Routine Maintenance Section for the selection of available pads.

Although the adjustment pads are available as a set, their price is prohibitive. It is suggested that pads are purchased individually, after an accurate assessment of requirements has been made. It is possible that some Suzuki Service Agents will be prepared to exchange used pads for others of the correct size, providing that the original pads are not worn.

4   Before inserting a replacement pad, lubricate both sides thoroughly with engine oil. Always fit the pads with the number downwards, so that it does not become obliterated by the action of the cam. Recheck the valve clearance after fitting the new adjuster pads.

5   After restoring the clearances on each valve refit the camshaft cover. Do not omit the semi-circular seals which are located at each end of the camshaft chambers. Replace the camshaft cover end caps.

46.2 Fit chain tensioner, using a new gasket

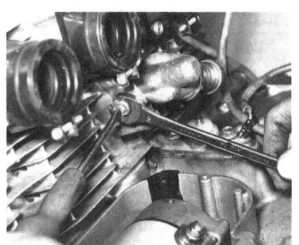

46.3 Hold adjuster screw when tightening locknut

47.5a Install the cam box end seals before ...

47.5b ... refitting the camshaft cover together with a new gasket

48 Engine reassembly: replacing the engine in the frame

1   The task of replacing the engine requires three people, two to lift the engine and one to hold the frame steady while the engine is lowered into position.
2   Lift the complete engine unit into the frame from the right-hand side and mount but do not secure the four engine mounting brackets, before inserting the engine bolts. Insert the three long bolts from the left-hand side of the machine and fit the two short central bolts and the special plate bolts. Do not force the bolts into position as this may damage the threads. Use a wooden lever between the frame and the casings, in order to lift the engine and align bolt holes. Tighten the engine mounting bracket bolts first and then the engine bolts.
3   Install the final drive sprocket to the engine with the chain already fitted to the sprocket, fit the lockwasher and tighten the locknut. Bend up the lockwasher to secure the nut.
4   Replace the starter motor in the compartment and fit and tighten the screws. Reconnect the starter motor lead with the terminal on the motor body. Remake the connections from the alternator, contact breaker, neutral indicator switch and oil pressure warning lamp leads. Ensure that the leads are routed correctly and secured as necessary. Ensure that the colour coding of the wires is followed exactly. Reconnect the main earth lead to the crankcase bolt.
5   Replace the final drive sprocket cover together with the two rubber spacer fillets (GS 750). Reconnect the clutch cable and adjust the cable and lifting mechanism as follows: Loosen the locknut on the adjuster screw and rotate the screw inwards until it can be felt to abut against the end of the pushrod. To gain the necessary running clearance unscrew the screw by $\frac{1}{4} - \frac{1}{2}$ a turn and then tighten the locknut. The cable should be adjusted so that there is 4mm ($\frac{1}{16}$ in) play measured between the stock and lever, before the clutch commences lifting.
6   Replace the breather cover on the cam box cover together with a new gasket, and then reconnect the HT leads with the spark plugs. Each HT cable is marked by a numbered sleeve, to aid correct positioning.
7   Position the air filter box to the rear of the engine and then lift the carburettor into place from the right-hand side. Ensure that the screw clips are fitted to the induction stubs and air hoses before installing the carburettors. Fit the air filter box

mounting bolts and then tighten the screw clips fully.
    Refit the two throttle cables to the wheel type control lever (one cable opens the throttles, and one cable closes them), making sure that the opening cable is fitted to the rear, and the closing cable is fitted to the front of the operating wheel.
8   Install the connecting hose between the breather cover and the airfilter box. Secure the hose by means of the spring clips. The carburettor drain hoses should be gathered together and retained by a strap to the engine right-hand upper rear mounting bracket. Allow the trailing ends of the hoses to pass between the swinging arm member and the rear of the engine. The air vent pipes from carburettors No. 2 and No. 4 should be passed through the clamp attached to the battery box (GS 750) or air filter box (GS 550).
9   Refit the exhaust pipes and also the silencers if they too were removed. Each pipe is identified by a letter 'L', 'R' or 'C' marked on the tail end of the pipe. Replace the kickstart lever and the gear change lever or link arm. Check that both controls are in the correct operating positions before tightening the pinch bolts.
10 Replace the rider's footrests, tightening the securing bolts fully.
11 Lower the petrol tank into place and refit the rear retaining bolt and rubber seat. Connect the petrol pipe and the vacuum tube to the petrol tap unions. Secure the petrol pipe by means of the spring clip.
12 Check that the crankcase drain plug has been secured, and then refill the engine with the correct amount of engine oil. The level can be checked through the sight window in the clutch cover which should be between the two marks. Replenish, using the specified quantity of SAE 20W/50 engine oil.

Oil capacity

GS 750	3.8 lit (4.0 US qt/6.7 Imp pint)
GS 550	2.7 lit (2.9 US qt/4.8 Imp pint)

Allow the engine to run for approximately 3 minutes after the initial start-up and then recheck the oil level. Ensure that the machine is standing vertically when checking the level because any angle of lean has a marked effect on the indicated level.
13 Replace the battery and remake the connections. Give the terminals a coat of petroleum jelly to inhibit corrosion. Fit the frame side covers.

48.3a Mesh sprocket with chain and fit on shaft

48.3b After tightening centre nut bend up tab washer

48.4a Insert the starter motor, securing it with the ...

48.4b ... two screws passing through the end flange

48.5a Do not omit rubber fillet when fitting sprocket cover (GS 750)

48.5b Insert the clutch cable through the top of the cover

48.5c Adjust the lifting mechanism free play before ...

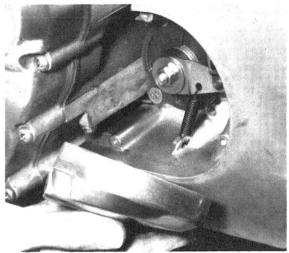

48.5d ... replacing the mechanism inspection cover

48.6a Check oil separator mesh is installed before ...

48.6b ... replacing the breather cover onto the cylinder head

48.8 Carburettor air vent pipes are secured by clip

48.9a Fit a new gasket ring to each exhaust port

48.9b Tighten the flange bolts and then ...

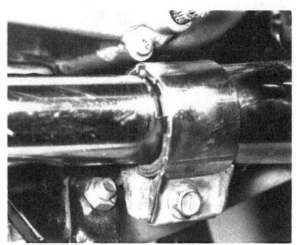

48.9c ... tighten the pipe/silencer joint clamps

49 Starting and running the rebuilt engine

1   Open the petrol tap, close the carburettor chokes and start the engine, using either the kickstarter or the electric starter. Raise the chokes as soon as the engine will run evenly and keep it running at a low speed for a few minutes to allow oil pressure to build up and the oil to circulate. If the red oil pressure indicator lamp is not extinguished, stop the engine immediately and investigate the lack of oil pressure.

2   The engine may tend to smoke through the exhausts initially, due to the amount of oil used when assembling the various components. The excess of oil should gradually burn away as the engine settles down.
   Check the exterior of the machine for oil leaks or blowing gaskets. Make sure that each gear engages correctly and that all the controls function effectively, particularly the brakes. This is an essential last check before taking the machine on the road.

50 Taking the rebuilt machine on the road

1   Any rebuilt machine will need time to settle down, even if parts have been replaced in their original order. For this reason it is advisable to treat the machine gently for the first few miles to ensure oil has circulated throughout the lubrication system and that any new parts fitted have begun to bed down.

2   Even greater care is necessary if the engine has been rebored or if a new crankshaft has been fitted. In the case of a rebore, the engine will have to be run-in again, as if the machine were new. This means greater use of the gearbox and a restraining hand on the throttle unit until at least 500 miles have been covered. There is no point in keeping to any set speed limit; the main requirement is to keep a light loading on the engine and to gradually work up performance until the 500 mile mark is reached. These recommendations can be lessened to an extent when only a new crankshaft is fitted. Experience is the best guide since it is easy to tell when an engine is running freely.

3   If at any time a lubrication failure is suspected, stop the engine immediately, and investigate the cause. If an engine is run without oil, even for a short period, irreparable engine damage is inevitable.

51 Fault diagnosis: Engine

Symptom	Cause	Remedy
Engine will not start	Defective spark plugs	Remove the plugs and lay on the cylinder head. Check whether spark occurs when ignition is on and engine rotated.
	Dirty or closed contact breaker points	Check the condition of the points and whether the points gap is correct.
	Faulty or disconnected condenser	Check whether the points arc when separated. Renew the condenser if there is evidence of arcing.

Engine runs unevenly	Ignition or fuel system fault	Check each system independently, as though engine will not start.
	Blowing cylinder head gasket	Leak should be evident from oil leakage where gas escapes.
	Incorrect ignition timing	Check accuracy and reset if necessary.
Lack of power	Fault in fuel system or incorrect ignition timing	Check fuel lines or float chambers for sediment. Reset ignition timing.
Heavy oil consumption	Cylinder block in need of rebore	Check bore wear, rebore and fit oversize pistons if required.

52 Fault diagnosis: clutch

Symptom	Cause	Remedy
Engine speed increases as shown by tachometer but machine does not respond	Clutch slip	Check clutch adjustment for free play, at handlebar lever, check thickness of inserted plates.
Difficulty in engaging gears, gear changes jerky and machine creeps forward when clutch is withdrawn, difficulty in selecting neutral	Clutch drag	Check clutch for too much free-play. Check plates for burrs on tongues or drum for indentations. Dress with file if damage not too great.
Clutch operation stiff	Damaged, trapped or frayed control cable	Check cable and replace if necessary. Make sure cable is lubricated and has no sharp bends.

53 Fault diagnosis: gearbox

Symptom	Cause	Remedy
Difficulty in engaging gears	Selector forks bent Gear clusters not assembled correctly	Replace with new forks. Check gear cluster for arrangement and position of thrust washers.
Machine jumps out of gear	Worn dogs on the ends of gear pinions	Renew worn pinions.
Gear change lever does not return to original position	Broken return spring	Renew spring.
Kickstart does not return when engine is turned over or started	Broken or wrongly tensioned return spring	Renew spring or retension.
Kickstart slips	Ratchet assembly worn	Dismantle engine and replace all worn parts.

Chapter 2 Fuel system and lubrication

For additional information relating to 1978 and 1979 GS750 models and 1978 through 1982 GS550 models, refer to Chapter 7.

Contents

Specifications

Fuel tank capacity

	GS 750	GS 550
Overall	18 lit (4.8/4.0 US/Imp gall)	17 lit (4.5/3.7 US/Imp gall)
Reserve	2.0 lit (4.2/3.6 US/Imp pints) After frame No. 20901 4.1 lit (8.6/7.2 US/Imp pints)	2.0 lit (4.2/3.6 US/Imp pints)

*Carburettors

	GS 750				GS 550
Engine No.	up to 11787	11788 to 19375	19376 to 20656	20657 on	
Make	Mikuni	Mikuni	Mikuni	Mikuni	Mikuni
Type	VM26SS	VM26SS	VM26SS	VM26SS	VM22SS
Main jet	105	97.5	100	100	80
Air jet	1.1	0.7	0.7	0.7	1.4
Needle jet	P–1	0–6	0–6	0–6	0–6
Jet needle	5F21–3	5F21–3	5F21–3	5F21–3	5DL35–3
Pilot jet	22.5	27.5	15	15	15
2nd pilot jet	NA	NA	NA	NA	50
Throttle valve cutaway	2.5	1.5	1.5	1.5	1.5
Pilot air jet	1.6	1.6	1.6	1.6	NA
Mixture screw setting	$1\frac{1}{4}$ turns out	$1\frac{3}{4}$	$1\frac{3}{4}$	1	2 turns out

Engine/transmission oil

	GS 750	GS 550
Capacity:		
At oil change	3.4 lit (3.6 US qt/6.0 Imp pt)	2.4 lit (2.5 US qt/4.2 Imp pt)
At oil and filter change	3.6 lit (3.8 US qt/6.3 Imp pt)	2.6 lit (2.8 US qt/4.6 Imp pt)
At engine rebuild (dry)	3.8 lit (4.0 US qt/6.7 Imp pt)	2.7 lit (2.9 US qt/4.8 Imp pt)
Specification	20W/50 engine oil	20W/50 engine oil

Oil pump

Oil pressure	0.1 kg cm^2 (1.42 psi)
Inner/outer rotor clearance	0.2 mm (0.008 in)
Outer rotor/housing clearance	0.25 mm (0.010 in)
Side clearance	0.15 mm (0.006 in)

*GS 750 specifications are dependent on engine No.

1 General description

The fuel system comprises a petrol tank from which petrol is fed by gravity to the float chamber of each of the four carburettors. A single petrol tap with a detachable gauze filter is located beneath the petrol tank, on the left-hand side. It contains provision for a reserve quantity of petrol, when the main supply is exhausted.

In both the ON and RES positions, fuel can only flow to the carburettors when the engine is running. This is due to the tap diaphragm which is controlled by the induction pressure. If there is no fuel in the float chambers, as may be the case after carburettor dismantling, the petrol tap should be turned to the PRIMING position, to allow an unrestricted flow of petrol to the float chambers. Return the tap to the ON position as soon as the engine is running.

Four Mikuni throttle slide carburettors are fitted, the GS 550 cc machines having VM22SS models and the larger machines VM26SS models. The carburettors are mounted as a unit on a cast aluminium alloy bracket. They are controlled by a push-pull cable arrangement secured to a cross-rod, which passes through the top of each carburettor, connecting each throttle valve by a bell-crank arrangement.

For cold starting, a hand-operated choke lever attached to the far left-hand carburettor is linked to the three other carburettors, so that the mixture can be enriched temporarily. When the engine has started, the choke can be opened gradually as the engine warms up, until full air is accepted under normal running conditions.

Lubrication is effected by the wet sump principle in which the reservoir of oil is contained within engine sump. This oil is shared by the engine, primary drive and transmission components. The oil pump is of the Eaton trochoid type and is driven from a pinion engaged with and to the rear of the clutch.

Oil is supplied under pressure, via a full flow oil filter with a replaceable element to the crankshaft and to the overhead camshaft and rocker gear. A secondary flow passes to the gearbox via the gearbox main bearings. All surplus oil drains to the sump and is returned to the oil tank by the scavenge section of the oil pump. The pump itself is protected by a gauze strainer in the base of the oil pick-up chamber.

2 Petrol tank: removal and replacement

1   The petrol tank is retained by two guide channels which locate with a circular rubber block on each side of the steering head and a bolt passing through a lug at the rear of the tank and into the frame.
2   To remove the tank, leave the petrol tap lever at the ON or RESERVE position and detach the diaphragm vacuum pipe and the larger bore petrol feed pipe. The latter pipe is secured at the union by a spring clip, the ears of which should be pinched together to release the tension on the pipe. Remove the bolt from the rear of the tank, after raising the dual seat to gain access.
3   Lift the tank up at the rear and then ease the unit backwards until the location cups leave the rubber blocks. At this stage the tank is obstructed by the location cups coming in contact with the ignition coils bolted to the frame. Lift the tank upwards off the machine.
4   Drainage of petrol is not strictly necessary when removing the tank, although the reduction in weight will facilitate the operation. A full tank will weigh approximately 50 lbs.
5   Replace the petrol tank by reversing the removal procedure. Take care not to trap control cables or stray wires between the tank and frame tubes. If the cups are a tight fit on the rubber blocks, apply a small amount of washing-up detergent to the blocks to ease refitting.

3 Petrol tap: removal and replacement

1   Removal of the complete petrol tap is required at regular intervals to gain access to the filter columns for cleaning. The tank should be drained of petrol by fitting a length of tubing to the petrol tap outlet and turning the lever to the Priming position.
2   The petrol tap is held to the underside of the petrol tank by two crosshead screws with washers. Note that there is an O ring seal between the petrol tap body and the petrol tank, which must be renewed if it is damaged or if petrol leakage has occurred. The filter screens which are integral with the plastic level pipes should be cleaned of any deposits using a soft brush and clean petrol. Because there is only a single tap to feed four carburettors, any restriction in petrol flow may lead to fuel starvation, causing missing and in extreme cases overheating, due to a weak mixture.
3   It is seldom necessary to remove the lever which operates the petrol tap, although occasions may occur when a leakage develops at the joint. Although the tank must be drained before the lever assembly can be removed, there is no need to disturb the body of the tap.
4   To dismantle the lever assembly, remove the two crosshead screws passing through the plate on which the operating positions are inscribed. The plate can then be lifted away, followed by a spring, the lever itself and the seal behind the lever. The seal will have to be renewed if leakage has occurred. Reassemble the tap in the reverse order. Gasket cement or any other sealing medium is NOT necessary to secure a petrol tight seal.

4 Carburettors: removal from the machine

1   To improve access to the carburettors it is suggested that the petrol tank is removed, as described in Section 2 of this Chapter, before dismantling proper commences.
2   Detach the engine breather hose from the unions at the air filter box and the breather cover on the cylinder head. The hose is secured at both ends by spring clips. Disconnect the throttle cables from the operating pulley at the carburettors. Both may be detached in a similar manner. Loosen the upper and lower locknuts on the cable adjuster screw and displace the adjuster and outer cable from the abutment bracket. Rotate the pulley until the inner cable nipple can be pushed out of the anchor point.
3   Loosen the screw clips which secure the air filter hoses and inlet stubs to the carburettors. Remove the air filter mounting bolts and ease the box rearwards, so that the hoses leave the carburettor mouths.
4   On GS 750 models, the air filter box should be removed from the machine towards the right-hand side, followed by removal of the carburettors as a complete unit. On GS 550 models, the carburettors must be detached without removing the air filter box, as the latter component is obstructed by the frame tubes. Before detaching the air filter box or carburettors from either model, displace the various vent and drain tubes from the securing clips.

5 Carburettors: dismantling and reassembly

1   The carburettors are mounted on a cast aluminium bracket which also serves as a support for the choke operating link rod and the cable anchor bracket. The bracket is so arranged that partial dismantling of all the carburettors is required before they can be removed from the bracket and attended to as individual items. Whenever possible, dismantle the carburettors separately, to prevent the accidental transposition of parts.
2   Remove the tops from the four carburettors. Each top is retained by three screws. Remove the bolt which passes through the forward end of each bellcrank and locates with the throttle link shaft. The throttle shaft is located longitudinally by a claw plate, secured by a single screw to a lug projecting from

the mounting bracket. Remove the claw plate and then prise out the outer blind grommets from the left-hand and right-hand carburettors. Using a pair of snipe nosed pliers, disconnect the throttle pulley return spring from the two anchor pegs. The shaft can now be pushed out of position to free the bell cranks and the pulley wheel. Note that the pulley cannot be removed completely until the carburettors are separated.

3   Place the carburettors rear face downwards and remove the two countersunk screws which hold each instrument to the mounting bracket. Lift the bracket away, if necessary moving the choke link rod slightly so that the operating arm forks clear the choke plungers.

4   The carburettors are now joined only by the fuel cross feed pipes, which are a push fit in the bodies. Before separating the individual units, mark each carburettor carefully so that on reassembly no confusion arises as to their correct positions.

5   Select one carburettor and continue dismantling as follows, following suit with the other three carburettors, in turn. Lift out the bell crank, link arm and throttle valve unit, taking care not to damage the throttle needle. The throttle valve and needle may be removed from the valve seat by removing the two tiny screws. Invert the valve and allow the needle and needle clip to fall out. Removal of the link arm from the bell crank requires that the throttle slide vertical position adjuster screw is unscrewed fully and hence the original adjustment will be lost. It is unlikely that the link arm and bell crank will require separation and it is therefore advised that these components are left as a sub-assembly.

6   Invert the carburettor and remove the four screws that hold the float chamber to its base. Remove the hinge pin that locates the twin float assembly in each carburettor, and lift away the float. This will expose the float needle. The needle is very small and should be put in a safe place so that it is not misplaced.

7   Make sure the float chamber gasket is in good condition. It should not be disturbed unless it shows sign of damage or has been leaking.

8   Unscrew the main jet from the jet holder, using a wide bladed screwdriver and then unscrew the holder itself. Note the O ring fitted above the holder threads. Invert the carburettor body and displace the needle jet from the central bore.

9   Unscrew the pilot jet from the boss to the side of the main jet housing. On GS 550 models, a second jet is fitted, in-line with the first. This too should be removed from the outside of the carburettor body. Unscrew the pilot air screw (mixture screw) and remove it, together with the spring. The yellow-painted fuel metering screws **MUST NOT** be disturbed because they are set at the factory to suit individual carburettors.

10   The starter plunger (choke) assembly is positioned in a tunnel to the side of the upper chamber. Unscrew the housing

cap and pull the starter plunger assembly out. This consists of the plunger rod, spring and plunger piece.

11   Check the condition of the floats. If they are damaged in any way, they should be renewed. The float needle and needle seating will wear after lengthy service and should be inspected carefully. Wear usually takes the form of a ridge or groove, which will cause the float needle to seat imperfectly. Always renew the seating and needle as a pair. An imperfection in one component will soon produce similar wear in the other.

12   After considerable service the throttle needle and the needle jet in which it slides will wear, resulting in an increase in petrol consumption. Wear is caused by the passage of petrol and the two components rubbing together. It is advisable to renew the jet periodically in conjunction with the throttle needle.

13   Before the carburettors are reassembled, using the reversed dismantling procedure, each should be cleaned out thoroughly using compressed air. Avoid using a piece of rag since there is always risk of particles of lint obstructing the internal passageways or the jet orifices. Pay particular attention to the starter jet (the long slim jet which projects into a separate bore in the float chamber) and the passage from the bottom of its bore to the float chamber. Over a period of time both will become blocked with fuel sediment with resultant poor starting. Clear the jet passages as described below (if necessary removing it from the casting) and use a proprietary carburettor cleaner to flush out any sediment.

14   Never use a piece of wire or any pointed metal object to clear a blocked jet. It is only too easy to enlarge the jet under these circumstances and increase the rate of petrol consumption. If compressed air is not available, a blast of air from a tyre pump will usually suffice.

15   Do not use excessive force when reassembling a carburettor because it is easy to shear a jet or some of the smaller screws. Furthermore, the carburettors are cast in a zinc-based alloy which itself does not have a high tensile strength. Take particular care when replacing the throttle valves to ensure the needles align with the jet seats.

16   Reassemble the carburettors by reversing the dismantling procedure. Before inserting the throttle link shaft, it should be lubricated with grease. Check the condition of the two O rings which seal each side of the fuel transfer pipes. Renew them if there is any doubt as to their efficiency. Fit and tighten the eight carburettor mounting screws before tightening fully the through bolts which secure the bell cranks to the throttle shaft. A small amount of locking fluid should be applied to the mounting screw threads before they are inserted.

17   Before replacing the carburettors on the machine and before refitting the carburettor tops, refer to the next section for details of carburettor synchronisation.

2.1 Petrol tank is retained at the rear by a single bolt

3.2 Petrol tap held to tank underside by two screws

3.3 Remove flange plate to detach tap lever

5.2a Remove bolt from each bellcrank and ...

5.2b ...detach the claw plate which secures the throttle rod

5.2c Prise out the blind end plugs and ...

5.2d ... withdraw the throttle rod

5.2e Lift the mounting bracket away to separate the carburettors

5.5a Withdraw the throttle valve unit

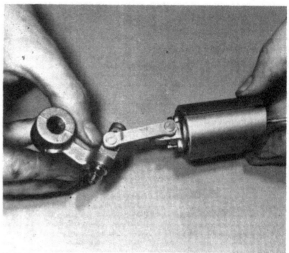

5.5b Crank link rod is secured by two tiny screws

5.5c Throttle needle is a sliding fit in the throttle valve

5.6a Float chamber bowl is held by four screws

5.6b Push out pivot pin to detach float assembly

5.6 Do not lose the minute float needle

5.6d The valve seat may be unscrewed for renewal

5.8 The main jet and holder

5.10 Choke plunger rarely gives trouble

5.16 Check condition of fuel transfer pipe 'O' rings

6 Carburettors: synchronisation and adjustment

1   Synchronisation of the carburettors should be carried out in two stages. The first stage as detailed in the following paragraph should be accomplished with the carburettors removed from the machine, at any time after the carburettors have been dismantled and reassembled. The second stage, which is synchronisation of the carburettors using vacuum gauges, should be carried out as a routine maintenance item. It is also necessary when rough idling or poor engine performance is encountered, or after the carburettors have been refitted to the machine.

2   Unscrew the remote throttle stop screw which is fitted with a nylon head, so that clearance can be seen between the end of the screw and the portion of the throttle pulley against which it normally abuts. The throttle slides should now be in the fully closed position, Make a visual check that all four throttle slides open and close at precisely the same time. If variations occur, each slide may be adjusted individually by means of the adjuster screw on the end of the bell crank. Loosen the locknut on the screw and make the required adjustment. Retighten the locknut without moving the screw. Rotate the throttle pulley so that the slides are in the fully open position and check that the lower

edge of the slides are at the position indicated in the accompanying diagram. Adjustment of this setting should be made by turning the single, spring secured screw, which is fitted to the rear face of the throttle cable anchor plate. After making the fully open and fully closed adjustments, replace the carburettor tops and refit the carburettors and controls to the machine.

3   Adjust the throttle cables by starting with the opening cable first. Loosen the locknut on the throttle opening cable, and use the adjuster to take up any slack in the cable before securing the locknut again. Loosen the locknut on the closing cable, and adjust it so there is about 2 mm ($\frac{1}{16}$ inch) of play in the throttle grip, then secure the locknut.

4   Screw in the pilot air screw on each carburettor until it can be felt to be seating lightly and then rotate the screw outwards the number of turns given in the specifications. The pilot air screws are now set at the correct datum for adjustment.

5   As stated above, running adjustment of the carburettors requires the use of a set of vacuum gauges or indicators, together with the appropriate adaptors, which screw into the inlet tracts and to which are attached the vacuum pipes. Unless the vacuum gauge set is to hand, it is recommended that the machine is returned to a Suzuki Service Agent who will carry out the synchronisation as a normal service task.

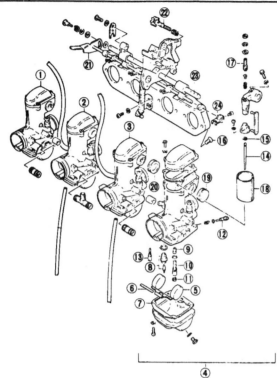

Fig. 2.1. Carburettors

1 LH carburettor
2 Centre left carburettor
3 Centre right carburettor
4 RH carburettor
5 Float assembly – 4 off
6 Pivot pin – 4 off
7 Gasket
8 Float needle valve assembly
9 Needle jet – 4 off
10 Jet holder – 4 off
11 Main jet – 4 off
12 Mixture adjustment (pilot air)
    screw – 4 off
13 Pilot jet – 4 off
14 Jet needle – 4 off
15 Needle clip - 4 off
16 Countersunk screw – 8 off
17 Adjuster screw – 2 off
18 Throttle valve (slide) – 4 off
19 Blind grommet – 4 off
20 Grommet – 6 off
21 Choke control shaft
22 Remote throttle adjuster
23 Throttle link rod
24 Choke operating fork – 4 off

6   Remove the blanking screws from the inlet tracts on the
cylinder head, fit the adaptors and connect up the vacuum
gauges. Start the engine and allow it to run until normal running
temperature has been reached. By means of the throttle stop
screw raise the engine speed to a steady 1,500 rpm. Select as a
datum the carburettor which shows the central reading. Make
adjustment using the bell-crank adjuster screw in each carburettor so that the three readings on the remaining gauges are
modified to correspond with that of the datum gauge. Using the
throttle stop screw reduce the engine speed to the specified
tick-over speed of 1,000 rpm. Disconnect the vacuum gauges
and refit the take-off blanking plugs, together with their sealing
washers.

7   Carburettors: checking the float chamber fuel level

1   If conditions of a continual weak mixture or flooding are
encountered on one or more carburettors, or if difficulty is
experienced in tuning the carburettors, the float levels should be
checked and, if necessary, adjusted. Although the float chambers may be removed with the carburettors in situ on the
machine, it is advised that the carburettors be removed to
facilitate inspection and adjustment.
2   The float level is correct when the distance between the
uppermost edge of the floats (with the carburettor inverted) and
the mixing chamber body flange is 26.00 mm (1.02 in). The
gasket must be removed from the mixing chamber body before
the measurement is taken. The floats should be in the closed
position when the measurement is taken. Adjustment is made
by bending the float assembly tang (tongue), which engages
with the float, in the direction required.

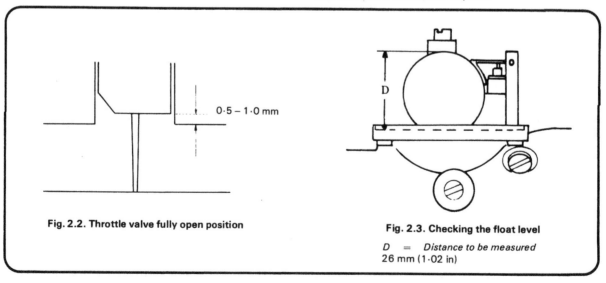

Fig. 2.2. Throttle valve fully open position

Fig. 2.3. Checking the float level

D = Distance to be measured
26 mm (1·02 in)

6.2 Throttle stop adjustment screw

6.4 Pilot air (mixture) adjustment screw

8   Carburettors: settings

1   Some of the carburettor settings, such as the sizes of the needle jets, main jets, and needle positions are pre-determined by the manufacturer. Under normal riding conditions it is unlikely that these settings will require modification. If a change appears necessary, it is often because of an engine fault, or an alteration in the exhaust system eg; a leaky exhaust pipe connection or silencer.

2   As an approximate guide to the carburettor settings, the pilot jet controls the engine speed up to 1/8th throttle. The throttle slide cut-away controls the engine speed from 1/8th to 1/4 throttle and the position of the needle in the slide from 1/4 to 3/4 throttle. The size of the main jet is responsible for engine speed at the final phase of 3/4 to full throttle. These are only guide lines; there is no clearly defined demarkation line due to a certain amount of overlap that occurs.

3   Always err slightly towards a rich mixture as one that is too weak will cause the engine to overheat and burn the exhaust valves. Reference to Chapter 3 will show how the condition of the spark plugs can be interpreted with some experience as a reliable guide to carburettor mixture strength.

4   Alterations to the mid-range mixture strength can be made by changing the position of the throttle needle in the throttle slide by moving the needle clip into a different groove. Raising the needle will richen the mixture and lowering the needle will weaken it.

9   Air cleaner: dismantling, servicing and reassembly

1   The air cleaner is mounted immediately behind the four carburettors into which the carburettor intakes fit. The air filter housing contains the element that is removable for cleaning or replacement, when necessary.

2   Access to the air filter element differs between the two models. On GS 550 models raise the dualseat and remove the air filter box lid, which is secured by two screws. The air filter element and carrier can be lifted out after removal of the single carrier screw. The air filter box on GS 750 models is fitted with a cover each side of the machine, both of which are retained by two screws. Detach both covers and remove the single carrier retaining screw from the left-hand side. The carrier and element may be pushed out.

3   Detach the element from the carrier after removing the two remaining screws. The element is of oil impregnated polyurethane sponge and should be cleaned thoroughly in petrol to remove all the old oil and dust. After cleaning, squeeze out the sponge to remove the petrol and then allow a short time for the remaining petrol to evaporate. Do not wring out the sponge as this will cause damage and will lead to the need for early renewal. Reimpregnate the sponge with engine oil and gently squeeze out the excess.

4   Reinstall the element and carrier by reversing the removal procedure.

5   The air filter should be removed for cleaning at approximately 3,000 mile intervals. If the sponge becomes damaged or hardened with age, it should be renewed as a matter of course.

6   Never run the machine without the element or with the air cleaner disconnected, otherwise the weak mixture that results will cause engine overheating and severe damage.

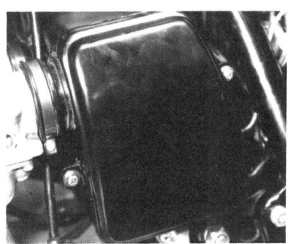

9.2a Remove air filter box cover to gain access to ...

9.2b ... filter element; secured by one screw (GS 750)

9.2c Filter carrier is a sliding fit in two channels

10 Engine and gearbox lubrication

1   As previously described at the beginning of the Chapter the lubrication system is of the wet sump type, with the oil being forceably pumped from the sump to positions at the gearbox bearings, the main engine bearings, and the cam box bearings, all oil eventually draining back to the sump. The system incorporates a gear driven oil pump, an oil filter, a safety by-pass valve, and an oil pressure switch. Oil vapours created in the crankcase are vented through a breather to the air cleaner box, where they are passed into the cylinder providing an oil-tight system.

2   The oil pump is an Eaton trochoid twin rotor unit which is driven from a gear engaged with and to the rear of the clutch. An oil strainer is fitted to the intake side of the pump, which serves to protect the pump mechanism from impurities in the oil which might cause damage.

3   A corrugated paper oil filter is included in the system and is fitted within an enclosed chamber in the front of the crankcase. Access to the filter is made through a finned cover. As the oil filter unit becomes clogged with impurities, its ability to function correctly is reduced, and if it becomes so clogged that it begins to impede the oil flow, a by-pass valve opens, and routes the oil flow through the filter core. This results in unfiltered oil being circulated throughout the engine, a condition which is avoided if the filter element is changed at regular intervals.

4   The oil pressure switch, which is situated at the top of the crankcase behind the cylinder block, serves to indicate when the oil pressure has dropped due to an oil pump malfunction, blockage in an oil passage, or a low oil content. The switch is not intended to be used as an indication of the correct oil level.

5   As previously mentioned an oil breather is incorporated into the system. It is mounted in the top of the camshaft cover and is essential for an engine of this size with so many moving parts. It serves to minimise crankcase pressure variations due to piston and crankshaft movement, and also helps lower the oil temperature, by venting the crankcase. Furthermore this system reduces the escape of unburnt oil into the atmosphere and so allows use of the machine in countries where stringent anti-pollution statutes are in operation. The breather tube carries the crankcase vapours to the air cleaner housing where they become mixed with the air drawn into the carburettors.

6   Excessive oil consumption indicated by blue smoke emitting from the exhaust pipes, coupled with a poor performance and fouling of spark plugs, is caused by either an excessive oil build-up in oil breather chamber, or by oil getting past the piston rings. First check the oil breather chamber and air cleaner for oil build-up. If this is the fault, check the passageway from the air/oil separator in the oil breather chamber to the lower half of the crankcase. Blockage here will prevent oil flowing back into the crankcase, resulting in oil build-up in the breather chamber and air cleaner tube.

7   Be sure to check the oil level in the sump before starting the engine. If the oil level is not seen between the two marks adjacent to the sight window at the bottom of the clutch cover, replenish with the correct amount of oil of the specified viscosity.

11 Oil pump: removal and examination

1   The oil pump is secured to the wall of the primary drive chamber behind the clutch unit. To gain access to the pump, the engine oil should be drained and the primary drive cover detached. The clutch should then be removed as described in Chapter 1, Section 12 paragraphs 3 – 5.

2   Unscrew the three screws retaining the oil pump and lift it from position. Displace the two O rings in the casing wall. The oil pump pinion is retained on the pump shaft. Remove the circlip, lift the pinion off the shaft and push out the drive pin.

3   Remove the single screw from the reverse side of the pump body. The two halves of the pump body are located by two tight fitting dowel pins. Rather than levering the cases apart, which would damage the mating surfaces, the dowels should be driven out. Use a parallel shanked punch of a suitable size, whilst resting the pump across two strips of wood of a thickness sufficient to raise the pump off the workbench surface.

4   Separate the outer casing (reverse side) from the pump, leaving the drive shaft and rotors in place at this stage. Push out the drive shaft, together with the drive pin and then lift out the two rotors.

5   Wash all the pump components with petrol and allow them to dry before carrying out a full examination. Before part reassembling the pump for the various measurements to be made, check the castings for cracks or other damage, especially the pump end covers.

6   Reassemble the pump rotors and measure the clearance between the outer rotor and the pump body, using a feeler gauge. If the clearance exceeds 0.25 mm (0.0098 in) the rotor or the body must be renewed, whichever is worn. Measure the clearance between the outer rotor and the inner rotor with a feeler gauge. If this clearance is greater than 0.2 mm (0.008 in) the rotors must be renewed as a set.

7   Using a small sheet of plate glass or a straight edge placed across the pump housing, check the rotor endfloat. If the endfloat exceeds 0.15 mm (0.006 in) the complete pump must be renewed.

8   Examine the rotors and the pump body for signs of scoring, chipping or other surface damage which will occur if metallic particles find their way into the oil pump assembly. Renewal of the affected parts is the only remedy under these circumstances, bearing in mind that rotors must always be replaced as a matched set.

9   Reassemble the pump by reversing the dismantling procedure. Make sure all parts of the pump are well lubricated before the end cover is replaced and that there is plenty of oil between the inner and outer rotors. Apply a small quantity of locking fluid to the thread of the single casing screw. **Do not** omit the two O rings when fitting the oil pump into the casing. Rotate the drive shaft as the screws are tightened down, to check that the oil pump revolves freely. A binding pump may be caused by dirt on the rotor faces or distortion of the cases, due to unequally tightened screws.

11.3a Remove single screw from oil pump and ...

11.3b ... separate the two halves of the pump

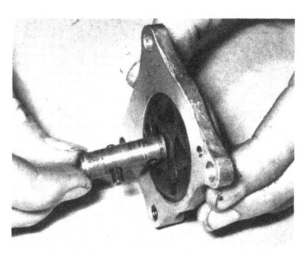

11.4a Withdraw the driveshaft and pin

11.7a Check rotor to rotor clearance and ...

11.7b ... rotor body clearance, with feeler gauge

12 Checking the oil pressure

1   Because of the predominant use of caged ball and roller
bearings in the GS series of engines, a low pressure lubrication
system is employed. If the condition of the oil pump is suspect,
the output pressure may be checked by connecting a suitable
pressure gauge to the engine.
2   A blanking plug is fitted to the right-hand end of the main
oil passage which runs across the crankcase below and to the
rear of the cylinder block. The blanking plug should be substituted by a suitable adaptor piece to which the pressure gauge
can be attached, via a flexible hose.
3   After connection of the pressure gauge, check that the oil
level in the crankcase is correct and then start the engine. The
engine should be run until the oil is at approximately 60°C
(140°F). Raise the engine speed to 3,000 rpm, when the pressure gauge should give a reading of 0.1 kg/cm^2 (1.42 psi). It can
be seen that the pressure gauge must be of high sensitivity and
of the correct calibration to give a useful reading. A pressure
reading lower than specified may be caused by a worn oil pump
or a blocked oil strainer or oil filter element. Before dismantling
the pump for inspection clean the oil strainer and renew the oil
filter, as described in Section 14 of this Chapter.

13 Oil pressure warning switch

1   An oil pressure failure warning switch is screwed in to a
holder bolted to the top of the crankcase. The switch is
interconnected with a warning light in the instrument console.
2   If the oil warning lamp comes on whilst the machine is
being ridden, the engine must be stopped immediately,
otherwise there is risk of severe engine failure due to a
breakdown of the lubrication system. The fault must be located
and rectified before the engine is re-started and run even for a
brief moment.
3   Oil pressure failure may be due to a blocked oil strainer
screen or a blocked filter and by-pass valve. A worn oil pump or

sheared drive shaft or pin will also produce the same symptoms.
4   Failure of the switch itself is possible, and may be due to
a sticking plunger. To check, remove the two bolts to free the
switch from the crankcase. Operate the switch plunger and
check that it returns smoothly under spring pressure. If the
oil pressure check described in Section 12 confirms the
lubrication system to be in order, and the warning lamp still
illuminates, renew the warning switch.
5   When the engine is operated at high temperatures, there
may be a tendency for the oil warning lamp to come on
occasionally, at idling speeds. This is quite in order if the light
extinguishes immediately the engine speed is increased.

14 Oil filter: renewing the element

1   The oil filter element is contained within a semi-isolated
chamber in the front of the lower crankcase, closed by a finned
cover retained by three domed nuts. Before removing the cover,
place a receptacle below the engine to catch the engine oil contained within the filter chamber. Drain the oil either by removing
the drain plug provided or as the cover is released.
     A coil spring is fitted between the cover and the filter
element to keep the element seated firmly in position. Be prepared for the cover to fly off after removal of the bolts.
2   No attempt should be made to clean the oil filter element; it
must be renewed. When renewing the filter element it is wise to
renew the filter cover O ring at the same time. This will obviate
the possibility of any oil leaks.
3   The by-pass valve which allows a continued flow of lubrication if the element becomes clogged is an integral part of the
filter. For this reason routine cleaning of the valve is not
required since it is renewed regularly.
4   Never run the engine without the filter element or increase
the period between the recommended oil changes or oil filter
changes. The oil should be changed every 1,500 miles and the
oil filter renewed at every second oil change.

13.1 Oil pressure warning switch is mounted on crankcase
top surface

13.4 Unbolt switch from the casing and check action of the
plunger

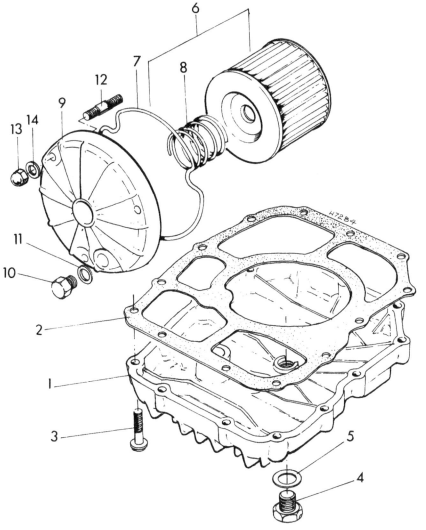

Fig. 2.4. Oil filter and sump

1 Oil sump
2 Gasket
3 Bolt – 13 off
4 Oil drain plug
5 Sealing washer
6 Engine oil filter set
7 'O' ring
8 Oil filter spring
9 Oil filter cover
10 Oil drain plug
11 Sealing washer
12 Stud – 3 off
13 Nut – 3 off
14 Washer – 3 off

15 Fault diagnosis: fuel system and lubrication

Symptom	Cause	Remedy
Engine gradually fades and stops	Fuel starvation	Check vent hole in filler cap. Sediment in filter bowl or float chamber. Dismantle and clean.
Engine runs badly. Black smoke from exhausts	Carburettor flooding	Dismantle and clean carburettor. Check for punctured float or sticking float needle.
Engine lacks response and overheats	Weak mixture Air cleaner disconnected or hose split Modified silencer has upset carburation	Check for partial block in carburettors. Reconnect or renew hose. Replace with original design.
Oil pressure warning light comes on	Lubrication system failure	Stop engine immediately. Trace and rectify fault before re-starting.
Engine gets noisy	Failure to change engine oil when recommended	Drain off old oil and refill with new oil of correct grade. Renew oil filter element.

Chapter 3/Ignition system

For additional information relating to 1978 and 1979 GS750 models and 1978 through 1982 GS550 models, refer to Chapter 7.

Contents

Specifications

Ignition timing

Retarded .... 17° BTDC
Advanced .... 37° BTDC
Advance commences .... 1,400 – 1,600 rpm
Advance completed .... 2,250 – 2,450 rpm
Contact breaker gap .... 0.3 – 0.4 mm (0.012 – 0.016 in)

Spark plugs

Type .... NGK B–8ES, Nippon Denso W24ES*
Gap .... 0.6 – 0.7 mm (0.024 – 0.028 in)
Alternative .... Motorcraft AGl

*manufacturers recommendation

1 General description

1 The spark necessary to ignite the petrol vapour in the combustion chambers is supplied by a battery and two ignition coils (one coil to two cylinders).

There are two sets of contact breaker points, two condensers, four spark plugs and an automatic ignition advance mechanism. The contact breaker cam, which is incorporated in the advance mechanism, opens each set of points once in 180° of crankshaft rotation, causing a spark to occur in two of the cylinders. The other set of points fires 180° later, so that in every 360° of crankshaft rotation each plug is fired once. One extra spark occurs during the time when there is no combustible material in the chamber.

Each set of points has one fixed and one movable contact, the latter of which pivots as the lobe of the cam separates them. The two condensers are wired in parallel, one with each set of contact points, and these function as electrical storage reservoirs, whilst also preventing arcing across the points. The condensers serve to absorb surplus current that tries to run back through the system when there is an overload situation, and feeds the current back to the ignition coils. They also help intensify the spark. When the points are closed, the current flows straight through them to earth. When they open, there is now an open circuit. If not for the condensers, the current would arc across the points causing them to burn and pit. When the condensers reach their capacity, they discharge the current back through the primary windings and eventually to the spark plug. Any time the points get badly burnt, it is advisable to renew them, and the condensers also.

Each of the two coils has two high voltage spark plug leads, and as in the case of points, one coil serves cylinders 1 and 4, and the other, cylinders 2 and 3.

The coils convert the low tension voltage into a high tension voltage sufficient to provide a spark strong enough to jump the spark plug air gap. If at any time a very weak or erratic spark occurs at the plug, and the rest of the ignition system is known to be in good condition, it is time to renew an ignition coil. Although coils normally have a long life they can sometimes be faulty, especially if the outer case has been damaged.

2 The automatic advance mechanism serves to advance the ignition timing as the engine rpm rises. The mechanism is made up of two spring loaded weights which, under the action of centrifugal force created by the rotation of the crankshaft, fly apart and cause the contact points to open earlier. If the mechanism does not operate smoothly, the timing will not advance smoothly, or it may stick in one position. This will result in poor running in any but that one position. Sometimes the springs are prone to stretching, which can cause the timing to advance too soon. It is best to check the automatic advance mechanism, by carrying out a static timing test on the ignition,

Electrode gap check - use a wire type gauge for best results

Electrode gap adjustment - bend the side electrode using the correct tool

Normal condition - A brown, tan or grey firing end indicates that the engine is in good condition and that the plug type is correct

Ash deposits - Light brown deposits encrusted on the electrodes and insulator, leading to misfire and hesitation. Caused by excessive amounts of oil in the combustion chamber or poor quality fuel/oil

Carbon fouling - Dry, black sooty deposits leading to misfire and weak spark. Caused by an over-rich fuel/air mixture, faulty choke operation or blocked air filter

Oil fouling - Wet oily deposits leading to misfire and weak spark. Caused by oil leakage past piston rings or valve guides (4-stroke engine), or excess lubricant (2-stroke engine)

Overheating - A blistered white insulator and glazed electrodes. Caused by ignition system fault, incorrect fuel, or cooling system fault

Worn plug - Worn electrodes will cause poor starting in damp or cold weather and will also waste fuel

followed by a strobe test. It is always best to check the motion of the weights by hand every 2000 miles and to clean and lubricate the unit at the same time.

3   The electrical system is powered by an AC generator (alternator) fitted to the extreme left-hand end of the crankshaft. The alternating current (AC) is passed through a full-wave rectifier where it is converted to direct current (DC) and used to charge the battery and provide current for the lights and ancillary components. Output of the alternator is controlled by a silicon-controlled regulator (SCR unit) to within a range 14 – 15.5 volts.

2   Crankshaft alternator: checking the output

1   If the charging performance of the alternator is suspect, it can be checked with a multi-meter test instrument that includes a voltmeter and ohmmeter. As most owner/riders are unlikely to possess equipment of this type it is advised that the machine be returned to a Suzuki Service Agent for testing.

2   If a multi-meter is available, an initial check on the alternator and the rectifier and regulator assemblies may be carried out as described in Chapter 6. As mentioned in Chapter 6, Section 3 the charging system should be considered as a whole, and should be tested accordingly.

3   Ignition coils: checking

1   Each ignition coil is a sealed unit, designed to give long service without need for attention. They are located within the top frame tubes, immediately to the rear of the steering head assembly. If a weak spark and difficult starting causes the performance of a coil to be suspect, it should be tested by a Suzuki Service Agent or an auto-electrical engineer who will have the appropriate test equipment. A faulty coil must be renewed; it is not possible to effect a satisfactory repair.

2   A defective condenser in the contact breaker circuit can give the illusion of a defective coil and for this reason it is advisable to investigate the condition of the condenser before condemning the ignition coil. Refer to Section 6 of this Chapter for the appropriate details.

3   Note that it is extremely unlikely that both ignition coils will prove faulty at the same time, unless the common electrical feed is in some way deranged. This can be checked by measuring the low tension voltage supplied to the coils, using a voltmeter.

4   Contact breaker: adjustments

1   To gain access to the contact breaker assembly, it is necessary to detach the aluminium cover retained by three crosshead screws at the right-hand end of the crankshaft. Note that the cover has a sealing gasket, to prevent the ingress of water.

2   Rotate the engine slowly by means of the engine turning hexagon until one set of points is in the fully open position. Examine the faces of the contacts. If they are blackened and burnt, or badly pitted, it will be necessary to remove them for further attention. See Section 5 of this Chapter. Repeat for the second set of contact points.

3   Adjustment is effected by slackening the screw through the plate of the fixed contact breaker point and moving the point either closer to or further from the moving contact until the gap is correct as measured by a feeler gauge. The correct gap with the points FULLY OPEN is 0.3 – 0.4 mm (0.012 – 0.016 in). Small projections on the contact breaker baseplate permit the insertion of a screwdriver to lever the adjustable point into its correct location. Repeat this operation for the second set of points, which must also be fully open.

4   Do NOT slacken the two screws through the extremities of the larger baseplate fitted to the right hand set of contact breaker points. They are used for adjusting the setting of the ignition timing and it will be necessary to re-time the engine if the baseplate is permitted to move. Only the centre screw should be slackened, to adjust the fixed contact breaker point.

5   Before replacing the cover and gasket, place a light smear of grease on the contact breaker cam and one or two drops of thin oil on the felt which lubricates the surface of the cam. It is better to under-lubricate rather than add excess because there is always chance of excess oil reaching the contact breaker points and causing the ignition circuit to malfunction.

5   Contact breaker points: removal, renovation and replacement

1   If the contact breaker points are burned, pitted or badly worn, they should be removed for dressing. If it is necessary to remove a substantial amount of material before the faces can be restored, the points should be renewed.

2   To remove the contact breaker points, detach the circlip which secures the moving contact to the pin on which it pivots. Remove the nut and bolt which secures the flexible lead wire to the end of contact return spring, noting the arrangement of the insulating washers so that they are replaced in their correct

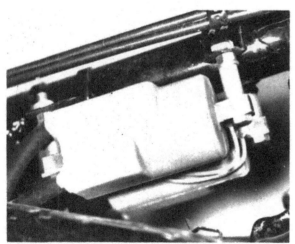

3.1 Each ignition coil serves two cylinders

4.3 Slacken single screw to adjust contact points

order during reassembly. Lift the moving contact off the pivot, away from the assembly.

3 The fixed contact is removed by unscrewing the screw which retains the contact to the contact breaker baseplate.

4 The points should be dressed with an oilstone or fine emery cloth. Keep them absolutely square throughout the dressing operation, otherwise they will make angular contact on reassembly, and rapidly burn away.

5 Replace the contacts by reversing the dismantling procedure, making sure that the insulating washers are fitted in the correct order. It is advantageous to apply a thin smear of grease to the pivot pin, prior to replacement of the moving contact arm.

6 Check, and if necessary, re-adjust the contact breaker gap when the points are fully open. Repeat the whole operation for the second set of points.

6 Condensers: removal and replacement

1 A condenser is included in each contact breaker circuit to prevent arcing across the contact breaker points as they separate. It is connected in parallel with each set of points and if

a fault develops, ignition failure is liable to occur.

2 If the engine proves difficult to start, or misfiring occurs, it is possible that the condenser is at fault. To check, separate the contact breaker points by hand when the ignition is switched on. If a spark occurs across the points and they have a blackened and burnt appearance, the condenser can be regarded as unserviceable.

3 It is not possible to check a condenser without the appropriate test equipment. In view of the low cost involved, it is preferable to fit a new one and observe the effect on engine performance.

4 Because each condenser and its associated set of contact breaker points is common to a pair of cylinders, a faulty condenser will not cause a misfire on one cylinder only. In such a case it is necessary to seek the cause of the trouble elsewhere, possibly in some other part of the ignition circuit or the carburettor. It also follows that both condensers are unlikely to fail at the same time unless damaged in an accident. If the cases are crushed or dented, electrical breakdown will occur.

5 The condensers are located at the base of the contact breaker assembly, parallel to each other. Each has an integral bracket and is attached to the contact breaker baseplate by a single crosshead screw, making renewal easy.

5.2 Note sequence of insulating washers before detaching lead

6.5 Condensers are held by a single screw each

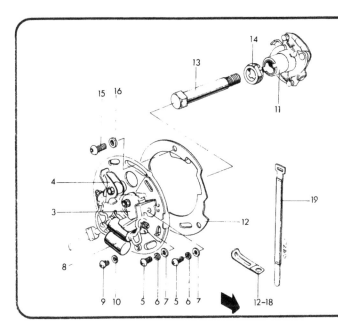

Fig. 3.1. Contact breaker assembly

1 Contact breaker assembly
2 Contact breaker plate
3 Right-hand contact breaker unit
4 Left-hand contact breaker unit
5 Screw – 4 off
6 Spring washer – 4 off
7 Plain washer – 4 off
8 Condenser – 2 off
9 Screw – 2 off
10 Spring washer – 2 off
11 Automatic timing unit (ATU)
12 Ignition timing index plate
13 Bolt
14 Engine turning hexagon
15 Screw – 3 off
16 Plain washer – 3 off
17 Cable clip – 3 off
18 Cable clip – 2 off
19 Cable strap

7   Ignition timing: checking and resetting

1   In order to check the accuracy of the ignition timing, it is necessary to remove the contact breaker cover from the right-hand side of the crankcase. Ignition timing checking and resetting should take place after resetting the contact breaker gaps, as described in Section 4.

2   Apply a spanner to the engine rotation hexagon and turn the engine in a forward direction, whilst viewing the ATU through the inspection aperture in the contact breaker stator plate. It will be seen that there is a set of three scribed lines on each side of the ATU.

3   Commence ignition timing checking on the left-hand contact breaker set, which controls cylinders No 1 and 4. To determine at which moment the points open connect a 12v bulb between the moving point and a suitable earthing point on the engine. With the ignition turned on, the bulb will light up when the points are open. Rotate the engine until the F1-4 mark on the ATU is in **exact** alignment with the index pointer mark on the plate fitted to the rear of the stator plate. If the ignition is correct, the points should be on the verge of opening when this position is reached. This will be indicated by the flickering of the bulb.

4   To adjust the ignition timing on No 1 and 4 cylinders slacken the three screws whichpass through the elongated holes in the stator plate periphery. Rotate the plate until the light flickers and then tighten the screws. Turn the engine backwards about 90° and then forwards again to check the setting.

5   Check the ignition timing on Nos 2 and 3 cylinders in a similar manner, using the F2-3 timing mark. If the timing is incorrect, slacken the two screws holding the right-hand contact breaker assembly mounting plate to the main stator plate. Move the plate to the correct position and tighten the screws. Recheck the timing.

6   Provided that the contact breakers are in good condition and care is taken, manual adjustment of the ignition timing should be acceptably accurate. If possible, however, the timing should be checked using a stroboscope lamp because not only can the accuracy of the timing be checked with the engine running but the correct performance of the ATU can be verified. The timing light should be connected to the low tension or high tension side of the ignition as instructed by the manufacturers of the light. Test the left-hand contact breaker and then the right-hand contact breaker. Start the engine and illuminate the ATU through the inspection aperture. With the engine running below 1,500 rpm the F mark should be in alignment with the index mark. Raise the engine speed slowly to 2,500 rpm when the advance mark should align with the index pointer.

7   The advance range of 1000 rpm peaks at 2,500 rpm, above which engine speed no more advance is possible. If, when increasing the engine speed from the commencement of advance at 1,500 rpm, the timing marks are seen to move erratically, or if the advance range has altered appreciably, the ATU should be inspected for wear or malfunctioning as described in the following Section.

8   Automatic timing unit: examination

1   The automatic timing unit rarely requires attention although it is advisable to examine it periodically.

2   To obtain access to the unit remove the inspection cover and the contact breaker back plate complete with contact breakers. The ATU centre bolt and engine turning hexagon should be removed before the stator plate. Before removal, the back plate and end cover should be marked so that the back plate can be replaced in exactly the same position,. This will ensure the ignition timing is not altered.

3   Pull the ATU from position, noting the drive pin with which it locates and is driven. The unit comprises balance weights which move outwards against spring tension as the centrifugal forces increase. The balance weights must move freely on their pivots, which should be lubricated. The tension springs must also be in good condition.

4   Check the surface of the contact breaker cam for pitting or obvious signs of wear. Damage to the cam cannot be rectified; the complete ATU must be renewed.

5   When replacing the ATU, check that the drive pin engages with the recess in the rear of the centre boss. Because there is a single recess only, the ATU cannot inadvertently be replaced in the incorrect position and so alter the timing marks in relation to the crankshaft.

9   Spark plugs: checking and resetting the gaps

1   All models are fitted with Nippon Denso type W24ES or NGK type B-8ES spark plugs as standard, gapped within the range 0.6 – 0.7 mm (0.024 – 0.028 in). Operating conditions may indicate a change in spark plug grade; the type recommended by the manufacturer gives the best, all round service.

2   Check the gap of the plug points during every three monthly or 3000 mile service. To reset the gap, bend the outer electrode to bring it closer to the centre electrode and check that a 0.6 mm (0.024 in) feeler gauge can be inserted. Never bend the central electrode or the insulator will crack, causing engine damage if the particles fall in whilst the engine is running.

3   With some experience, the condition of the spark plug electrodes and insulator can be used as a reliable guide to engine operating conditions. See accompanying illustrations.

4   Beware of overtightening the spark plugs, otherwise there is risk of stripping the threads from the aluminium alloy cylinder heads. The plugs should be sufficiently tight to sit firmly on their copper sealing washers, and no more. Use a spanner which is a good fit to prevent the spanner from slipping and breaking the insulator.

5   If the threads in the cylinder head strip as a result of over tightening the spark plugs, it is possible to reclaim the head by the use of a Helicoil thread insert. This is a cheap and convenient method of replacing the threads; most motorcycle dealers operate a service of this kind.

6   Make sure the plug insulating caps are a good fit and have their rubber seals. They should also be kept clean to prevent tracking. These caps contain the suppressors that eliminate both radio and TV interference.

7.2a Index marks on back plate align with ...

7.2 b ... marks on ATU. Unmarked line is full advance mark

7.5a Timing adjustment screws for cylinders 2 and 3

7.5b Use slot provided to alter plate position

8.3 Check bob-weights, pivots and springs on ATU

10 Fault diagnosis

Symptom	Cause	Remedy
Engine will not start	Faulty ignition switch	Operate switch several times in case contacts are dirty. If lights and other electrics function, switch may need renewal.
	Starter motor not working	Discharged battery. Use kickstart until battery is recharged.
	Short circuit in wiring	Check whether fuse is intact. Eliminate fault before switching on again.
	Completely discharged battery	If lights do not work, remove battery and recharge.
Engine misfires	Faulty condenser in ignition circuit	Renew condenser and re-test.
	Fouled spark plug	Renew plug and have original cleaned.
	Poor spark due to generator failure and discharged battery	Check output from generator. Remove and recharge battery.
Engine lacks power and overheats	Retarded ignition timing	Check timing and also contact breaker gap. Check whether auto-advance mechanism has jammed.
Engine 'fades' when under load	Pre-ignition	Check grade of plugs fitted; use recommended grades only.

Chapter 4 Frame and forks

For additional information relating to 1978 and 1979 GS750 models and 1978 through 1982 GS550 models, refer to Chapter 7.

Contents

Specifications

Front forks

Type	Telescopic, one-way hydraulically damped
Damping fluid capacity:	
GS 750	170 cc (5.75/5.98 US/Imp fl oz)
GS 550	165 cc (5.58/5.81 US/Imp fl oz)
Type	50/50 mixture of ATF and 10W/30 engine oil

Rear suspension

Swinging arm supported on hydraulically damped 5-way adjustable suspension units

1 General description

The Suzuki GS 750 and GS 550 models share a frame of similar design and characteristics. The frame is of the duplex cradle type; that is, with the engine not comprising any part of the frame.

Rear suspension is of the swinging arm type, using oil filled suspension units to provide the necessary damping action. The units are adjustable so that the spring ratings can be effectively changed within certain limits to match the load carried.

The front forks are of the conventional telescopic type, having internal, oil-filled dampers. The fork springs are contained within the fork stanchions and each fork leg can be detached from the machine as a complete unit, without dismantling the steering head assembly.

2 Front forks: removal from the frame

1 It is unlikely that the front forks will need to be removed from the frame as a complete unit, unless the steering head bearings require attention or the forks are damaged in an accident. In the event of damage to one or both of the fork legs, they may be removed from the steering head and lower fork yoke, whilst leaving the two latter components in situ on the frame.

2 Commence complete fork removal operations by removing the control cables from the handlebar levers or by removing the levers complete with cables. The shape of the handlebars fitted and the length of control cables will probably dictate the method used. Remove the front brake lever master cylinder unit, which is retained by a clamp held by two bolts. Tie the master cylinder to some part of the machine not to be dismantled, so that it is secure and resting in an upright position.

3 Detach the handlebars from their mounting points on the fork upper yoke. The handlebars are held by two U clamps, retained by two bolts and spring washers each. Remove the headlamp unit from the headlamp shell and disconnect the electrical leads at the snap connectors. No difficulty should be encountered in replacement, as the connections are mainly of the block type and the wiring is colour coded.

4 Disconnect the speedometer and tachometer cables at the instrument, where they are retained by knurled rings. Detach the wiring connections from the instrument bulb holders and from the warning lamp console at the two separate block connectors. Undo the two bolts which pass through the instrument mounting bracket and lift the complete unit from the machine.

5 Remove the front wheel as described in Chapter 5, Section 3. Where two caliper units are fitted, both should be detached from the fork legs. Temporarily, tie each to the frame down tubes so that their weight is not taken by the hydraulic hoses.

6 Remove the front mudguard, which is retained by two bolts passing into each fork leg.

7   Loosen the clamp bolts which retain the fork legs in the upper and lower yokes. The fork legs can now be eased downwards, out of position. If the clamps prove to be excessively tight, they may be gently sprung, using a large screwdriver. This must be done with great care, in order to prevent breakage of the clamps, necessitating renewal of the complete yoke. Support the headlamp as the second leg is removed, and lift it away from the machine, once freed.

8   Remove the single bolt which secures the hydraulic hose union to the fork lower yoke. The complete front brake assembly, including the master cylinder, hoses and calipers, may be lifted away from the machine without the need to drain the fluid. By following this procedure, draining, refilling, and bleeding of the system is not required.

9   Loosen the clamp bolt located at the rear of the upper yoke, and from the top of the yoke remove the large chrome bolt together with the washer. From the underside, tap the upper yoke upwards until it frees the steering column. Support the weight of the lower yoke and, using a C spanner, remove the steering head bearing adjuster ring. If a C spanner is not available, a soft brass drift and hammer may be used to slacken the nut.

10   Remove the dust excluder and outer race (cone) once the adjuster nut has been detached. The bottom yoke, complete with steering column, can now be lowered from position. Make provision to catch the ball bearings as they are released; only the lower bearings will drop free since the upper bearings will most probably remain seated in the cup race retaining them.

3   Front forks: dismantling

1   It is advisable to dismantle each fork leg separately, using an identical procedure. There is less chance of unwittingly exchanging parts if this approach is adopted. Commence by draining each fork leg of damping oil; there is a drain plug in each lower leg above and to the rear of the wheel spindle housing. Remove the chromium plated bolt at the top of each fork leg. The fork has a one or two piece spring, depending on the model. On the latter type, the two springs are separated by a small spacer.

2   Clamp the fork lower leg in a vice fitted with soft jaws, or wrap a length of rubber inner tube around the leg to prevent damage. Unscrew the socket screw, recessed into the housing which carries the front wheel spindle. Prise the dust excluder from position and slide it up the fork upper tube. The upper tube (stanchion) can be pulled out of the lower fork leg. Pull the damper rod seat off the rod, invert the upper tube and push the damper rod out of position towards the top end of the tube.

3   The oil seal fitted to the top of the lower leg should be removed only if it is to be renewed, because damage will almost certainly be inflicted when it is prised from position. The seal is retained by a spring clip.

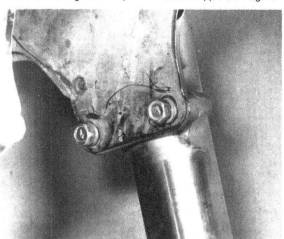

2.6 The mudguard is held by four bolts

2.7a Slacken the pinch bolts and ...

2.7b ... withdraw each fork leg individually

3.1a Remove drain screw to allow damping fluid to escape

3.1b Unscrew the chromed cap bolt and ...

3.1c ... withdraw the fork spring(s)

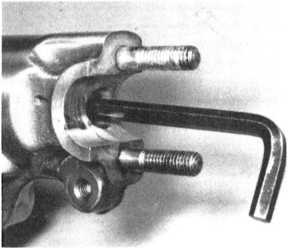

3.2a Unscrew the socket bolt from the lower leg

3.2b Prise off the dust cover ...

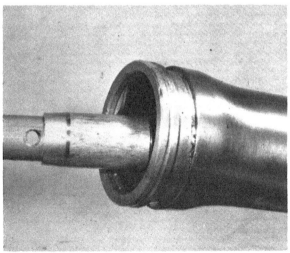

3.2c ... pull the damper rod seat off the rod and ...

3.2d ... remove the damper rod from the stanchion

3.3 Oil seal is retained by a spring clip

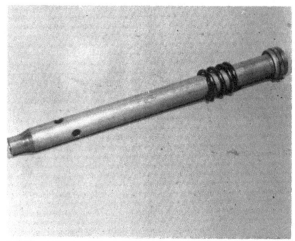

4.5 Check the condition of the damper piston ring

4   Front forks: examination and renovation

1   The front forks do not contain bushes. The fork legs slide directly against the inner hard chrome surface by the fork tubes. If wear occurs, indicated by slackness, the fork leg complete will have to be renewed, possibly also the fork stanchion. Wear on the fork stanchion is indicated by scuffing and penetration of the hard chrome surface.

2   After an extended period of service the fork springs may take a permanent set. If the spring lengths are suspect, they should be compared with a new set. It is wise to fit new components if the overall length has decreased. Always fit new springs as a pair, NEVER separately.

3   Check the outer surface of the stanchion for scratches or roughness. It is only too easy to damage the oil seal during reassembly, if these high spots are not eased down. The stanchions are unlikely to bend unless the machine is damaged in an accident. Any significant bend will be detected by eye, but if there is any doubt about straightness, roll the stanchion tubes on a flat surface. If the stanchions are bent, they must be renewed. Unless specialised repair equipment is available, it is rarely practicable to effect a satisfactory repair to a damaged stanchion.

4   The piston ring fitted to the damper rod may wear if oil changes at the specified intervals are neglected. If damping has become weakened and does not improve as a result of an oil change, the piston ring should be renewed. Check also that the oilways in the damper rod have not become obstructed.

5   Steering head bearings: examination and renovation

1   Clean and examine the cups and cones of the steering head bearings. They should have a polished appearance and show no signs of indentation. Renew the set if necessary.

2   Clean and examine the ball bearings which should also be polished and show no signs of surface cracks or blemishes. If any require replacement the whole set must be renewed.

3   Eighteen balls are fitted both in the top and bottom races. This arrangement will leave a gap but an extra ball must not be fitted otherwise the balls will press against each other, accentuating wear and making the steering stiff.

4   The outer races are a drive fit in the steering head lug and may be drifted out, using a suitable long handled drift passed through the centre of the lug. The lower inner race may be levered from position on the steering stem. When driving the new inner races into place, ensure that they remain square to the housing in the lug or the housing may be damaged.

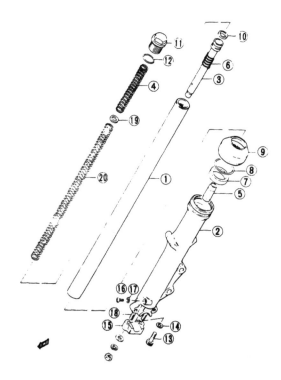

Fig. 4.1. Front forks

1 Stanchion (upper tube) – 2 off	11 Bolt – 2 off
2 Left-hand fork lower leg	12 O ring – 2 off
3 Damper rod – 2 off	13 Socket screw – 2 off
4 Short spring – 2 off	14 Sealing washer – 2 off
5 Damper rod seat – 2 off	15 Spindle clamp – 2 off
6 Rebound spring – 2 off	16 Screw
7 Oil seal – 2 off	17 Sealing washer cap
8 Circlip – 2 off	18 Stud – 4 off
9 Dust excluder	19 Washer – 2 off
10 Piston ring – 2 off	20 Long spring

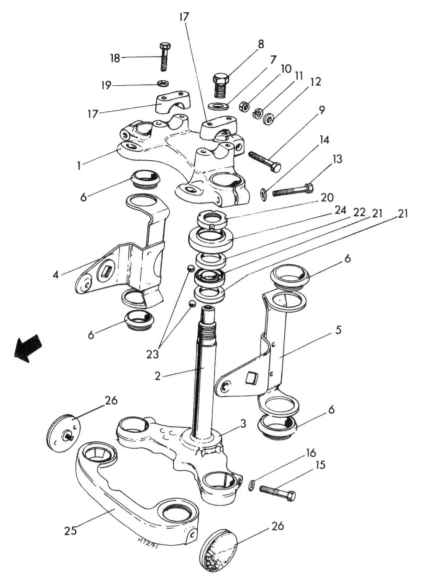

Fig. 4.2. Steering head assembly

1 Fork upper yoke
2 Steering stem/lower yoke
3 Lower bearing cone
4 Headlamp bracket
5 Headlamp bracket
6 Rubber cushion
7 Crown washer
8 Crown bolt
9 Pinch bolt
10 Nut
11 Spring washer
12 Plain washer
13 Pinch bolt – 2 off
14 Spring washer – 2 off
15 Pinch bolt – 2 off
16 Spring washer
17 Handlebar clamp – 2 off
18 Bolt – 4 off
19 Spring washer – 4 off
20 Bearing adjuster ring
21 Upper bearing/lower bearing
   cup – 2 off
22 Upper bearing cone
23 Steel ball – 36 off
24 Dust seal
25 Front fork cover
26 Reflector – 2 off

6   Front forks: replacement

1   Replace the front forks by following in reverse the dismantling procedures described in Sections 2 and 3 of this Chapter. Before fully tightening the front wheel spindle clamps and the fork yoke pinch bolts, bounce the forks several times to ensure they work correctly and settle down into their original settings. Complete the final tightening from the wheel spindle upwards.
2   Refill each fork leg with the correct quantity and specification of fork oil before replacing the handlebars. The handlebars obstruct access to the filler orifices.

Fork oil quantity (per leg)

GS750   170 cc (5.75/5.98 US/Imp fl oz)
GS550   165 cc (5.58/5.81 US/Imp fl oz)

   Suzuki recommend that the damping fluid be a 50/50 mixture of fork oil or ATF and 10W/30 motor oil. Check that the drain plugs have been re-inserted and tightened before the oil is added.

3   If the fork stanchions prove difficult to relocate through the fork yokes, make sure their outer surfaces are clean and polished so that they will slide more easily. It is often advantageous to use a screwdriver blade to open up the clamps, as the tubes are moved upwards into position.
4   Before the machine is used on the road, check the adjustment of the steering head bearings. If they are too slack, judder will occur especially during braking. There should be no detectable play in the head races when the handlebars are pulled and pushed with the front brake applied hard.
5   Overtight head races are equally undesirable. It is possible to unwittingly apply a loading of several tons on the head races when they have been overtightened, even though the handlebars appear to turn quite freely. Overtight bearings will make the machine roll at low speeds and give generally imprecise handling with a tendency to weave. Adjustment is correct if there is no perceptible play in the bearings and the handlebars will swing to full lock in either direction, when the machine is on the centre stand with the front wheel clear of the ground. Only a slight tap should cause the handlebars to swing.

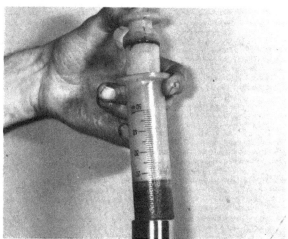

6.2 Fill each leg with the correct quantity of fluid

6.5 Adjust the head race bearings by means of a 'C' spanner

7 Steering head lock

1   On GS 750 models the steering head lock is attached to the underside of the lower yoke of the forks by a single screw and washer. When in a locked position, a tongue extends from the body of the lock when the handlebars are on full lock in either direction and abuts against a plate welded to the base of the steering head. In consequence, the handlebars cannot be straightened until the lock is released.

2   The steering head lock on GS 550 models is incorporated in the ignition switch mounted on the fork upper yoke between the speedometer and tachometer. The lock, which functions in a manner similar to that of the GS 750, is operated when the ignition is turned to the lock or park position.

3   If the lock malfunctions, it must be renewed. A repair is impracticable. When the lock is changed the key must be changed too, to match the new lock.

8   Frame: examination and renovation

1   The frame is unlikely to require attention unless accident damage has occurred. In some cases, replacement of the frame is the only satisfactory course of action if it is badly out of alignment. Only a few frame repair specialists have the jigs and mandrels necessary for resetting the frame to the required standard of accuracy and even then there is no easy means of assessing to what extent the frame may have been over-stressed.

2   After the machine has covered a considerable mileage, it is advisable to examine the frame closely for signs of cracking or splitting at the welded joints. Rust can also cause weakness at these joints. Minor damage can be repaired by welding or brazing, depending on the extent and nature of the damage.

3   Remember that a frame which is out of alignment will cause handling problems and may even promote speed wobbles. If misalignment is suspected, as the result of an accident, it will be necessary to strip the machine completely so that the frame can be checked to and, if necessary, renewed.

9   Swinging arm fork: dismantling and renovation

1   The rear fork of the frame is of the swinging arm type. It pivots on a shaft that passes through the crossmember and both sides of the main frame assembly, with a spacing collar, two inner bushes, and two needle roller bearings. The whole assembly is held together with a pivot shaft that is bolted up

with a nut one end.

Worn swinging arm bushes can be detected by placing the machine on its centre stand and pulling and pushing vigorously on the rear wheel in a horizontal direction. Any play will be noticeable by the leverage effect.

2   When wear develops in the swinging arm, necessitating renewal of the bearings, the renovation procedure is quite straightforward. Commence by removing the rear wheel as described in Chapter 5, Section 10.

3   On GS 750 models suspend the caliper unit from the right-hand rear indicator stalk using a length of wire or string. If care is taken during dismantling, disconnection of the rear brake hydraulic pipe will not be required. This will facilitate reassembly. Remove the brake pipe protector plate and carefully ease the hydraulic pipe and the grommet through which it passes from position in the locating clip welded to the swinging arm.

4   Remove the lower two bolts that hold the suspension units to the swinging fork, so that the fork swings down. Leave the suspension units hanging from the frame, but slacken the top nut so that they are free to move. This facilitates reassembly.

5   Take out the swinging arm pivot shaft by undoing the nut on the left-hand side of the machine. This may need a gentle tap with a rawhide mallet and drift to displace it. Pull the final drive chain across so that it clears the swinging arm fork left-hand end. The swinging arm is now free and can be lifted out to the rear.

6   Remove the dust cap and thrust washer from each side of the swinging arm cross-member and then pull out the two short bushes. Push out the long central spacer, using a long shanked screwdriver. A circlip fitted to the spacer on original assembly will be displaced as the spacer is removed. The circlip served a useful purpose only during factory assembly and therefore may be discarded.

7   The caged needle roller bearings may be drifted out of position, using a suitable length of steel rod. Do not remove the bearings merely for inspection as the cages will be damaged by the drift. Lubricate the outside of the new bearing cages before driving them into place, and ensure that they are fitted with the punch marked face outwards.

8   Check that the swinging arm pivot shaft is straight. A bent shaft may be straightened in a jig. If this cannot be accomplished, the shaft should be renewed.

9   Reassemble the swinging arm fork by reversing the dismantling procedure. Grease the pivot shaft and bearings liberally prior to reassembly, bearing in mind that no provision is given for subsequent lubrication on the GS 550 model when the swinging arm is fitted to the machine.

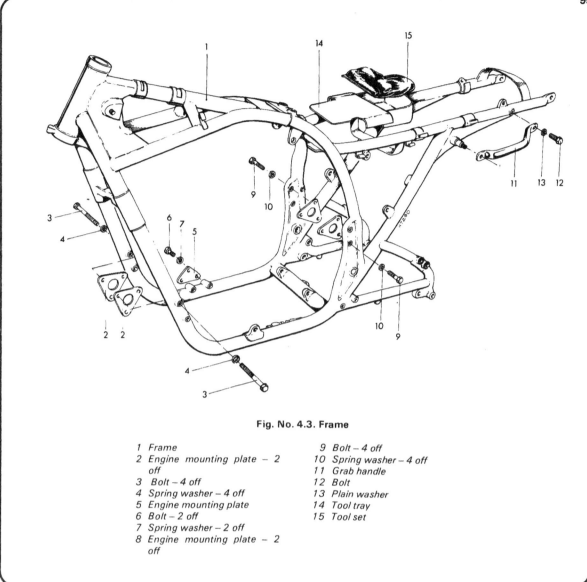

Fig. No. 4.3. Frame

1 Frame
2 Engine mounting plate – 2 off
3 Bolt – 4 off
4 Spring washer – 4 off
5 Engine mounting plate
6 Bolt – 2 off
7 Spring washer – 2 off
8 Engine mounting plate – 2 off
9 Bolt – 4 off
10 Spring washer – 4 off
11 Grab handle
12 Bolt
13 Plain washer
14 Tool tray
15 Tool set

9.3a Detach the hydraulic pipe protector plate and ...

9.3b ... ease the pipe and grommet from the clip

9.4 Release the suspension unit lower mounting bolts

9.5a After removal of the pivot shaft and nut ...

9.5b ... lift the swinging arm fork out towards the rear

9.6a Remove the dust cap and shim from the cross-member

9.6b Pull out the short inner bush and ...

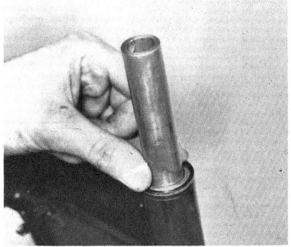

9.6c ... the longer central spacer

9.7 The bearing must be driven from position, for renewal

10 Rear suspension units: examination

1   Rear suspension units of the hydraulically damped type are fitted to the Suzuki GS models. They can be adjusted to give five different spring loadings, without removal from the machine.

2   Each rear suspension unit has two peg holes immediately above the adjusting notches, to facilitate adjustment. Either a C spanner or the screwdriver supplied with the original tool kit can be used to turn the adjusters. Turn clockwise to increase the spring tension and stiffen up the rear suspension.
    The recommended settings are:-
    Position 1 (least tension) for normal solo riding and
    Position 5 (greatest tension) for high speed riding or when carrying a heavy load. The intermediate settings may be used for varying conditions, as required.

3   The suspension units are sealed and there is no means of topping up or changing the damping fluid. If the damping fails or if the unit leaks, renewal is necessary.

4   In the interests of good roadholding it is essential that both suspension units have the same load setting. If renewal is necessary, the units must be replaced as a matched pair.

11 Centre stand: examination

1   The centre stand is retained on the underside of the frame by two bolts which serve as pivot shafts. A bush is fitted to each shaft. The pivot assemblies on centre stands are often neglected with regard to lubrication and this will eventually lead to wear. It is prudent to remove the pivot bushes from time to time and grease them thoroughly. This will prolong the effective life of the stand.

2   Check that the return spring is in good condition. A broken or weak spring may cause the stand to fall whilst the machine is being ridden, and catch in some obstacle, unseating the rider.

12 Prop stand: examination

1   The prop stand bolts to a lug attached to the rear of the left-hand lower frame tube. An extension spring ensures that the stand is retracted when the weight of the machine is taken off the stand.

2   Check that the pivot bolt is secure and that the extension spring is in good condition and not over-stretched. An accident is almost inevitable if the stand extends whilst the machine is on the move.

13 Footrests: examination and renovation

1   The front footrests on all models are of the bolt-on type, with fixed rubber pads. If they are bent in a spill or through the machine falling over, they can be removed and straightened in a vice whilst heated to a dull red with a blow lamp, or welding torch. The pillion footrests are hinged and therefore are less likely to become damaged than the front footrests. Each peg pivots on a clevis pin secured by a washer and split pin.

14 Brake pedal: examination

1   The rear brake pedal is secured by a single pinch bolt to the splined brake pivot shaft. In the event of damage, the pedal may be removed and treated similarly to a bent footrest, as described in the previous section.

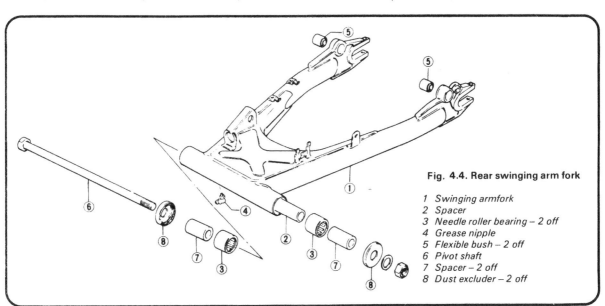

Fig. 4.4. Rear swinging arm fork

1 Swinging armfork
2 Spacer
3 Needle roller bearing – 2 off
4 Grease nipple
5 Flexible bush – 2 off
6 Pivot shaft
7 Spacer – 2 off
8 Dust excluder – 2 off

2   The pedal may be pulled off the shaft after removing completely the pinch bolt. The outer end of the brake return spring, which shares the pivot shaft, should be displaced from the anchor peg on the frame, so that it may be removed at the same time as the pedal.

15 Dualseat: removal and replacement

1   The dualseat is attached to two lugs on the left side of the frame by two clevis pins secured with split pins. If it is necessary to remove the dualseat, withdraw the two split pins, take out the clevis pins, and the seat will lift off as a complete unit.

16 Speedometer and tachometer heads: removal and replacement

1   The speedometer and tachometer are both mounted together on a single panel on top of the front forks. They are secured in position by nuts on two studs projecting from the base of each instrument and passing through the shared mounting bracket and the base cover.
2   The instruments may be detached from the machine as a unit, after disconnecting the drive cables and the warning bulb leads at the block connector. After removing the base plate, the bulb holders may be pulled from position.
3   If either instrument fails to record, check the drive cable first before suspecting the head. If the instrument gives a jerky response it is probably due to a dry cable, or one that is trapped or kinked.
4   The speedometer and tachometer heads cannot be repaired by the private owner, and if a defect occurs a new instrument has to be fitted. Remember that a speedometer in correct working order is required by law on a machine in the UK and also in many other countries.
5   Speedometer and tachometer cables are only supplied as a complete assembly. Make sure the cables are routed correctly through the clamps provided on the top fork yoke, brake branch pipe, and the frame.

17 Speedometer and tachometer drives: location and examination

1   The speedometer is driven from a gearbox fitted to the front

wheel spindle on the left-hand side of the hub. Drive is transmitted through a dog plate fixed to the hub which engages with the drive gear in the gearbox.
2   Provided that the gearbox is repacked with grease from time to time, very little wear should be experienced. In the event of failure, the complete gearbox should be renewed. The tachometer drive is taken from the cylinder head cover, between number three and four cylinders. The drive is taken from the overhead camshaft by means of skew-cut pinions, and then by a flexible cable to the tachometer head. It is unlikely that the drive will give trouble during the normal service life of the machine, especially since it is fully enclosed and effectively lubricated.

18 Cleaning the machine

1   After removing all surface dirt with a rag or sponge which is washed frequently in clean water, the machine should be allowed to dry thoroughly. Application of car polish or wax to the cycle parts will give a good finish, particularly if the machine receives this attention at regular intervals.
2   The plated parts should require only a wipe with a damp rag, but if they are badly corroded, as may occur during the winter when the roads are salted, it is permissible to use one of the proprietary chrome cleaners. These often have an oily base which will help to prevent corrosion from recurring.
3   If the engine parts are particularly oily, use a cleaning compound such as Gunk or Jizer. Apply the compound whilst the parts are dry and work it in with a brush so that it has an opportunity to penetrate and soak into the film of oil and grease. Finish off by washing down liberally, taking care that water does not enter the carburettors, air cleaners or the electrics. If desired, the now clean aluminium alloy parts can be enhanced still further when they are dry by using a special polish such as Solvol Autosol. This will restore the full lustre.
4   If possible, the machine should be wiped down immediately after it has been used in the wet, so that it is not garaged under damp conditions which will promote rusting. Make sure that the chain is wiped and re-oiled, to prevent water from entering the rollers and causing harshness with an accompanying rapid rate of wear. Remember there is less chance of water entering the control cables and causing stiffness if they are lubricated regularly as described in the Routine Maintenance Section.

19 Fault diagnosis: frame and forks

Symptom	Cause	Remedy
Machine is unduly sensitive to road conditions	Forks and/or rear suspension units have defective damping	Check oil level in front forks. Renew rear suspension units.
Machine tends to roll at low speeds	Steering head bearings overtight or damaged	Slacken bearing adjustment. If no improvement, dismantle and inspect bearings.
Machine tends to wander, steering is imprecise	Worn swinging arm bearings	Check and if necessary renew bearings.
Fork action stiff	Fork legs have twisted in yokes or have been drawn together at lower ends	Slacken off spindle nut clamps, pinch bolts in fork yokes and fork top nuts. Pump forks several times before retightening from bottom
Forks judder when front brake is applied	Worn fork legs and stanchions Steering head bearings too slack	Renew one or both items. Readjust to take up play.
Wheels out of alignment	Frame distorted as result of accident damage	Check frame alignment after stripping out. If bent, specialist repair is necessary.

Chapter 5 Wheels, brakes and tyres

For additional information relating to 1978 and 1979 GS750 models and 1978 through 1982 GS550 models, refer to Chapter 7.

Contents

Specifications

Tyres:

Front	19 x 3.25 in H 19
Rear	18 x 4.00 in H 18 (18 x 3.75 in, GS 550 model)

Tyre pressures

	Solo	Pillion
Front	25 psi (1.75 kg – cm^2)	25 psi (1.75 kg – cm^2)
Rear	28 psi (2.0 kg – cm^2)	32 psi (2.25 kg – cm^2)

At continuous high speeds the pressure in both tyres should be raised an additional 3 psi (0.25 kg – cm^2)

Brakes

Front	*Double 297 mm (11.7 in) hydraulically operated disc
Rear	Single 297 mm (11.7 in) hydraulically operated disc

Model GS 750B has a single disc

Brake fluid specifications . . . .   DOT 3 or 4 (USA) SAE J1703a, b or c

1   General description

1   All models within the range are fitted with a 19 inch diameter wheel at the front and an 18 inch diameter wheel at the rear. The front tyre has a section of 3.25 inches and the rear tyre 3.75 inch on GS 550 and 4.00 inch on GS 750 models. The wheels are of traditional design having steel rims laced to an aluminium hub by butted and chromed spokes.

The GS 750B model, fitted with a single hydraulically-operated front disc brake, has been superseded by the 750DB model, which together with all the GS 550 models, has twin front disc brakes. The rear brake on the GS 750 model is a single disc, and on GS 550 models is a single leading shoe internally expanding drum brake.

2   Front wheel: examination and renovation

1   Place the machine on the centre stand so that the front

wheel is raised clear of the ground. Spin the wheel and check the rim alignment. Small irregularities can be corrected by tightening the spokes in the affected area although a certain amount of experience is necessary to prevent over-correction. Any flats in the wheel rim will be evident at the same time. These are more difficult to remove and in most cases it will be necessary to have the wheel rebuilt on a new rim. Apart from the effect on stability, a flat will expose the tyre bead and walls to greater risk of damage if the machine is run with a deformed wheel.

2   Check for loose and broken spokes. Tapping the spokes is the best guide to tension. A loose spoke will produce a quite different sound and should be tightened by turning the nipple in an anticlockwise direction. Always check for run out by spinning the wheel again. If the spokes have to be tightened by an excessive amount, it is advisable to remove the tyre and tube as detailed in Section 20 of this Chapter. This will enable the protruding ends of the spokes to be ground off, thus preventing them from chafing the inner tube and causing punctures.

3 Front wheel: removal and replacement

1   Place the machine on the centre stand so that it is resting securely on firm ground with the front wheel well clear of the ground. If necessary, place wooden blocks below the crankcase to raise the wheel.

2   Where two brake calipers are utilised, one must be detached from the fork leg to allow clearance for the wide section tyre. Remove the caliper as a complete unit – without disconnecting the hydraulic fluid hose – by unscrewing the two bolts which pass through the caliper support bracket and fork leg.

3   Disconnect the speedometer at the gearbox by unscrewing the knurled ring. Pull the cable through the guide clip. Displace the split pin from the wheel spindle nut and slacken the nut slightly. The wheel may be removed either by detaching the two spindle clamps or by slackening the clamp bolts and withdrawing the spindle. In the latter case the speedometer gearbox and wheel spacer will fall free as the wheel is lowered from place.

4   When refitting the wheel into the forks, ensure that the speedometer gearbox is fitted with the embossed arrow-mark pointing upwards. Tighten the wheel spindle nut fully before tightening the two spindle clamps, and do not omit the split pin. The two nuts holding each spindle clamp should be tightened down evenly so that the gap between the clamp and fork leg is equal either side of the wheel spindle.

4 Front brake assembly: examination and brake pad renewal

1   Check the front brake master cylinder, hoses and caliper units for signs of leakage. Pay particular attention to the condition of the hoses, which should be renewed without question if there are signs of cracking, splitting or other exterior damage. Check the hydraulic fluid level by referring to the upper and lower level lines visible on the exterior of the transparent reservoir body.

2   Replenish the reservoir after removing the cap on the brake fluid reservoir and lifting out the diaphragm plate. The condition of the fluid can be checked at the same time. Checking the fluid level is one of the maintenance tasks which should **never be neglected.** If the fluid is below the lower level mark, brake fluid of the correct specification must be added. **Never** use engine oil or any fluid other than that recommended. Other fluids have unsatisfactory characteristics and will rapidly destroy the seals.

3   The two sets of brake pads should be inspected for wear. Each has a red groove, which marks the wear limit of the friction material. When this limit is reached, both pads in the set must be renewed, even if only one has reached the wear mark. In normal use both sets of pads will wear at the same rate and therefore both sets must be renewed.

4   If the brake action becomes spongy, or if any part of the hydraulic system is dismantled (such as when a hose has been renewed) it is necessary to bleed the system in order to remove all traces of air. Follow the procedure in Section 6 of this Chapter.

5   To gain access to the pads for renewal, the caliper assembly must be detached from the front fork. Removal of the wheel is not required, nor is separation of the caliper from the hydraulic hose.

Remove the two bolts which pass through the fork leg into the caliper support bracket and lift the complete caliper unit upwards, off the disc.

6   Remove the single screw and the convolute backing plate from the inner side of the caliper unit. The inner pad is now free and may be displaced towards the centre of the caliper and lifted out. The outer pad which abuts against the caliper piston is not retained positively and may be lifted out.

7   Refit the new pads and replace the caliper by reversing the dismantling procedure. The caliper piston should be pushed inwards slightly so that there is sufficient clearance between the brake pads to allow the caliper to fit over the disc. It is recommended that the outer periphery of the outer (piston) pad is lightly coated with disc brake assembly grease (silicon grease). Use the grease sparingly and ensure that grease **DOES NOT** come in contact with the friction surface of the pad.

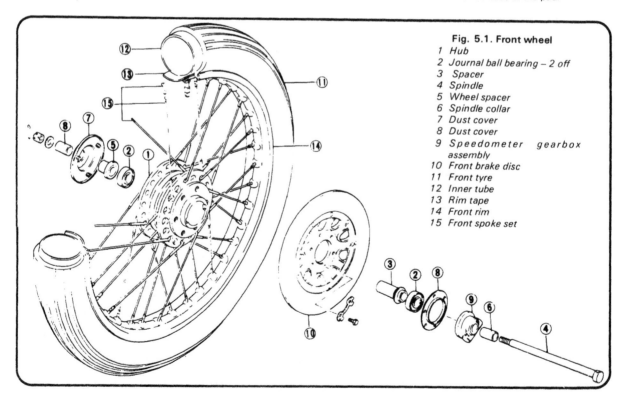

Fig. 5.1. Front wheel

1   Hub
2   Journal ball bearing – 2 off
3   Spacer
4   Spindle
5   Wheel spacer
6   Spindle collar
7   Dust cover
8   Dust cover
9   Speedometer gearbox assembly
10 Front brake disc
11 Front tyre
12 Inner tube
13 Rim tape
14 Front rim
15 Front spoke set

3.3a Disconnect the speedometer cable at the drive gearbox

3.3b Remove the nut and withdraw the spindle

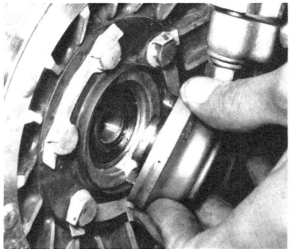

3.3c Speedometer gearbox will fall free as will ...

3.3d ... wheel spacer, as wheel is removed

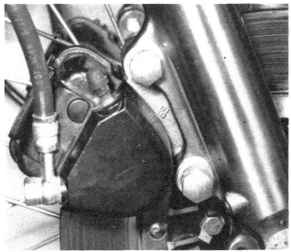

4.5 The caliper is secured by two chromed bolts

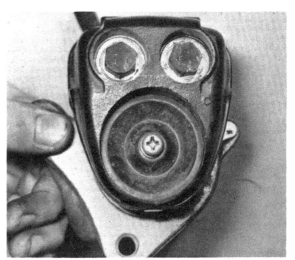

4.6a Remove screw and plate and ...

4.6b ... displace inner pad towards the piston pad

4.6c Piston pad is located by spring clip

5 Front brake caliper: examination and overhaul

1   Select a suitable receptacle into which may be drained the
hydraulic fluid. Remove the banjo bolt holding the hydraulic
hose at the caliper and allow the fluid to drain. Repeat this
operation with the second caliper unit (where fitted). Take great
care not to allow hydraulic fluid to spill onto paintwork; it is a
very effective paint stripper. Hydraulic fluid will also damage
rubber and plastic components.
2   Remove the caliper from the fork leg and displace the brake
pads as described in the preceding Section. Where two calipers
are fitted they should be dismantled and reassembled
individually, to prevent the accidental interchange of components.
3   Remove the two bolts (socket screws on the GS 550
models) which pass through the caliper body, and separate the
body from the caliper support bracket. Prise out the piston boot,
using a small screwdriver, taking care not to scratch the surface
of the cylinder bore. The piston can be displaced most easily by
applying an air jet to the hydraulic fluid feed orifice. Be prepared
to catch the piston as it falls free. Displace the annular piston
seal from the cylinder bore groove.
4   Clean the caliper components thoroughly in a fine solvent
or in hydraulic brake fluid. **CAUTION**: Never use petrol for

cleaning hydraulic brake parts otherwise the rubber components will be damaged. Discard all the rubber components as
a matter of course. The replacement cost is relatively small and
does not warrant re-use of components vital to safety. Check
the piston and caliper cylinder bore for scoring, rusting or
pitting. If any of these defects are evident it is unlikely that a
good fluid seal can be maintained and for this reason the components should be renewed.
5   To assemble the caliper, reverse the removal procedure.
When assembling pay attention to the following points. Apply
Suzuki caliper grease (high heat resistance) to the caliper
spindles. Apply a generous amount of brake fluid to the inner
surface of the cylinder and to the periphery of the piston, then
assemble. Do not assemble the piston with it inclined or
twisted. When installing the piston push it slowly into the
cylinder while taking care not to damage the piston seal. Apply
Suzuki brake pad grease around the periphery of the moving
pad. Bleed the brake after refilling the reservoir with new
hydraulic brake fluid, then check for leakage while applying the
brake lever tightly. After a test run, check the pads and brake
disc.
6   Note that any work on the hydraulic system must be
undertaken under ultra-clean conditions. Particles of dirt will
score the working parts and cause early failure of the system.

5.5 Support bracket must slide freely on the two spindles

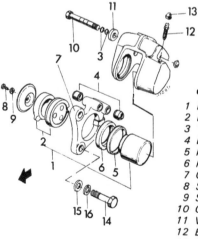

Fig. 5.2. Front brake caliper assembly

1 Piston/pad set
2 Pad set
3 'O' ring – 4 off
4 Dust cover – 4 off
5 Piston seal
6 Piston boot
7 Caliper support bracket
8 Screw
9 Spring washer
10 Caliper spindle – 2 off
11 Washer – 2 off
12 Bleed nipple
13 Dust cap
14 Bolt – 2 off
15 Plain washer – 2 off
16 Spring washer – 2 off

6 Front disc brake master cylinder: examination and renovation

1   The master cylinder and hydraulic reservoir take the form of a combined unit mounted on the right-hand side of the handlebars, to which the front brake lever is attached. The master cylinder is actuated by the front brake lever, and applies hydraulic pressure through the system to operate the front brake when the handlebar lever is manipulated. The master cylinder pressurises the hydraulic fluid in the brake pipe which, being incompressible, causes the piston to move in the caliper unit and apply the friction pads to the brake. If the master cylinder seals leak, hydraulic pressure will be lost and the braking action rendered much less effective.
2   Before the master cylinder can be removed the system must be drained. Place a clean container below the caliper unit and attach a plastic tube from the bleed screw on top of the caliper unit to the container. Open the bleed screw one complete turn and drain the system by operating the brake lever until the master cylinder reservoir is empty. Close the bleed screw and remove the pipe.
3   Remove the front brake stop lamp switch from the master cylinder (USA and Canadian specification). Unscrew the union bolt and disconnect the connection between the brake hose and the master cylinder. Unscrew the two master cylinder fastening bolts and remove the master cylinder body from the handlebar. Empty any surplus fluid from the reservoir.
4   Remove the brake lever from the body, remove the boot stopper (taking care not to damage the boot) and then remove the boot. Remove the circlip that was hidden by the boot, the piston, primary cup, spring and check valve. Place the parts in a clean container and wash them in new brake fluid. Examine the cylinder bore and piston for scoring. Renew if scored. Check also the brake lever for pivot wear, cracks or fractures and the hose union threads and brake pipe threads for cracks or other signs of deterioration.
5   When assembling the master cylinder follow the removal procedure in reverse order. Pay particular attention to the following points: Make sure the primary cup is fitted the correct way round. Renew the split pin of the brake lever pivot nut and fit it securely. Mount the master cylinder to the handlebar so the gap between it is 2 mm (0.08 in) and the reservoir is horizontal when the motorcycle is on the centre stand with the steering in the straight ahead direction. Fill with fresh fluid and bleed the system. Be sure to check the brake reservoir by removing the reservoir cap. If the level is below the ring mark inside the reservoir, refill to the level with the prescribed brake fluid.
6   The component parts of the master cylinder assembly and the caliper assembly may wear or deteriorate in function over a long period of use. It is however, generally difficult to foresee how long each component will work with proper efficiency and from a safety point of view it is best to change all the expendable parts every two years on a machine that has covered a normal mileage.

7 Bleeding the hydraulic brake system

1   If the hydraulic system has to be drained and refilled, if the front brake lever travel becomes excessive or the lever operates with a soft or spongy feeling, the brakes must be bled to expel air from the system. The procedure for bleeding the hydraulic brake is best carried out by two persons.
2   First check the fluid level in the reservoir and top up with fresh fluid.
3   Keep the reservoir at least half full of fluid during the bleeding procedure.
4   Screw the cap on to the reservoir to prevent a spout of fluid or the entry of dust into the system. Place a clean glass jar below the caliper bleed screw and attach a clear plastic pipe from the caliper bleed screw to the container. Place some clean hydraulic fluid in the jar so that the pipe is always immersed

below the surface of the fluid.
5   Unscrew the bleed screw one half turn and squeeze the brake lever as far as it will go but do not release it until the bleeder valve is closed again. Repeat the operation a few times until no more air bubbles come from the plastic tube.
6   Keep topping up the reservoir with new fluid. When all the bubbles disappear, close the bleeder valve. Remove the plastic tube and install the bleeder valve dust cap. Check the fluid level in the reservoir, after the bleeding operation has been completed.
7   Reinstall the diaphragm and tighten the reservoir cap securely. Do not use the brake fluid drained from system, since it will contain minute air bubbles.
8   Never use any fluid other than that recommended. Oil must not be used under any circumstances.

8 Front wheel bearings: examination and replacement

1   Access to the front wheel bearings can be made after removal of the speedometer gearbox and spindle spacer.
2   The wheel bearings can be drifted out of position, using a suitable drift. Support the wheel so the exit of the bearing is not obstructed. When the first bearing has been removed the spacer that lies between the two bearings can be removed. Insert the drift and drive out the opposite bearing.
3   Remove all the old grease from bearings and hub. Wash the bearings in petrol and dry them thoroughly. Check the bearings for roughness by spinning them whilst holding the inner track with one hand and rotating the outer track with the other. If there is the slightest sign of roughness renew them.
4   Before driving bearings back into the hub, pack the hub with new grease and also grease the bearings. Use the same double diameter drift to place them in position. Refit any oil seals or dust covers which have been displaced.

9 Removing and replacing the disc

1   It is unlikely that the brake discs will require attention unless bad scoring has developed or the discs have warped. To detach the discs first remove the wheel as described in Section 3 of this Chapter. Each disc is retained by six bolts screwed into the hub, which are linked in pairs by tab washers. Bend down the ears of the tab washers and remove the bolts. The discs can then be eased off the hub bosses.
2   Replace the discs by reversing the dismantling procedure. Ensure that the twelve nuts are tightened fully and that the tab washer ears are bent up against the bolt head flats.

Fig. 5.3. Front brake master cylinder

1 Piston and seal set
2 Master cylinder assembly
3 Fluid reservoir cap
4 Diaphragm ring
5 Diaphragm
6 Reservoir clamp plate
7 Reservoir
8 O ring
9 Screw – 2 off
10 Bolt – 2 off

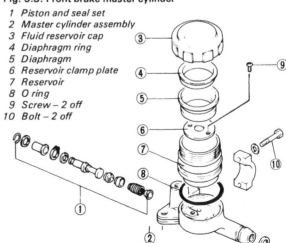

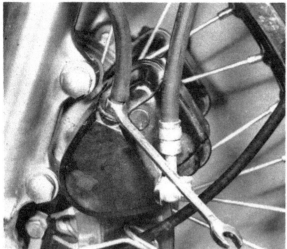

7.4 Fit a length of tube to caliper nipple when bleeding brakes

8.2 Drift bearings out carefully

8.3a Do not omit bearing spacer on reassembly

8.3b Bearings incorporating seals should be fitted seal outwards

8.3c Check condition of seals before reinstalling

9.1 The disc is retained by bolts secured by locking plates

10 Rear wheel: examination , removal and renovation

1   Place the machine on the centre stand so that the rear wheel is raised clear of the ground. Check for rim alignment, damage to the rim and loose or broken spokes by following the procedure relating to the front wheel, as described in Section 2 of this Chapter.

2   To remove the rear wheel first detach the plastic chain-guard which is retained by two bolts.

GS 550 models

3   It is recommended that both silencers are removed to improve access. Each is retained by a single bolt passing through a lug on the underside of the silencer body. It will be necessary also to slacken the two clamps at the silencer/exhaust pipe joints.

4   Detach the torque arm from the brake back plate after removing the nut secured by a split pin. Unscrew the brake rod adjuster nut fully and depress the brake pedal so that the rod leaves the trunnion in the brake operating arm. Refit the nut to secure the rod spring.

5   Remove the wheel spindle nut after displacing the split pin. Withdraw the wheel spindle from the left-hand side and catch the right-hand spacer as it falls free. The sprocket, still meshed with the chain, can be pulled out, away from the hub to free the wheel. The cush drive hub will come away with the sprocket, leaving the cush drive rubber inserts in position. Tilt the wheel slightly and remove it from between the fork arms.

GS 750 models

6   Unscrew the bolt passing vertically through each chain adjuster block. The right-hand bolt also secures the hydraulic hose guide clamp. Remove the split pin and nut securing the torque arm rod to the top of the caliper support bracket. Detach the caliper from the support bracket by removing the two mounting bolts. Suspend the caliper from the rear right-hand indicator stalk so that it does not obstruct further dismantling and does not become damaged.

7   After loosening the locknuts, unscrew the two wheel adjuster bolts so that the adjuster brackets can be swung

downwards below the fork ends. Remove the R spring securing the spindle nut and slacken the nut. Push the wheel forwards fully and lift the chain off the sprocket, pulling to the outside of the fork end and then forwards to clear the wheel spindle head. The wheel can now be moved rearwards, tilted and removed from between the fork arms.

All models

8   Refit the wheel by reversing the dismantling procedure. Ensure that the torque arm is secure and that the securing split pins are fitted. Likewise do not omit the wheel spindle nut securing pin. Before tightening the spindle nut, the final drive chain should be adjusted so that there is 20 – 30 mm (0.8 – 1.2 inch) up and down play measured in the centre of the chain lower run. Refer to the index marks on the fork ends when tightening the adjuster bolts, to ensure that wheel alignment is maintained.

11 Rear disc brake: examination and pad renewal

1   In general, remarks concerning the front disc brake as described in Section 4 of this Chapter apply equally to the rear disc brake. The rear brake master cylinder/reservoir unit is fitted to the right-hand side of the machine, behind and below the frame cover.

2   To inspect the brake pads for wear, prise off the inspection cap fitted to the top of the caliper. Each pad is stepped slightly, the step nearer the backing plate being painted red. If either pad is worn down to the red line, the pads must be renewed as a set.

3   Pad removal may take place without displacing the caliper unit or the wheel. Pull out the stop pin which passes through each of the two pad mounting pins. Displace one mounting pin and remove the two hair springs. Push out the final pin and lift each pad out individually, removing the outer pad first.

4   Install new pads by reversing the dismantling procedure. If necessary, push back each piston to give the required clearance between the piston and the disc. The shim fitted to the piston side of each pad must be positioned with the punched arrow mark pointing in the direction of wheel travel.

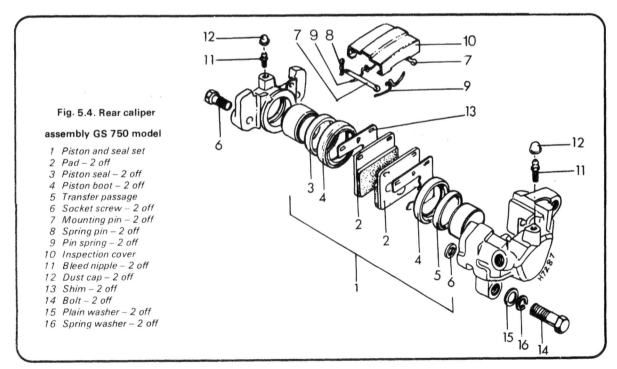

Fig. 5.4. Rear caliper

assembly GS 750 model

1 Piston and seal set
2 Pad – 2 off
3 Piston seal – 2 off
4 Piston boot – 2 off
5 Transfer passage
6 Socket screw – 2 off
7 Mounting pin – 2 off
8 Spring pin – 2 off
9 Pin spring – 2 off
10 Inspection cover
11 Bleed nipple – 2 off
12 Dust cap – 2 off
13 Shim – 2 off
14 Bolt – 2 off
15 Plain washer – 2 off
16 Spring washer – 2 off

10.6a Detach the caliper unit from the support bracket after ...

10.6b ... removing the torque rod nut and bolt

10.7a Loosen the spindle nut and ...

10.7b ... pull the wheel rearwards out of the fork ends

10.8a On refitting rear wheel check spindle nut spring pin and

10.8b ... torque nut split pin are fitted securely

11.2a Prise the caliper inspection cap off the caliper

11.3a Remove the mounting pin stop pins and ...

11.3b ... withdraw the pins to free the pads

11.4a Each pad can then be lifted out

11.4b The triangular arrow on pad shim must face direction of wheel

12 Rear disc brake caliper: examination and overhaul

1   Unlike the front brake caliper, which has only one piston. The rear brake caliper has two pistons and two moving brake pads. The general procedure however for dismantling and overhaul is similar to that described for the front brake in Section 5 of this Chapter.

2   After reassembling the caliper, the hydraulic circuit should be bled of all air as described in Section 7. Both sides of the caliper unit should be bled simultaneously by fitting separate bleed pipes to the two nipples provided.

13 Rear brake master cylinder: removal and overhaul

1   In common with the unit fitted to the front brake system, the rear brake master cylinder and fluid reservoir are a combined unit. The master cylinder is fitted inboard of the rear frame right-hand triangulation and is operated via a pushrod from the foot brake pedal.

2   To detach the master cylinder, remove the split pin and clevis pin from the lower end of the operating pushrod. Disconnect the hydraulic hose at the master cylinder by removing the

banjo bolt, and allow the hose fluid to drain into a suitable container. The master cylinder is secured to the frame by two bolts passing through lugs on the master cylinder body.

3   Remove the reservoir cap and diaphragm and allow the fluid to drain. Pull the gaiter along the pushrod and remove the circlip to allow detachment of the pushrod assembly. Using a wood dowel inserted through the hydraulic fluid inlet orifice push out the piston/seal assembly.

4   Refer to the procedure given in Section 6 for inspection and reassembly details.

14 Rear wheel drum brake: examination and renovation (GS 550 models)

1   After removal of rear wheel the brake plate complete with brake shoes can be removed from the wheel hub.

2   Examine the brake linings for oil, dirt or grease. Surface dirt can be removed with a stiff brush but oil soaked linings should be replaced. High spots can be carefully eased down with emery cloth.

3   Examine the condition of the brake linings and if they have worn thin they should be renewed. The brake linings are bonded to the brake shoes and thus separate linings are not available.

4   To remove the shoes, pull them away from the cam and then pull them away from the plate in a V formation so that they can be removed together, complete with the return springs. When they are well clear of the brake plate, the springs can be removed. Check the springs for any signs of wear or stretching and renew, if necessary. Check the surface of the brake drum for wear or scoring.

5   Whilst the brake plate is off, the brake cam spindle should be lubricated sparingly with grease. Mark the relative position of the brake operating arm and the splined end of the cam shaft. Remove the pinch bolt and pull off the arm. The cam shaft may be pushed out towards the inside of the back plate. Note the O ring on the cam shaft, which prevents the escape of grease. When refitting the cam shaft and arm, realign the marks to restore the original position.

6   The brake drum should be checked for scoring. This happens if the brake shoe linings have been allowed to get too thin. The drums should be quite smooth. Remove all traces of lining dust and wipe with a clean rag soaked in petrol to remove all traces of grease and oil.

7   To reassemble the brake shoe on the brake plate, fit the return springs and pull the shoes apart, holding them in a V formation. If they are now located with the cam they can be pushed back into position. Do not use excessive force or there is a risk of distorting the shoes or over-stretching the springs.

15 Adjusting the rear brake

GS 550 models only

1   Adjustment of the rear brake is correct when there is 20 – 30 mm ($\frac{3}{4}$″ – 1″ approx) up and down movement measured at the rear brake pedal foot piece, between the fully off and on position.

2   If, when the brake is fully applied, the angle between the brake arm and the operating rod is more than 90° the brake arm should be pulled off the camshaft, after loosening the pinch bolt. Reset the brake arm so that the right angle is produced.

3   Note that it may be necessary to adjust the height-setting of the stop lamp switch after adjustment of the brake pedal position.

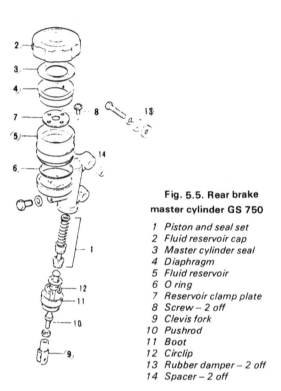

Fig. 5.5. Rear brake master cylinder GS 750

1 Piston and seal set
2 Fluid reservoir cap
3 Master cylinder seal
4 Diaphragm
5 Fluid reservoir
6 O ring
7 Reservoir clamp plate
8 Screw – 2 off
9 Clevis fork
10 Pushrod
11 Boot
12 Circlip
13 Rubber damper – 2 off
14 Spacer – 2 off

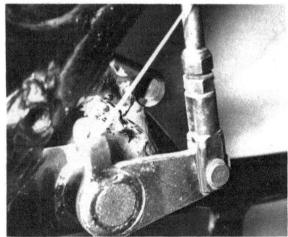

13.2a Rear master cylinder pushrod is secured by clevis pin

13.2b Master cylinder is retained by two bolts

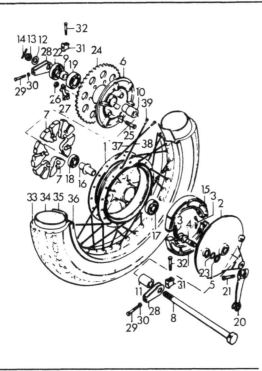

Fig. 5.6. Rear wheel assembly – GS 550

1 Hub	21 Clamp bolt
2 Brake plate	22 Oil seal
3 Return spring – 2 off	23 O ring
4 Camshaft	24 Rear wheel sprocket
5 Washer	25 Bolt – 6 off
6 Cush drive hub	26 Nut – 6 off
7 Cush drum rubbers	27 Locking plate – 3 off
8 Wheel spindle	28 Adjuster – 2 off
9 Spacer	29 Draw bolt – 2 off
10 Distance piece	30 Locknut – 2 off
11 Spacer	31 Fillet – 2 off
12 Washer	32 Bolt
13 Nut	33 Tyre
14 Split pin	34 Inner tube
15 Brake shoe – 2 off	35 Rim tape
16 Bearing spacer	36 Rim
17 Bearing	37 Spoke
18 Bearing	38 Spoke
19 Bearing	39 Spoke nipple
20 Operating lever	

16 Rear wheel bearings: removal and replacement

1   The rear wheel assembly has three journal ball bearings. One bearing lies each side of the wheel hub and the third bearing is fitted in the cush drive assembly to which is attached the sprocket.

On GS 550 models, the cush drive sprocket unit can be removed from engagement with the final drive chain after the rear wheel spindle has been withdrawn and the wheel lifted over to the right-hand side of the swinging arm fork. On GS 750 models, the rear wheel must be removed completely before the cush drive hub can be lifted from the wheel hub.

2   Drift the wheel bearings from position using the same method as described for the front wheel. Before the cush drive bearing is tapped out, the hollow spindle should be removed. It is not necessary to remove the sprocket.

The cush drive hub bearing oil seal may be drifted out at the same time as the bearing.

17 Rear cush drive: examination and renovation

1   The cush drive assembly is contained in the left-hand side of the wheel hub. It takes the form of six triangular rubber pads incorporating slots, that fit within the vanes of the hub. A heavily ribbed plate bolted to the rear sprocket engages with the slots to form a shock absorber which permits the sprocket to move within certain limits. This absorbs any surge or roughness in the transmission. The rubbers should be renewed when movement of the sprocket indicates bad compaction of the rubbers or if they commence to break up.

18 Rear wheel sprocket: examination and replacement

1   The rear wheel sprocket is held to the cush drive hub by six bolts locked by three tab washers. To remove the sprocket, bend back the locking tabs and undo the bolts. The sprocket need only be renewed if the teeth are worn or chipped. It is always a good policy to change both sprockets at the same time, together with the chain, otherwise the worn component will cause rapid wear of the new component(s).

17.1a Cush drive hub is a push fit in rubber inserts

17.1b Do not omit spacer when replacing hub

19 Final drive chain: examination and lubrication

1   As the final drive chain is fully exposed on all models it requires lubrication and adjustment at regular intervals. To adjust the chain, take out the split pin from the rear wheel spindle and slacken the spindle nut. Undo the locknut on the chain adjusters and turn the adjuster bolts inwards to tighten the chain. Marks on the adjusters must be in line with identical marks on the frame fork to align the rear wheel correctly. A final check can be made by laying a straight wooden plank alongside the wheels, each side in turn. Chain tension is correct if there is 15 – 20 mm (0.6 – 0.8 in) of slack in the middle of the chain run betweeen the two sprockets.
2   Do not run the chain too tight to try to compensate for wear as it will absorb a surprising amount of engine power. Also it can damage the gearbox and rear wheel bearings.

A chain that is run exceptionally slack may strike the gear indicator switch which is retained on the gearbox wall. If the switch body breaks, lubricant loss from the gearbox may endanger the continued good health of the gearbox components.
3   The chain fitted to the Suzuki GS 550 and GS 750 models is of unusual design in that when the chain is lubricated on initial assembly, the lubricant is sealed in for the life of the component by O rings placed on each end of the rollers. Although the internal bearing surfaces of the chain are permanently lubricated, the outside of the rollers and the sprockets with which they mesh are not. Lubricant should be applied at regular intervals to prevent wear of the sprockets and rollers. One of the proprietary chain lubricants applied cold, should be used. The chain should not be immersed in a molten lubricant as is usual with chains because the O rings will suffer damage caused by the heat. Nor should aerosol lubricants or solvents other than paraffin be used. These too may damage the O rings.
4   If the chain is of the original endless type, it is necessary to remove the complete swinging arm assembly in order to detach the chain for renewal. Refer to Chapter 4, Section 9.
5   To check if the chain is due for renewal, lay it lengthwise in a straight line and compress it endwise until all play is taken up. Anchor one end, then pull in the opposite direction to take up the play which has developed. If the chain extends by more than $\frac{1}{4}$ inch per foot, it should be renewed with the sprockets.

20 Tyres: removal and replacement

1   At some time or other the need will arise to remove and replace the tyres, either as a result of a puncture or because replacements are necessary to offset wear. To the inexperienced, tyre changing represents a formidable task, yet if a few simple rules are observed and the technique learned, the whole operation is surprisingly simple.
2   To remove the tyre from either wheel, first detach the wheel from the machine. Deflate the tyre by removing the valve insert and when it is fully deflated, push the bead from the tyre away from the wheel rim on both sides so that the bead enters the centre well of the rim. Remove the locking cap and push the tyre valve into the tyre itself.
3   Insert a tyre lever close to the valve and lever the edge of the tyre over the outside of the wheel rim. Very little force should be exerted; if resistance is encountered it is probably due to the fact that the tyre beads have not entered the well of the wheel rim all the way round the tyre.
4   Once the tyre has been edged over the wheel rim, it is easy to work around the wheel rim so that the tyre is completely free on one side. At this stage, the inner tube can be removed.
5   Working from the other side of the wheel, ease the other edge of the tyre over the outside of the wheel rim that is furthest away. Continue to work around the rim until the tyre is free completely from the rim.
6   If a puncture has necessitated the removal of the tyre, reinflate the inner tube and immerse in a bowl of water to trace the source of the leak. Mark its position and deflate the tube. Dry the tube and clean the area around the puncture with a petrol soaked rag. When the surface has dried, apply rubber solution and allow this to dry before removing the backing from the patch and applying the patch to the surface.
7   It is best to use a patch of self-vulcanising type, which will form a very permanent repair. Note that it may be necessary to remove a protective covering from the top surface of the patch, after it has sealed into position. Inner tubes made from synthetic rubber may require a special type of patch and adhesive, if a satisfactory bond is to be achieved.
8   Before refitting the tyre, check the inside to make sure that the agent which caused the puncture is not trapped. Check the outside of the tyre, particularly the tread area, to make sure nothing is trapped that may cause a further puncture.
9   If the inner tube has been patched on a number of past occasions, or if there is a tear or large hole, it is preferable to

19.1 Align rear wheel by means of index marks on fork ends

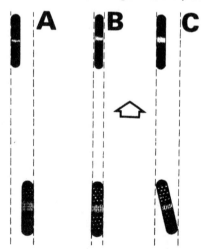

Fig. 5.7. Checking wheel alignment

A and C incorrect

B correct

Tyre changing sequence - tubed tyres

A Deflate tyre. After pushing tyre beads away from rim flanges push tyre bead into well of rim at point opposite valve. Insert tyre lever adjacent to valve and work bead over edge of rim.

Use two levers to work bead over edge of rim. Note use of rim protectors

B

C Remove inner tube from tyre

When first bead is clear, remove tyre as shown

D

E When fitting, partially inflate inner tube and insert in tyre

Work first bead over rim and feed valve through hole in rim. Partially screw on retaining nut to hold valve in place.

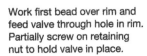

F

G Check that inner tube is positioned correctly and work second bead over rim using tyre levers. Start at a point opposite valve.

Work final area of bead over rim whilst pushing valve inwards to ensure that inner tube is not trapped

H

discard it and fit a new one. Sudden deflation may cause an accident, particularly if it occurs with the front wheel.

10 To replace the tyre, inflate the inner tube sufficiently for it to assume a circular shape but only just. Then push it into the tyre so that it is enclosed completely. Lay the tyre on the wheel at an angle and insert the valve through the rim tape and the hole in the wheel rim. Attach the locking cap on the first few threads, sufficient to hold the valve captive in its correct location.

11 Starting at the point furthest from the valve, push the tyre bead over the edge of the wheel rim until it is located in the central well. Continue to work around the tyre in this fashion until the whole of one side of the tyre is on the rim. It may be necessary to use a tyre lever during the final stages.

12 Make sure that there is no pull on the tyre valve and again commencing with the area furthest from the valve, ease the other bead of the tyre over the edge of the rim. Finish with the area close to the valve, pushing the valve up into the tyre until the locking cap touches the rim. This will ensure the inner tube is not trapped when the last section of the bead is edged over the rim with a tyre lever.

13 Check that the inner tube is not trapped at any point. Reinflate the inner tube, and check that the tyre is seating correctly around the wheel rim. There should be a thin rib moulded around the wall of the tyre on both sides, which should be equidistant from the wheel rim at all points. If the tyre is unevenly located on the rim, try bouncing the wheel when the tyre is at the recommended pressure. It is probable that one of the beads has not pulled clear of the centre well.

14 Always run the tyres at the recommended pressures and never under or over-inflate. The correct pressures for solo use are given in the Specifications Section of this Chapter.

15 Tyre replacement is aided by dusting the side walls, particularly in the vicinity of the beads, with a liberal coating of french chalk. Washing-up liquid can also be used to good effect, but this has the disadvantage of causing the inner surfaces of the wheel rim to rust.

16 Never replace the inner tube and tyre without the rim tape in position. If this precaution is overlooked there is good chance of the ends of the spoke nipples chafing the inner tube and causing a crop of punctures.

17 Never fit a tyre that has a damaged tread or side walls. Apart from the legal aspects, there is a very great risk of a blowout, which can have serious consequences on any two-wheel vehicle.

18 Tyre valves rarely give trouble, but it is always advisable to check whether the valve itself is leaking before removing the tyre. Do not forget to fit the dust cap, which forms an effective second seal.

21 Tyre valve dust caps

1 Tyre valve dust caps are often left off when a tyre has been replaced, despite the fact that they serve an important two-fold function. Firstly they prevent dirt or other foreign matter from entering the valve and causing the valve to stick open when the tyre pump is next applied. Secondly, they form an effective second seal so that in the event of the tyre valve sticking, air will not be lost.

2 Isolated cases of sudden deflation at high speeds have been traced to the omission of the dust cap. Centrifugal force has tended to lift the tyre valve off its seating and because the dust cap is missing, there has been no second seal. Racing inner tubes contain provision for this happening because the valve inserts are fitted with stronger springs, but standard inner tubes do not, hence the need for the dust cap.

3 Note that when a dust cap is fitted for the first time, the wheel may have to be rebalanced.

22 Front wheel: balancing

1 It is customary on all high performance machines to balance the front wheel complete with tyre and tube. The out of balance forces which exist are eliminated and the handling of the machine is improved in consequence. A wheel which is badly out of balance produces through the steering a most unpleasant hammering effect at high speeds.

2 Some tyres have a balance mark on the sidewall, usually in the form of a coloured dot. This mark must be in line with the tyre valve, when the tyre is fitted to the inner tube. Even then, the wheel may require the addition of balance weights, to offset the weight of the tyre valve itself.

3 If the front wheel is raised clear of the ground and is spun, it will probably come to rest with the tyre valve or the heaviest part downward and will always come to rest in the same position. Balance weights must be added to a point diametrically opposite this heavy spot until the wheel will come to rest in ANY position after it is spun.

4 Balance weights which clip around the wheel spokes are normally available in 20 or 30 gramme sizes. If they are not available, wire solder, wrapped around the spokes close to the spoke nipples, forms a good substitute.

5 There is no necessity to balance the rear wheel under normal road conditions, although it is advisable to replace the rear wheel tyre so that any balance mark is in line with the tyre valve.

23 Fault diagnosis: wheels, brakes and tyres

Symptom	Cause	Remedy
Handlebars oscillate at low speed	Buckle or flat in wheel rim, most probably front wheel Tyre not straight on rim	Check rim alignment by spinning the wheel. Correct by retensioning spokes or having wheel rebuilt on new rim. Check tyre alignment.
Machine lacks power and accelerates poorly	Brakes binding (rear brake) Wrongly adjusted caliper	Hot brake drum provides best evidence. Readjust caliper.
Brakes grab when applied gently	Ends of brake shoes not chamfered (internal expanding brake) Eliptical brake drum (internal expanding brake) Faulty caliper, on disc brake Warped disc	Chamfer with a file. Lightly skim in a lathe by a specialist. Replace with a new caliper. Replace disc if beyond skimming limit.
Brake squeal	Glazed pads Extremely dirty and dusty front brake caliper and disc assembly	Lightly sand the pads, and use the brake gently for a hundred miles or so until they have a chance to bed in properly. Clean with water; do not use high pressure spray equipment.
Excessive lever travel on front brake	Air in system, or leak in master clyinder or caliper; worn disc pads	Bleed the brake. Renew the cylinder seals. Renew the pads.

Chapter 6 Electrical system

For additional information relating to 1978 and 1979 GS750 models and 1978 through 1982 GS550 models, refer to Chapter 7.

Contents

Specifications

	GS 750	GS 550
Battery		
Make	Furukawa	Yuasa
Type	12N14 – 3A	YB 10L – A2
Voltage	12	12
Capacity	14 AH	10 AH
Earth or ground	Negative	Negative
Alternator		
Make	Nippon Denso or Kokusan	Nippon Denso or Kokusan
Type	Permanent magnet rotor 12 coil stator	Permanent magnet rotor 12 coil stator
No load voltage	17 volts	17 volts
Stator coil resistance	0.65 ohm ± 0.05%	0.65 ohm ± 0.05%
Starter motor		
Make	Mitsuba or Nippon Denso	Mitsuba or Nippon Denso
Brush length	12 – 13 mm (0.47 – 0.51 in)	14 mm (0.55 in)
Service limit	6 mm (0.24 in)	9 mm (0.35 in)
Commutator under cut	0.6 mm (0.020 in)	0.6 mm (0.020 in)
Service limit	0.2 mm (0.008 in)	0.2 mm (0.008 in)
Bulbs		
Headlamp	50/35 watt (USA) 50/40 watt (UK)	50/35 watt (USA) 50/40 watt (UK)
Tail/stop lamp	8/23 watt (3.32 cp)	8/23 watt (3.32 cp)
Pilot lamp	3.4 watt	3.4 watt
Instrument lights	3.4 watt	3.4 watt
High beam indicator light	3.4 watt	3.4 watt
Oil pressure warning light	3.4 watt	3.4 watt
Neutral indicator light	3.4 watt	3.4 watt
Flashing indicator lamps	23 watt	23 watt
Indicator warning light	3.4 watt	3.4 watt

All bulbs rated at 12 volt

1 General description

The Suzuki GS 750 and GS 550 models are fitted with a 12 volt electrical system, powered by an alternator mounted on the extreme left-hand end of the crankshaft. The alternator, which produces alternating current, is of the three-stage type, having a permanent magnet rotor and a twelve-coil stator. During daylight running, when no lights are being used, only two of the three output stages are utilised. The third stage remains out of circuit until the lighting switch is operated, when additional current is required to meet the demands of the lighting circuit.

The AC current produced by the alternator is converted into DC current by a full-wave silicon rectifier and is controlled to meet the voltage demands of the system by a solid state regulator (SCR).

2 Testing the electrical system: general

1 Checking the electrical output and the performance of the various components within the charging system requires the use of test equipment of the multi-meter type. When carrying out checks, care must be taken to follow the procedures laid down and so prevent inadvertent incorrect connections or short circuits. Irreparable damage to individual components may result if reversal of current or shorting occurs. It is advised that unless some previous experience has been gained in auto-electrical testing, the machine be returned to a Suzuki Service Agent or auto-electrician, who will be qualified to carry out the work and have the necessary test equipment.

2 If the performance of the charging system is suspect, the system as a whole should be checked first, followed by testing of the individual components to isolate the fault. The three main components are the alternator, the rectifier, and the regulator. Before commencing the tests, ensure that the battery is fully charged, as described in Section 7.

3 Charging system: checking the output

1st test
1 The first test is performed in a no-load state, with the regulator disconnected, and will verify whether the alternator and rectifier are functioning. Raise the dualseat so that the access may be made to the wiring harness.

2 Disconnect the yellow wire running from the regulator. Disconnect the white/green wire running from the alternator and the white/red wire from the rectifier. Connect these two wires together to by-pass the lighting switch. Turn the lighting switch off. Connect a 0-20v DC voltmeter across the battery terminals. Start the engine and increase the speed to 5,000 rpm. At this speed the indicated voltage should be 17v (16.5 on GS 550 models) or over. If the voltage is below 17v (16.5 on GS 550 models) the alternator or the rectifier is faulty. To eliminate the faulty component refer to Section 4 or 5 of this Chapter.

2nd test
3 If the first test proved that both the alternator and rectifier are functioning correctly, the second test should be carried out to determine the performance of the regulator. Reconnect the wires so that they are restored to their original positions. Turn the lighting switch off so that only two of the three output stages are in circuit. On models supplied to the USA, where the lighting switch is locked in the On position, remove the switch knob and turn the switch off.

4 Start the engine and again check the voltage at 5,000 rpm. If the indicated voltage is within the range 14.0 – 15.5 volts the regulator is functioning correctly. A reading above or below this range indicates that the regulator is faulty. Before consigning the regulator to the scrap bin, check that all the wiring connections are clean and tight. Again check that the battery is fully charged and repeat the test. A replacement regulator must be of the same make as the alternator.

4 Rectifier: location and testing

1 The rectifier is fitted behind the left-hand side cover on GS 550 models and behind the right-hand side cover on GS 750 models. If the rectifier is suspected of being faulty after carrying out test No 1 in the preceding Section, it may be tested in situ using a multi-meter set to the resistance function.

2 Disconnect the battery to isolate the electrical system and then disconnect all five wires which lead to the rectifier unit. Connect the negative ohmmeter lead to the regulator earth terminal (black/white) and then test the continuity between the earth and the following terminals: yellow, white/red, red/blue. Continuity should be indicated on each. Reverse the polarity of the ohmmeter and repeat the test. No continuity should be indicated. Carry out the same series of tests but with the output terminal (red) used as the common test terminal, in place of the earth terminal. The correct results should be the reverse of those given for the first part of the test. If one or more incorrect readings is found, the rectifier must be renewed.

5 Alternator: testing

1 If after carrying out test No 1 in Section 3 of this Chapter it was found that the alternator or rectifier was not functioning correctly, as indicated by the voltage reading, the alternator may be tested after removal of the stator from the machine, using a multi-meter set to the resistance function.

2 Disconnect the leads running from the alternator and check the continuity between the three wires, making the test in pairs. The correct resistance is 0.65 ohms ± 0.05%. If there is found to be no continuity between any two of the wires, or if the resistance is too low, a short-circuit or open-circuit is evident, and the stator must be renewed. Two makes of alternator are utilised, Denso and Kokusan. When renewing the stator, ensure that the replacement component is of the same manufacture as the rotor. Note also that after engine No GS 750 – 44985 the GS 750 was fitted with a modified alternator. The stator from one type will not fit the rotor of the other.

3 Check the resistance between each wire and the stator core. No continuity should be found.

6 Battery: examination and maintenance

1 Both models are fitted with a 12 volt battery of which the GS 750 has a 14 ampere hour capacity and the GS 550 a 10 ampere hour capacity.

2 The transparent plastic case of the battery permits the upper and lower levels of the electrolyte to be observed without disturbing the battery by removing the left-hand side cover. Maintenance is normally limited to keeping the electrolyte level between the prescribed upper and lowerlimits and making sure that the vent tube is not blocked. The lead plates and their separators are also visible through the transparent case, a further guide to the general condition of the battery.

3 Unless acid is spilt, as may occur if the machine falls over, the electrolyte should always be topped up with distilled water to restore the correct level. If acid is spilt onto any part of the machine, it should be neutralised with an alkali such as washing soda or baking powder and washed away with plenty of water, otherwise serious corrosion will occur. Top up- with sulphuric acid of the correct specific gravity (1.260 to 1.280) only when spillage has occurred. Check that the vent pipe is well clear of the frame or any of the other cycle parts.

4 It is seldom practicable to repair a cracked battery case because the acid present in the joint will prevent the formation of an effective seal. It is always best to renew a cracked battery, especially in view of the corrosion which will be caused if the acid continues to leak.

5   If the machine is not used for a period, it is advisable to remove the battery and give it a refresher charge every six weeks or so from a battery charger. If the battery is permitted to discharge completely, the plates will sulphate and render the battery useless.

6   Occasionally, check the condition of the battery terminals to ensure that corrosion is not taking place and that the electrical connections are tight. If corrosion has occurred, it should be cleaned away by scraping with a knife and then using emery cloth to remove the final traces. Remake the electrical connections whilst the joint is still clean, then smear the assembly with petroleum jelly (NOT grease) to prevent recurrence of the corrosion. Badly corroded connections can have a high electrical resistance and may give the impression of a complete battery failure.

7   Battery: charging procedure

1   The normal charging rate for batteries of up to 14 amp. hour capacity is $1\frac{1}{2}$ amps. It is permissible to charge at a more rapid rate in an emergency but this shortens the life of the battery, and should be avoided. Always remove the vent caps when recharging a battery, otherwise the gas created within the

battery when charging takes place will explode and burst the case with disastrous consequences.

8   Fuse: location and replacement

1   A fuse is incorporated in the electrical system. It is contained in a plastic holder and clips to the side of the battery holder. The fuse is incorporated in the system to give protection from a sudden overload such as could happen with a short circuit. The fuse is rated at 15 amps.

2   If the fuse blows it should not be renewed until the cause of the short is found. This will involve checking the electrical circuit to correct the fault. If this rule is not observed, the fuse will almost certainly blow again.

3   When a fuse blows and no spare is available a, "get you home" remedy is to wrap the fuse in silver paper before replacing it in the fuse holder. The silver paper will restore electrical continuity by bridging the broken wire within the fuse. Replace the doctored fuse at the earliest opportunity to restore full circuit protection. Make sure any short circuit is eliminated first.

4   Always carry two spare fuses of the correct rating.

4.1 The rectifier is the finned component behind the frame side cover

5.1. Alternator stator is secured to the alternator cover

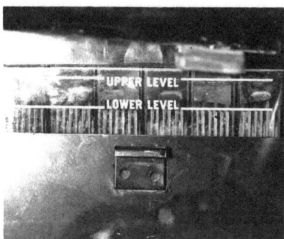

6.2 Electrolyte level must fall between the two lines

6.6 Ensure that the terminal screws are tight

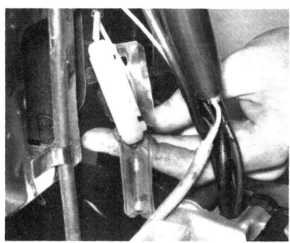

8.1 In-line fuse holder, with spare fuse

9 Starter motor: removal, examination and replacement

1 An electric starter motor, operated from a small push-button on the right-hand side of the handlebars, provides an alternative and more convenient method of starting the engine, without having to use the kickstart. The starter motor is mounted within a compartment at the rear of the cylinder block, closed by an oblong, chromium plated cover. Current is supplied from the battery via a heavy duty solenoid switch and a cable capable of carrying the very high current demanded by the starter motor on the initial start-up.

2 The starter motor drives a free running clutch immediately behind the generator rotor. The clutch ensures the starter motor drive is disconnected from the primary transmission immediately the engine starts. It operates on the centrifugal principle; spring loaded rollers take up the drive until the centrifugal force of the rotating engine overcomes their resistance and the drive is automatically disconnected.

3 To remove the starter motor from the engine unit, first disconnect the positive lead from the battery, to isolate the electrical system. Remove the cover plate which encloses the starter motor and detach the heavy duty cable from the terminal on the starter motor body. Temporarily detach the oil pressure switch lead from the switch. The starter motor is secured to the crankcase by two bolts which pass through the left-hand end of the motor casting. When these bolts are withdrawn, the motor can be prised out of position and lifted out of its compartment.

4 The parts of the starter motor most likely to require attention are the brushes. The end cover is retained by the two long screws which pass through the lugs cast on both end pieces. If the screws are withdrawn, the end cover can be lifted away and the brush gear exposed.

5 Lift up the spring clips which bear on the end of each brush and remove the brushes from their holders. The standard length and wear limit of the brushes depends on the make of starter motor employed, as follows:

	standard length	service limit
Mitsuba	12–13 mm	6 mm
	(0.47–0.51 in)	(0.24 in)
Denso	14 mm	9 mm
	(0.55 in)	(0.35 in)

6 Before the brushes are replaced, make sure the commutator is clean, on which they bear. Clean with a strip of fine glass paper cloth pressed against the commutator whilst the latter is revolved by hand.

Emery paper should **NOT** be used because abrasive fragments may embed themselves in the soft metal of the commutator and cause excessive wear of the brushes. Finish off the commutator with metal polish to give a smooth surface and finally wipe the segments over with a methylated spirits soaked rag to ensure a grease free surface. Check that the mica insulators, which lie between the segments of the commutator, are undercut. The standard groove depth is 0.6 mm (0.02 in) but if the average groove depth is less than 0.2 mm (0.008 in) the armature should be renewed or returned to a Suzuki Service Agent for re-cutting.

7 Replace the brushes in their holders and check that they slide quite freely. Make sure the brushes are replaced in their original positions because they will have worn to the profile of the commutator. Replace and tighten the end cover, then replace the starter motor and cable in the housing, tighten down and re-make the electrical connection to the solenoid switch. Check that the starter motor functions correctly before replacing the compartment cover and sealing gasket.

10 Starter motor free running clutch: construction and renovation

1 Although a mechanical and not an electrical component, it is appropriate to include the free running clutch in this Chapter because it is an essential part of the electric starter system.

2 As mentioned in Chapter 1, the free running clutch is built into the alternator rotor assembly and will be found in the back of the rotor when the latter is removed from the left-hand end of the crankshaft. The only parts likely to require attention are the rollers and their springs, or the bush in the centre of the driven sprocket. Access to the rollers is gained by removing the three countersunk crosshead screws which retain the clutch body to the rear of the alternator rotor. Signs of wear or damage will be obvious and will necessitate renewal of the worn or damaged parts.

3 The bush in the centre of the driven sprocket behind the clutch will need renewal only after very extensive service.

4 To check whether the clutch is operating correctly, turn the driven sprocket anticlockwise. This should force the spring loaded rollers against the crankshaft and cause it to tighten on the crankshaft as the drive is taken up.

5 If the starter clutch has been dismantled, make sure the three crosshead screws are staked over after reassembly, to prevent them working loose.

11 Starter solenoid switch: function and location

1 The starter motor switch is designed to work on the electro-magnetic principle. When the starter motor button is depressed, current from the battery passes through windings in the switch solenoid and generates an electro-magnetic force which causes a set of contact points to close. Immediately the points close, the starter motor is energised and a very heavy current is drawn from the battery.

2 This arrangement is used for at least two reasons. Firstly, the starter motor current is drawn only when the button is depressed and is cut off again when pressure on the button is released. This ensures minimum drainage on the battery. Secondly, if the battery is in a low state of charge, there will not be sufficient current to cause the solenoid contacts to close. In consequence, it is not possible to place an excessive drain on the battery which, in some circumstances, can cause the plates to overheat and shed their coatings. If the starter will not operate, first suspect a discharged battery. This can be checked by trying the horn or switching on the lights. If this check shows the battery to be in good shape, suspect the starter switch which should come into action with a pronounced click. It is located under the dualseat, close to the battery, and can be identified by the heavy duty starter cable connected to it. It is

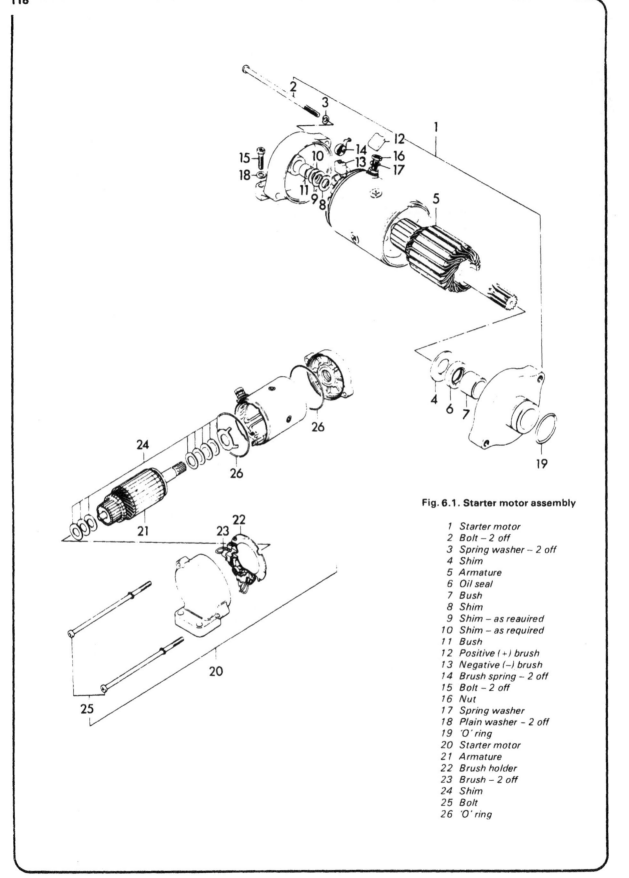

Fig. 6.1. Starter motor assembly

1 Starter motor
2 Bolt – 2 off
3 Spring washer – 2 off
4 Shim
5 Armature
6 Oil seal
7 Bush
8 Shim
9 Shim – as reauired
10 Shim – as required
11 Bush
12 Positive (+) brush
13 Negative (–) brush
14 Brush spring – 2 off
15 Bolt – 2 off
16 Nut
17 Spring washer
18 Plain washer – 2 off
19 'O' ring
20 Starter motor
21 Armature
22 Brush holder
23 Brush – 2 off
24 Shim
25 Bolt
26 'O' ring

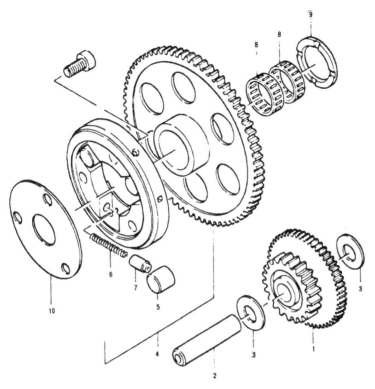

Fig. 6.2. Starter clutch assembly

1 *Starter idle gear*
2 *Shaft*
3 *Thrust washer – 2 off*
4 *Starter clutch assembly*
5 *Roller – 3 off*
6 *Spring – 3 off*
7 *Plunger – 3 off*
8 *Needle roller bearing – 2 off*
9 *Washer*
10 *End plate*

not possible to effect a satisfactory repair if the switch malfunctions; it must be renewed.

12 Headlamp: replacing bulbs and adjusting beam height

1   In order to gain access to the headlamp bulbs it is necessary first to remove the rim, complete with the reflector and headlamp glass. The rim is retained by three crosshead screws equally spaced around the headlamp shell. Remove the screws completely and draw the rim from the headlamp shell.
2   UK models have a main headlamp bulb which is a push fit into the central bulb holder of the reflector. The bulb holder can be replaced in one position only to ensure the bulb is always correctly focussed. It is retained by a rubber boot. A bulb of the twin filament type is fitted which has a 50/40W rating. The pilot lamp bulb is bayonet fitting and fits within a bulb holder which has the same form of attachment to the headlamp reflector. This bulb has a 6W rating.
3   US models have a sealed beam headlamp unit, rated at 50/35W with no provision for a pilot lamp. If one filament blows, the complete unit must be renewed. To release the lamp unit, remove the horizontal adjusting screw, the upper and lower retaining lock pins and screws from the collar which clamps the light unit to the headlamp rim. Make a note of the setting of the adjusting screw, otherwise it will be necessary to re-adjust the beam height after installing the new light unit by reversing the dismantling procedure.
4   Beam height is adjusted by turning the adjusting screw fitted in the nine o'clock position when the headlamp is viewed from the front. Turn anticlockwise to lower the beam and clockwise to raise the beam.
5   UK lighting regulations stipulate that the lighting system must be arranged so that the light will not dazzle a person standing at a distance greater than 25 feet from the lamp, whose eye level is not less than 3 feet 6 inches above that plane. It is easy to approximate this setting by placing the machine 25 feet away from a wall, on a level road, and setting the beam height so that it is concentrated at the same height as

the distance of the centre of the headlamp from the ground. The rider must be seated normally during this operation and also the pillion passenger, if one is carried regularly.

13 Stop and tail lamp: replacing bulbs

1   The tail lamp has a twin filament bulb of 8/23W (3/32 cp) to illuminate the rear number plate and to indicate when the rear brake is applied. On some models the stop lamp also operates in conjunction with the front brake; a stop lamp switch is incorporated in the front brake cable to meet the statutory requirements of the country or state to which the machine is exported.
2   To gain access to the stop and tail lamp bulb, unscrew the four crosshead screws which retain the plastic lens cover in position. The bulb has a bayonet fitting and offset pins so that the stop lamp filament cannot be inadvertently connected with the tail lamp and vice versa.

14 Flashing indicator lamps: replacing bulbs

1   Flashing indicator lamps are fitted to the front and rear of the machine. They are mounted on short stalks through which the wires pass. Access to each bulb is gained by removing the two screws holding the plastic lens cover. The bulbs are of 23W rating and are retained by a bayonet fixing.

15 Instrument and warning bulbs: replacement

1   The bulbs fitted to the instrument heads and the warning light panel (late models) are of the small bayonet type, the holders being a push fit in the underside of the brackets. Replacement of bulbs in the warning panel first requires that the lower cover be removed. It is retained by the two sets of two nuts which secure the instruments to the mounting bracket.

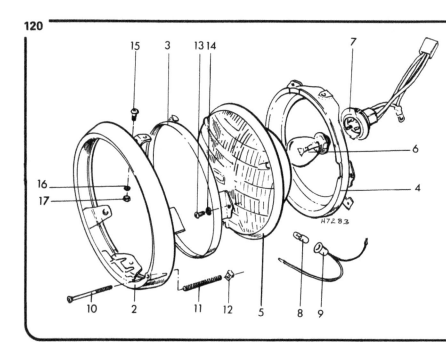

Fig. 6.3. Headlamp assembly

1 Headlamp assembly
2 Headlamp rim
3 Outer retaining rim
4 Mounting ring
5 Reflector unit
6 Bulb
7 Bulb socket
8 Bulb
9 Bulb socket
10 Adjusting screw
11 Spring
12 Adjuster block nut
13 Screw – 3 off
14 Lockwasher – 3 off
15 Screw – 2 off
16 Lockwasher – 2 off
17 Nut – 2 off

12.1 Remove screws from headlamp shell to free reflector/rim unit

12.2a Main bulb holder is secured by a rubber boot

12.2b Bulb is a three pin bayonet fit

12.2c Pilot bulb holder has bayonet fixing as has the bulb

13.2 Stop/tail lamp lens is held by four screws

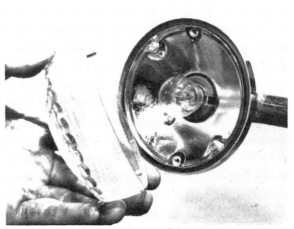

14.1 Indicator bulbs have a bayonet fixing

16 Horn: adjustments

1   On some models the horn is adjustable by means of a small grub screw at the back of the body so that the volume can be varied if necessary. To adjust the volume, turn the screw about half a turn either way until the desired tone is required.
2   The horn button is located on the left side of the handlebars, below the dipper switch.

17 Handlebar switches, ignition and lighting switches: examination

1   The arrangement of the handlebar switches is the same on all models. The switches seldom give any trouble; they can be separated by removing the two screws that hold the two halves together. It is not advisable to take the switches apart as the parts are small and difficulties can occur during reassembly. If a switch fails, it is best to fit a new replacement.
2   The ignition switch is located in the centre of the instrument panel. It can be removed by undoing the locking ring or bezel on the body. The wires can be pulled out of the socket and the new switch plugged in. New keys are supplied with a new switch. A defective switch is not repairable.

18 Stop lamp switch: adjustment

1   The stop lamp switch is located in a bracket above the rear brake pedal and is operated by an expansion spring linked to the rear brake pedal. The body of the switch is threaded to permit it to be adjusted.
2   If the stop lamp is late in operating, slacken the locknuts and raise the switch body. When the adjustment seems correct tighten locknuts and test. If the stop lamp is too early in operation, slacken the locknuts and lower the body in relation to the bracket.
3   As a guide, the light should come on when the rear brake pedal has been depressed about 2 cm ($\frac{3}{4}$ in).

19 Gear selection indicator: location and operation

1   A gear selection indicator is fitted to all models in addition to the neutral warning light. In this system, a switch on the change drum illuminates a single digit display unit fitted in a console between the speedometer and tachometer heads. The display unit is similar to that used on pocket calculators and indicates which of the gears has been selected. If a malfunction occurs, the unit in question must be renewed as both components are sealed. On all models, the neutral warning bulb can be replaced as with the other warning bulbs fitted to the instrument heads.

20   Fault diagnosis: Electrical system

Symptom	Cause	Remedy
Complete electrical failure	Blown fuse	Check wiring and electrical components for short circuit before fitting new 15 amp fuse.
	Isolated battery	Check battery connections, also whether connections show signs of corrosion.
Dim lights, horn and starter in-operative	Discharged battery	Remove battery and charge with battery charger. Check generator output and voltage regulator settings.
Constantly blowing bulbs	Vibration or poor earth connection	Check security of bulb holders. Check earth return connections.
Starter motor sluggish	Worn brushes	Remove starter motor. Renew brushes.
Parking lights dim rapidly	Battery will not hold charge	Renew battery at earliest opportunity.
Flashing indicators do not operate	Blown bulb	Renew bulb.
	Damaged flasher unit	Renew flasher unit.

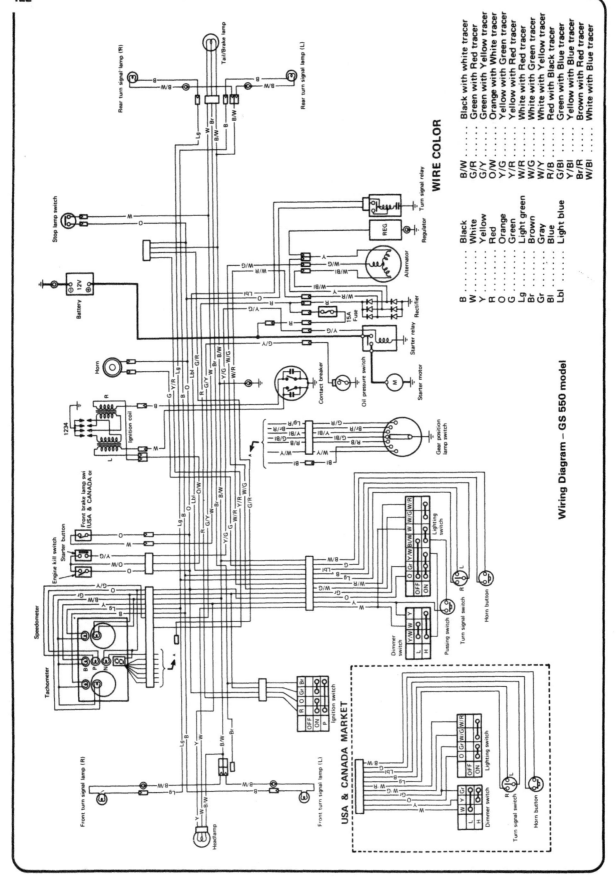

WIRE COLOR

B/W	.....	Black with white tracer
G/R	.....	Green with Red tracer
G/Y	.....	Green with Yellow tracer
O/W	.....	Orange with White tracer
Y/G	.....	Yellow with Green tracer
Y/R	.....	Yellow with Red tracer
W/R	.....	White with Red tracer
W/G	.....	White with Green tracer
W/Y	.....	White with Yellow tracer
R/B	.....	Red with Black tracer
G/Bl	.....	Green with Blue tracer
Y/Bl	.....	Yellow with Blue tracer
Br/R	.....	Brown with Red tracer
W/Bl	.....	White with Blue tracer

B	.....	Black
W	.....	White
Y	.....	Yellow
R	.....	Red
O	.....	Orange
G	.....	Green
Lg	.....	Light green
Br	.....	Brown
Gr	.....	Gray
Bl	.....	Blue
Lbl	.....	Light blue

Wiring Diagram – GS 550 model

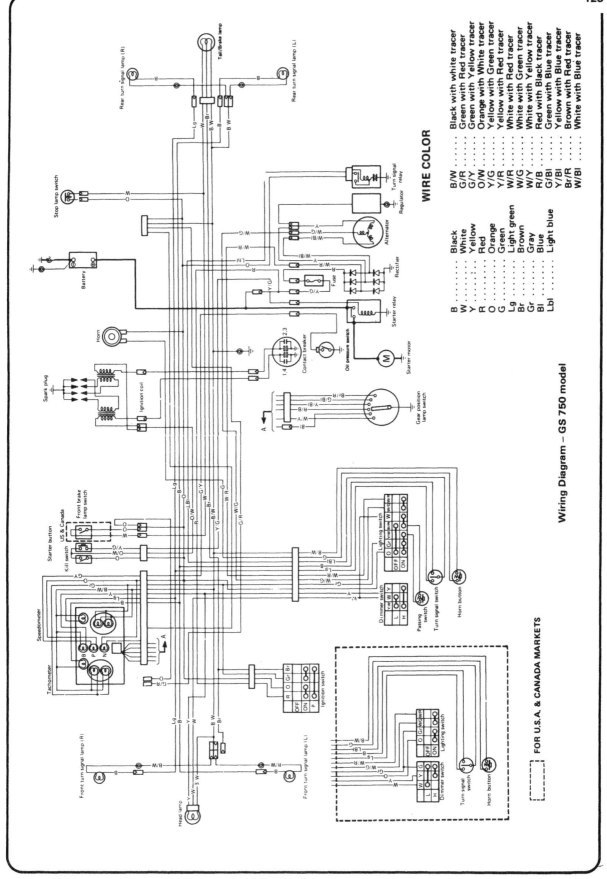

WIRE COLOR

B	....	Black
W	....	White
Y	....	Yellow
R	....	Red
O	....	Orange
G	....	Green
Lg	....	Light green
Br	....	Brown
Gr	....	Gray
Bl	....	Blue
Lbl	....	Light blue

B/W	....	Black with white tracer
G/R	....	Green with Red tracer
G/Y	....	Green with Yellow tracer
O/W	....	Orange with White tracer
Y/G	....	Yellow with Green tracer
Y/R	....	Yellow with Red tracer
W/R	....	White with Red tracer
W/G	....	White with Green tracer
W/Y	....	White with Yellow tracer
R/B	....	Red with Black tracer
G/Bl	....	Green with Blue tracer
Y/Bl	....	Yellow with Blue tracer
Br/R	....	Brown with Red tracer
W/Bl	....	White with Blue tracer

Wiring Diagram – GS 750 model

FOR U.S.A. & CANADA MARKETS

Chapter 7 Supplement: Revisions and information on later models

Contents

1 Introduction

This supplementary Chapter covers changes made to the GS750 line for 1978 and 1979 and to the GS550 line during the 1978 through 1982 model years, as well as the procedures affected by these changes.

Operations that are not included in this Chapter are the same as or similar to those described in the first six Chapters of this manual.

Although there have not been extensive mechanical changes during this period, there have been considerable styling alterations made. Some of the major changes include the following.

In 1978, designated by C in the model number, the E series was introduced, which was basically the standard GS with cast wheels, a double disc front brake (on some models) and a rear disc brake for GS550 models.

The 1979 models are designated by the letter N, and featured the introduction of the "customized" L series. These models are equipped with a two-step seat, "teardrop" style tank, swept-back handlebars, cast wheels, leading axle forks and a rear disc brake. Due to extensive revisions of the 750 cc engine in the following year, which places it beyond the scope of this manual, 1979 was also the last model year for coverage of the GS750 in this book.

1980, designated by the letter T, saw the introduction of

numerous mechanical changes, notably, the elimination of the kick starter, a high performance alternator, a cable-operated choke system, a redesign of the charging system to incorporate the regulator and rectifier into one unit, a redesign of the steering head, front brake master cylinder and caliper and replacement of the conventional ccarburetors with constant velocity types.

In 1981, designated by the letter X, the radical looking GS550M, more popularly termed the Katana, was introduced in the UK. Although for the most part mechanically unchanged, this model received a total styling redesign with a larger forward sloping tank, along with streamlined seat, fenders and side covers. During this year a semi-custom version of the GS550, termed the T series, was also released in the USA and Canada. This is basically a toned down version of the L.

In 1982, designated by the letter Z, the Katana was brought to the USA and Canada. Both the M and L models received modifications including air forks, a handlebar mounted choke, another redesign of the front brake master cylinder and a return to rear drum brakes for the L.

The recommended way of using this supplement is, prior to any operation, check here first for any relevant information pertaining to your model. After noting any model differences, particularly in the Specifications Section, you can then follow the appropriate procedure, either listed in this Chapter or one of the preceding six.

2 Specifications

Note: *The specifications listed here are revisions of or supplementary to the main specifications given at the beginning of each Chapter. Specifications not listed here are the same as those listed in Chapters 1 through 6.*

Dimensions and steering geometry

GS750L

Overall length	2230 mm (87.8 in)
Overall width	890 mm (35.0 in)
Overall height	1245 mm (49.0 in)
Wheelbase	1510 mm (59.4 in)
Ground clearance	160 mm (6.3 in)
Dry weight	233 kg (514 lbs)
Caster	62° 30'
Trail	100 mm (3.9 in)
Turning radius	2.5 m (8.2 ft)

GS550L (1979 and 1980)

Overall length	2190 mm (86.2 in)
Overall width	890 mm (35.0 in)
Overall height	1215 mm (47.8 in)
Wheelbase	1480 mm (58.3 in)
Ground clearance	165 mm (6.5 in)
Dry weight	206 kg (454 lbs)
Caster	
1979	62° 00'
1980	60° 00'
Trail	
1979	118 mm (4.6 in)
1980	114 mm (4.5 in)

GS550E (1981)

Overall length	2150 mm (84.6 in)
Wheelbase	1440 mm (56.7 in)
Dry weight	203 kg (448 lbs)
Caster	61° 30'
Trail	116 mm (4.5 in)

GS550T (1981)

Overall length	2200 mm (86.6 in)
Overall height	1180 mm (46.4 in)
Dry weight	200 kg (441 lbs)
Caster	61° 30'
Trail	116 mm (4.5 in)

GS550L (1981)

	UK models	USA and Canada models
Overall length	2185 mm	2215 mm (87.2 in)
Overall width	870 mm	870 mm (34.3 in)
Overall height	1200 mm	1180 mm (46.4 in)
Wheelbase	1455 mm	1460 mm (57.5 in)
Dry weight	202 kg	205 kg (452 lbs)
Seat height	800 mm	775 mm (30.5 in)
Caster	61° 00'	60° 00'
Trail	122 mm	112 mm (4.4 in)

GS550L (1982 USA only)

Overall length	2205 mm (86.8 in)
Wheelbase	1450 mm (57.1 in)
Dry weight	199 Kg (439 lbs)

GS550M

Overall length	2145 mm (84.4 in)
Overall width	730 mm (28.7 in)
Overall height	1110 mm (43.7 in)
Wheelbase	1455 mm (57.3 in)
Ground clearance	160 mm (6.3 in)
Dry weight	205 kg (452 lbs)
Caster	61° 50'
Trail	115 mm (4.5 in)

Engine *(GS750 models)*

Valve guide-to-stem clearance	
Intake (service limit)	0.35 mm (0.014 in)

Engine *(GS750 models)* (continued)

Exhaust
    Standard .... 0.040 to 0.070 mm
    (0.0016 to 0.0028 in)
    Service limit .... 0.35 mm (0.014 in)
Valve stem diameter
    Intake .... 6.960 to 6.975 mm
    (0.2740 to 0.2746 in)
    Exhaust .... 6.945 to 6.960 mm
    (0.2734 to 0.2740 in)
Cam lobe height (service limits)
    Intake .... 35.970 mm (1.4161 in)
    Exhaust .... 35.440 mm (1.3953 in)
Camshaft bearing holder inner diameter (all) .... 22.012 to 22.025 mm
    (0.8666 to 0.8671 in)
Cylinder bore (service limit) .... 64.070 mm (2.5618 in)
Piston diameter (service limit) .... 64.880 mm (2.5543 in)
Piston ring free end gap (service limit — 1st and 2nd rings) ... 6.4 mm (0.25 in)
Piston ring end gap (service limit — 1st and 2nd rings) ...... 0.7 mm (0.03 in)
Connecting rod small end bore-to-piston pin clearance
    Standard .... 0.006 to 0.019 mm
    (0.0002 to 0.0007 in)
    Service limit .... 0.080 mm (0.0031 in)
Crankshaft runout .... 0.05 mm (0.002 in) max.

Engine *(GS550 models)*

Valve guide-to-stem clearance
    Intake
        Standard (1981 and 1982) .... 0.020 to 0.050 mm (0.0008 to 0.0020 in)
        Service limit .... 0.35 mm (0.014 in)
    Exhaust
        Standard (1979 and 1980) .... 0.040 to 0.070 mm (0.0016 to 0.0028 in)
        Standard (1981 and 1982) .... 0.030 to 0.060 mm (0.0012 to 0.0024 in)
        Service limit .... 0.35 mm (0.014 in)
Valve stem diameter
    Intake (1979 and 1980) .... 6.960 to 6.975 mm (0.2740 to 0.2746 in)
    Intake (1981 and 1982) .... 6.965 to 6.980 mm (0.2742 to 0.2748 in)
    Exhaust (1979 and 1980) .... 6.945 to 6.960 mm (0.2734 to 0.2740 in)
    Exhaust (1981 and 1982) .... 6.955 to 6.970 mm (0.2738 to 0.2744 in)
Cam lobe height
    Intake
        Standard .... 35.485 to 35.515 mm (1.3970 to 1.3982 in)
        Service limit .... 35.190 mm (1.3854 in)
    Exhaust
        Standard .... 35.285 to 35.315 mm (1.3892 to 1.3904 in)
        Service limit .... 34.990 mm (1.3776 in)
Camshaft bearing oil clearance (standard)
    1980 .... 0.032 to 0.066 mm (0.0013 to 0.0026 in)
    1981 and 1982 .... 0.020 to 0.054 mm (0.0008 to 0.0021 in)
    Service limit – all models .... 0.150 mm (0.0059 in)
Camshaft bearing holder inner diameter (standard) .... 22.000 to 22.013 mm (0.8661 to 0.8667 in)
Piston-to-cylinder clearance (1981 and 1982) .... 0.045 to 0.055 mm (0.0018 to 0.0022 in)
Piston diameter (1981 and 1982) .... 55.950 to 55.965 mm (2.2028 to 2.2033 in)
Piston ring end gap (service limit) .... 0.7 mm (0.03 in)
Connecting rod small end bore-to-piston pin clearance
    Standard .... 0.006 to 0.019 mm (0.0002 to 0.0007 in)
    Service limit .... 0.080 mm (0.0031 in)
Crankshaft runout
    1979 and 1980 .... 0.05 mm (0.002 in) max.
    1981 and 1982 .... 0.10 mm (0.004 in) max.

Clutch

Clutch plate warpage (GS750L) .... 0.2 mm (0.008 in) max.
Clutch spring free length (GS550)
    1979 and 1980 .... 35.9 mm (1.41 in) min.
    1981 and 1982 .... 36.5 mm (1.44 in) min.

Final drive

Final reduction ratio (1981 and 1982 GS550L)
    UK 3.400 (51/15)
    USA and Canada 3.266 (49/15)

Drive chain length
   1981 and 1982 GS550L (USA and Canada) . . . .   108 links
   GS550M . . . .   112 links

Final drive torque specifications
Countershaft sprocket nut (1980 through 1982) . . . .   5.0to 7.0 M-kg (36 to 50 Ft-lb)

Fuel system and lubrication

Carburetor (GS750 models)
  UK and Canada
    Air screw . . . .   1-1/4 turns out
    Jet needle 5DL36-2
    Pilot air jet 1.2
    Main jet 102.5
    Float height . . . .   24.0 mm (0.95 in)
  USA
    Main jet 102.5
    Air screw . . . .   Preset
    Pilot screw . . . .   Preset
    Needle jet   0-4
    Jet needle 5DL36-2
Carburetor (GS550 models)
  1979 USA models
    ID number   47110
    Float height . . . .   24.0 ± 1.0 mm (0.95 ± 0.04 in)
    Fuel level . . . .   4.0 ± 1.0 mm (0.16 ± 0.04 in)
    Air screw . . . .   Preset
    Pilot screw . . . .   Preset
    Pilot outlet 0.6
    Needle jet   0-4
    By-pass 0.7
  1979 Canada models (same as USA except for the following)
    ID number   47120
    Air screw . . . .   2.0 turns out
    Pilot screw 1.0
    Needle jet   0-6
    By-pass 1.0
  1980 through 1982 UK and Canada models
    Type . . . .   Mikuni BS32SS
    Bore size . . . .   32 mm (1.26 in)
    ID number (1980 and 1981)   47090
    ID number (1982)   47170
    Idle speed . . . .   1100 ± 100 rpm
    Fuel level . . . .   5.0 ± 0.5 mm (0.20 ± 0.02 in)
    Float height . . . .   22.4 ± 1.0 mm (0.88 ± 0.04 in)
    Main jet 92.5
    Main air jet 1.6
    Jet needle 5F42-3
    Needle jet X-6
    Pilot jet   40
    By-pass 1.0, 0.8, 0.8
    Pilot outlet 0.7
    Valve seat 2.0
    Starter jet   35
    Pilot screw (1980) . . . .   3-1/2 turns out
    Pilot screw (1981 and 1982) . . . .   Preset
    Throttle cable play . . . .   0.5 to 1.0 mm (0.02 to 0.04 in)
    Throttle valve (1981 and 1982)   135
    Pilot air jet (1981 and 1982)   120
  1980 through 1982 USA models (same as above except for the following)
    ID number (1980 and 1981)   47070
    ID number (1982)   47160
    Jet needle 4BEL2
    By-pass 0.9, 0.7, 0.7
    Pilot screw . . . .   Preset
    Pilot air jet (1981 and 1982)   150
    Throttle valve (1981 and 1982)   140
Fuel tank capacity
  GS750L
    Total, including reserve . . . .   13 L (3.4 US gal) (2.9 Imp gal)
    Reserve . . . .   3 L (3.2 US qt) (2.6 Imp qt)
  1979 and 1980 GS550L
    Total, including reserve . . . .   13 L (3.4 US gal) (2.9 Imp gal)
    Reserve . . . .   3 L (3.2 US qt) (2.6 Imp qt)

Fuel system and lubrication (continued)

1980 GS550E
  Total, including reserve............................ 16 L (4.2 US gal) (3.5 Imp gal)
  Reserve .... 4 L (4.2 US qt) (3.5 Imp qt)
1981 GS550T
  Total, including reserve............................ 12 L (3.2 US gal) (2.6 Imp gal)
  Reserve .... 4 L (4.2 US qt) (3.5 Imp qt)
1981 and 1982 GS550L
  Total, including reserve............................ 12 L (3.2 US gal) (2.6 Imp gal)
  Reserve .... 4 L (4.2 US qt) (3.5 Imp qt)
1981 and 1982 GS550M
  Total, including reserve............................ 23 L (6.1 US gal) (5.1 Imp gal)
  Reserve .... 4 L (4.2 US qt) (3.5 Imp qt)

Fuel system torque specifications (constant velocity carburetors)	M-kg	Ft-lb
Float chamber screws	0.25 to 0.45	1.8 to 3.0
Upper retaining plate screws	0.25 to 0.45	1.8 to 3.0
Lower retaining plate screws	0.4 to 0.6	3.0 to 4.5
Vacuum chamber screws	0.25 to 0.45	1.8 to 3.0

Ignition system *(1980 USA and Canada models and all 1981 and 1982 models)*

Type .... Transistorized
Ignition timing .... 15° BTDC below 1500 rpm; 40° BTDC above 2350 rpm

Frame and forks

Front fork oil capacity (per fork)
  GS750L .... 280 ml (9.46 US oz) (9.86 Imp oz)
  1979 and 1980 GS550L .... 217 ml (7.33 US oz) (7.64 Imp oz)
  1981 GS550E (UK) .... 204 ml (6.90 US oz) (7.18 Imp oz)
  1981 GS550T and GS550E (USA and Canada) .... 190 ml (6.42 US oz) (6.69 Imp oz)
  1981 GS550L (UK) .... 196 ml (6.62 US oz) (6.90 Imp oz)
  1981 GS550L (USA and Canada) .... 249 ml (8.42 US oz) (8.77 Imp oz)
  1981 GS550M (UK) .... 195 ml (6.59 US oz) (6.87 Imp oz)
  1982 GS550L (USA) .... 239 ml (8.08 US oz) (8.41 Imp oz)
  1982 GS550M (USA and Canada) .... 223 ml (7.54 US oz) (7.85 Imp oz)
Fork oil level (measured from upper end with forks fully compressed)
  GS750L .... 202 mm (8.0 in)
  1979 GS550L .... 229 mm (9.02 in)
  1980 GS550E .... 204 mm (8.03 in)
  1981 GS550E and T
    UK .... 174.8 mm (6.88 in)
    USA and Canada .... 201 mm (7.91 in)
  1981 GS550L
    UK .... 219.6 mm (8.65 in)
    USA and Canada .... 208 mm (8.19 in)
  1981 GS550M (UK) .... 194 mm (7.64 in)
  1982 GS550L (USA) .... 144 mm (5.7 in)
  1982 GS550M (USA and Canada) .... 140 mm (5.5 in)
Fork oil type
  GS750L .... SAE 10W/20 motor oil
  1979 and 1980 GS550 .... 1:1 mixture of 10W/30 and 5W/20 motor oil
  1981 and 1982 .... 15W fork oil or 1:1 mixture of 10W/30 motor oil and ATF
Fork air pressure (1982) .... 7.11 psi (0.5 kg/cm$_2$)

Fork spring free length (min.)	Upper spring	Lower spring
GS750L	154 mm (6.1 in)	460 mm (18.1 in)
1979 GS550L	153 mm (6.02)	451 mm (17.76 in)
1980 GS550E (USA and Canada)	93 mm (3.66 in)	393 mm (15.47 in)
1980 GS550E (UK)	121 mm (4.80 in)	365 mm (15.47 in)
1981 GS550E and T		
UK	54.9 mm (2.16 in)	434.4 mm (17.10 in)
USA and Canada	92.9 mm (3.66 in)	396.4 mm (15.61 in)
1981 GS550L		
UK	152.4 mm (6.00 in)	373.4 mm (14.70 in)
USA and Canada	159.1 mm (6.26 in)	448.7 mm (17.67 in)
1981 GS550M (UK)	57.1 mm (2.25 in)	423.2 mm (16.66 in)
1982 GS550L (USA)	528 mm (20.8 in) (one spring only)	
1982 GS550M (USA and Canada)	494 mm (19.4 in) (one spring only)	

Frame and forks torque specifications

	M-kg	Ft-lb
Fork slider-to-axle pinch bolt (1982)	1.5 to 2.5	11 to 18
Damper rod bolt (1982)	1.5 to 2.5	11 to 18
Steering stem pinch bolt	1.5 to 2.5	11 to 18
Steering stem head nut..............................	3.6 to 5.2	26 to 37
Steering stem nut	4.0 to 5.0	30 to 36
Lower bracket pinch bolts	2.0 to 3.0	15 to 21
Upper bracket pinch bolts (1980 and 1981)	2.0 to 3.0	15 to 21
Upper bracket pinch bolts (1982)	3.5 to 5.5	25 to 40
Handlebar mounting bolts (1982)	1.2 to 2.0	8.5 to 14.5

Wheels, brakes and tires *(GS750 models)*

Brake disc thickness	
Front (single disc)	
Standard	6.7 mm (0.264 in)
Service limit	6.00 mm (0.236 in)
Front (dual disc)	
Standard	6.0 mm (0.24 in)
Service limit	5.5 mm (0.22 in)
Rear disc	
Standard	6.7 mm (0.264 in)
Service limit	6.0 mm (0.236 in)
Brake disc runout	0.3 mm (0.012 in) max.
Brake caliper piston diameter	
Front (single disc)	
Standard	42.82 mm (1.686 in)
Service limit	42.77 mm (1.684 in)
Front (dual disc)	
Standard	38.116 to 38.148 mm (1.5006 to 1.5019 in)
Service limit	38.105 mm (1.5002 in)
Rear disc	
Standard	38.18 mm (1.503 in)
Service limit	38.13 mm (1.501 in)
Brake caliper bore diameter	
Front (single disc)	
Standard	42.85 mm (1.687 in)
Service limit	42.89 mm (1.689 in)
Front (dual disc)	
Standard	38.180 to 38.219 mm (1.5031 to 1.5047 in)
Service limit	38.230 mm (1.5051 in)
Rear disc	
Standard	38.15 mm (1.502 in)
Service limit	38.19 mm (1.504 in)
Brake master cylinder piston diameter	
Front (dual disc)	
Standard	13.96 mm (0.550 in)
Service limit	13.94 mm (0.549 in)
Front(dual disc)	
Standard (except L models)	15.811 to 15.838 mm (0.6225 to 0.6235 in)
Standard (L models)	15.827 to 15.854 mm (0.623 to 0.624 in)
Service limit	15.799 mm (0.6220 in)
Rear disc	
Standard	13.96 mm(0.550 in)
Service limit	13.94 mm (0.549 in)
Brake master cylinder bore diameter	
Front (single disc)	
Standard	14.00 mm (0.551 in)
Service limit	14.05 mm (0.553 in)
Front (dual disc)	
Standard	15.870 to 15.913 mm (0.6248 to 0.6265 in)
Service limit	15.925 mm (0.6270 in)
Rear disc	
Standard	14.00 mm (0.551 in)
Service limit	14.05 mm (0.553 in)

Wheels, brakes and tires *(GS550 models)*

Brake disc thickness	
Front (single disc)	
Standard	6.7 mm (0.26 in)
Service limit	6.0 mm (0.24 in)

Wheels, brakes and tires *(GS550 models)* (continued)

Front (dual disc — 1979 only)
  Standard .... 6.0 mm (0.24 in)
  Service limit .... 5.5 mm (0.22 in)
Front (dual disc — 1980 through 1982)
  Standard .... 5.0 mm (0.20 in)
  Service limit .... 4.5 mm (0.18 in)
Rear disc
  Standard .... 6.7 mm (0.26 in)
  Service limit .... 6.0 mm (0.24 in)
Brake disc runout .... 0.30 mm (0.012 in) max.
Brake caliper piston diameter
  Front (single disc — except 1981 and 1982 UK models)
    Standard .... 42.790 to 42.810 mm (1.6846 to 1.6854 in)
    Service limit .... 42.690 mm (1.6807 in)
  Front (single disc — 1981 and 1982 UK models) .... 38.098 to 38.148 mm (1.4999 to 1.5019 in)
  Front (dual disc)
    Standard .... 38.025 to 38. 050 mm (1.4970 to 1.4980 in)
    Service limit .... 37.925 mm (1.4931 in)
  Rear disc
    Standard .... 38.116 to 38.148 mm (1.5006 to 1.5019 in)
    Service limit .... 38.016 mm (1.4967 in)
Brake caliper cylinder bore diameter
  Front (single disc — except 1981 and 1982 UK models)
    Standard .... 42.860 to 42.899 mm (1.6874 to 1.6889 in)
    Service limit .... 42.999 mm (1.6929 in)
  Front (single disc — 1981 and 1982 UK models) .... 38.180 to 38.256 mm (1.5031 to 1.5061 in)
  Front (dual disc)
    Standard .... 38.180 to 38.219 mm (1.5031 to 1.5047 in)
    Service limit .... 38.319 mm (1.5086 in)
  Rear disc
    Standard .... 38.180 to 38.230 mm (1.5031 to 1.5051 in)
    Service limit .... 38.330 mm (1.5091 in)
Brake master cylinder piston diameter
  Front (single disc)
    Standard .... 13.941 to 13.968 mm (0.5489 to 0.5499 in)
    Service limit .... 13.920 mm (0.5480 in)
  Front (dual disc)
    Standard (1981 and 1982 UK models)............... 15.827 to 15.854 mm (0.6231 to 0.6242 in)
    Standard (all others) .... 15.811 to 15.838 mm (0.6225 to 0.6235 in)
    Service limit (except 1981 and 1982 UK models) .... 15.799 mm (0.6220 in)
  Rear (all disc models)
    Standard (1979)............................. 13.941 to 13.968 mm (0.5489 to 0.5499 in)
    Standard (1980 through 1982).................. 13.957 to 13.984 mm (0.5495 to 0.5506 in)
    Service limit (1979 only) .... 13.929 mm (0.5484 in)
Brake master cylinder bore diameter
  Front (single disc)
    Standard .... 13.900 to 14.043 mm (0.5472 to 0.5529 in)
    Service limit .... 14.07 mm (0.5547 in)
  Front (dual disc)
    Standard .... 15.870 to 15.913 mm (0.6248 to 0.6265 in)
    Service limit .... 15.925 mm (0.6270 in)
  Rear (all disc models)
    Standard .... 14.000 to 14.043 mm (0.5512 to 0.5529 in)
    Service limit .... 14.055 mm (0.5533 in)
Rear drum brakes
  Brake drum inner diameter .... 180.7 mm (7.11 in) max.
  Brake lining thickness .... 1.5 mm (0.06 in) min.

Wheels, brakes and tires torque specifications

	M-kg	Ft-lb
Front caliper bracket mounting bolts (1980 through 1982)....	2.5 to 4.0	18 to 29
Front brake caliper-to-bracket bolts (1980 through 1982).....	4.0 to 5.5	29 to 40
Brake disc mounting bolts	1.5 to 2.5	11 to 18
Rear master cylinder bolts............................	1.5 to 2.5	11 to 18
Rear torque link nut	2.0 to 3.0	14.5 to 21.5
Rear brake caliper mounting bolts	2.0 to 3.0	14.5 to 21.5
Rear brake caliper axle bolt	2.5 to 3.5	18 to 25
Front master cylinder mounting bolts...................	0.5 to 0.8	3.5 to 6.0
Front axle shaft	3.6 to 5.2	26 to 37
Front axle holder nuts................................	1.5 to 2.5	11 to 18

Electrical system

	UK	USA and Canada
Generator voltage (no load) (1980 through 1982 GS550 models)	Over 80V AC at 5000 rpm	
Starter motor brush length (1981 and 1982 GS550 models) ..	6 mm (0.24 in) min.	

Light bulbs (GS750L)
Headlight

	UK	USA and Canada
High beam	60W	60W
Low beam	55W	55W
Tail/brake light	5/21W	8/23W
Turn signal light	21W	23W
Parking or city light	4W	—

Light bulbs (1980 and 1981 GS550 UK models)
Headlight (1980 GS550E only)

	UK
High beam	45W
Low beam	45W

Headlight (1981)

High beam	60W
Low beam	55W
Parking or city light	4W
Parking or city light (M only)	3.4W
Tail/brake light	5/21W
Turn signal light	21
License light (M only)	5W

Light bulbs (1981 GS550 USA and Canada models)
Headlight

High beam	60W
Low beam	55W
Gear position indicator light	1.4W

Light bulbs (1982 GS550 USA and Canada models)

Fuel meter light (L and M only)	1.7W
Tail/brake light (M only)	8/23W
License light (M only)	8W
Turn signal light (M models)	23W

---

3   Routine maintenance schedule

After initial break-in; 600 miles (1000 km) or two months

Check torque on cylinder head nuts and exhaust pipe bolts
Check and adjust valve clearances
Change engine oil and filter
Check and adjust carburetor idle speed
Check and adjust clutch
Check, adjust and lubricate drive chain
Inspect brake pad and/or shoe wear
Check tire wear
Check steering stem bearing wear
Tighten all visible chassis bolts and nuts
Check battery condition and state of charge
Check engine compression
Check ignition timing

Every 600 miles (1000 km)

Clean, adjust and lubricate drive chain

Every 6 months

Check and adjust fork air pressure (air fork models)

Every two years

Replace fuel line
Replace brake hoses
Change brake fluid

Every 3500 miles following initial break-in (USA models) or every 5000 km (UK and Canada models)

Clean air filter element
Clean spark plugs
Have oil pressure checked by dealer
Plus all items listed above under initial break-in

Every 7500 miles (USA models) or 10000 km (UK) and Canada models)

Replace spark plugs
Change fork oil
Clean oil sump filter

---

4   Engine, clutch and gearbox

Crankshaft (GS750L) — disassembly and reassembly

The left crankcase shaft circlip has been eliminated for these models. Other than this minor difference, the servicing procedures are the same as described in Chapter 1.

---

5   Fuel system and lubrication

Carburetor adjustments (USA only; 1978 on)

1   All motorcycles produced after January 1, 1978, are required to meet specific exhaust emissions limitations. To ensure that the correct air/fuel mixture needed to meet the emissions levels is maintained, both the air screw and pilot screw are set at the factory and sealed to prevent readjustment. Tampering with these settings, besides being illegal, may also adversely affect the performance of the carburetors.

Carburetors (1979 through 1982) — servicing

2   The choke on these models has been changed from lever operated to cable operated with the choke operating knob mounted on the handlebars. Other than disconnecting the choke cable from the carburetors, removal and installation of the carburetors is the same as described in Chapter 2.

3   Except for the absence of the choke lever, the disassembly and reassembly procedures are also the same as described in Chapter 2.

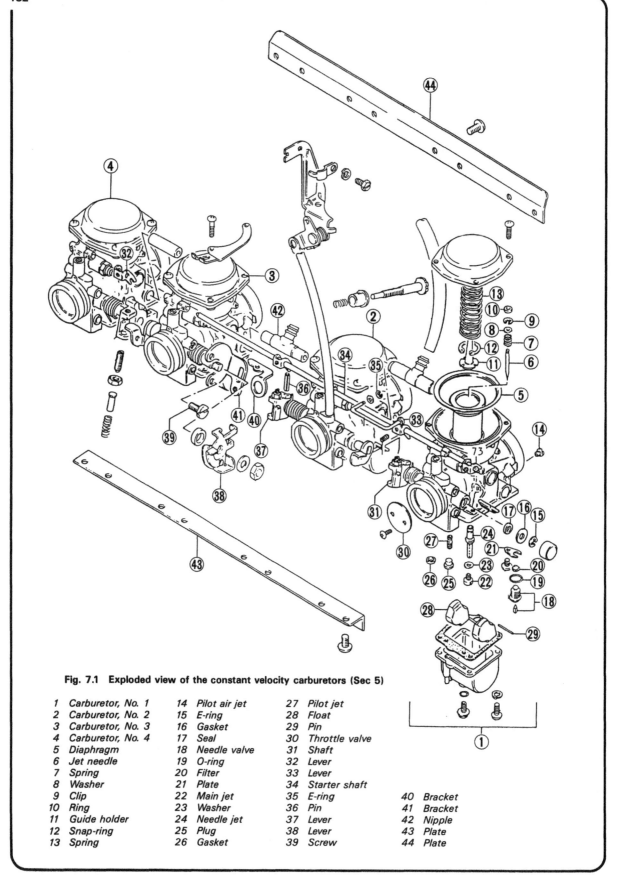

Fig. 7.1 Exploded view of the constant velocity carburetors (Sec 5)

1	Carburetor, No. 1	14	Pilot air jet
2	Carburetor, No. 2	15	E-ring
3	Carburetor, No. 3	16	Gasket
4	Carburetor, No. 4	17	Seal
5	Diaphragm	18	Needle valve
6	Jet needle	19	O-ring
7	Spring	20	Filter
8	Washer	21	Plate
9	Clip	22	Main jet
10	Ring	23	Washer
11	Guide holder	24	Needle jet
12	Snap-ring	25	Plug
13	Spring	26	Gasket

27	Pilot jet		
28	Float		
29	Pin		
30	Throttle valve		
31	Shaft		
32	Lever		
33	Lever		
34	Starter shaft		
35	E-ring	40	Bracket
36	Pin	41	Bracket
37	Lever	42	Nipple
38	Lever	43	Plate
39	Screw	44	Plate

Constant velocity carburetors—general information

4   All 1980 through 1982 models come equipped with constant velocity carburetors in place of the conventional carburetors supplied on earlier models. With this type of carburetor, the throttle cable is hooked directly to a throttle valve, which controls the air flow to the combustion chamber. A rubber diaphragm is attached to the top of the slide, which seals off the upper chamber except for a single air port downstream from the needle. This port allows the slide to be sensitive to venturi vacuum. The further the throttle valve is opened, the greater the downstream vacuum and the higher the slide will rise. This set up ensures that the air flow at the needle jet is always the same, allowing for optimal atomization of the fuel.

5   The removal and installation procedures for these carburetors are basically the same as for the earlier types. Refer to Chapter 2.

Constant velocity carburetors — disassembly, inspection and reassembly

6   **Note:** *If the vacuum chamber covers are to be removed, it is easier, though not necessary, to break the cover screws loose while the carburetors are still mounted on the engine.*

7   The vacuum and float chamber components can be disassembled and inspected without separating the carburetors from each other. In fact, it is a good idea not to separate the carburetors unless absolutely necessary (such as to replace a carburetor body, a leaking fuel pipe or a choke valve). Keeping The carburetors attached eliminates the need to synchronize them after the following operation. If separation is necessary, refer to the following subsection.

8   Be sure to keep the components of each carburetor separate as they should not be interchanged.

9   Before disassembling the carburetor, thoroughly clean the exterior with solvent to remove any accumulated dirt and grime, then let it dry. As the carburetor is disassembled, lay the parts out in the order removed on a clean shop rag.

Vacuum chamber disassembly

10   Remove the four screws that retain the vacuum chamber cover and lift it off (photo). **Note:** *When working on the number 3 carburetor, remove the throttle cable bracket prior to removing the vacuum chamber cover.*

11   Withdraw the spring and lift out the slide/diaphragm assembly.

12   If there is any damage to the needle, it can be removed from the slide by first removing the snap-ring from inside the slide (photo) and lifting out the guide holder and needle. Do not lose the needle spring, washer, E-ring or clip.

13   Repeat the procedure for the other three carburetors.

5.10   The vacuum chamber components can be overhauled without separating the carburetors

5.12   The slide needle is retained in the slide by a snap-ring (arrow) and guide holder

5.15   After starting it out with a small pin punch, the float pivot pin can be withdrawn with pliers

5.16   Float chamber components (A — Starter jet plug; B — Main jet; C — Float valve seat retaining plate; D — Float valve; E — Float valve seat)

Float chamber disassembly

14 Turn the carburetors over and remove the float chamber. It is attached to the carburetor body with four screws.

15 Use needle-nose pliers to withdraw the float pin (photo), then lift out the float.

16 Lift out the float valve from its seat (photo).

17 To remove the float valve seat, first remove the single screw that secures the retaining plate, then lift out the seat and detach the filter from the top of it. It is a good idea to replace the O-ring whenever the seat is removed (photo).

18 Unscrew the main jet and lift it out along with its washer.

19 Remove the rubber plug and unscrew the pilot jet.

20 After removing the main jet, the needle jet can be removed by gently tapping it in with a small pin punch (photo).

Choke valve removal

21 Although the removal of all four choke valves requires the separation of the carburetors, the choke valve in the number 1 carburetor can be removed and inspected and will indicate the general condition of all of the choke valves.

22 Loosen the starter lever screw that secures it to the starter shaft (photo). Loosen the choke valve nut until the choke valve assembly and starter lever can be withdrawn from the carburetor body (photo).

General cleaning

23 Submerge the metal components in carburetor cleaner and allow them to soak for approximately 30 minutes. *Do not place any plastic or rubber parts in the cleaning solution, as they will be damaged or dissolved. Also, do not allow excessive amounts of carburetor cleaner to get on your skin.*

24 If the carburetors are attached, use a soft bristle brush and solvent to clean the carburetor body as thoroughly as possible.

25 After the parts have soaked long enough for the cleaner to loosen and dissolve the varnish and other deposits, rinse them thoroughly in solvent and blow them dry with compressed air. Also, blow out all the fuel and air passages in the float bowl and carburetor body with compressed air.

Vacuum chamber component inspection

26 Inspect the carburetor slide and its bore for evidence of excessive wear, nicks and scratches. Make sure that the slide moves freely up and down in the bore. If wear is excessive, a new carburetor is the only solution. If the slide binds in the bore at all, it may be loosened up by sanding lightly with a very fine piece of emery or crocus cloth.

27 Check the jet needle and its corresponding jet in the carburetor body for wear and make sure the needle is not bent or nicked. If the machine has a lot of miles on it, the needle and

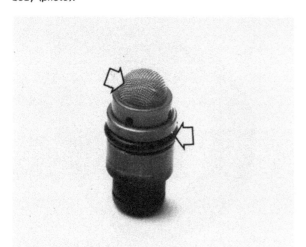

5.17   Whenever the float valve seat is removed, the screen filter should be cleaned and the O-ring replaced with a new one (arrows)

5.20   After removal of the main jet, the needle jet is removed by tapping it in with a small punch

5.22a   Location of the starter lever screw for the number 1 carburetor

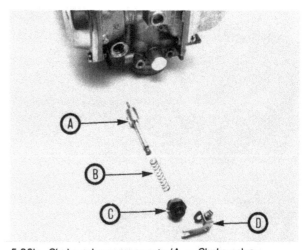

5.22b   Choke valve components (A — Choke valve; B — Choke valve spring; C — Choke valve nut; D — Starter lever)

jet may be worn enough to require replacement with new parts.
28 Check the slide diaphragm for tears or deterioration (photo) and replace the assembly with a new one if necessary.

Float chamber component inspection
29 Check the float valve and valve seat for nicks and a pronounced groove or ridge on the sealing surfaces. If there is evidence of wear, the valve and seat can be replaced with new ones. Also check the valve seat filter for deposits or damage and replace it if necessary.
30 Check the float pivot pin and its bores for wear. If the pin is a sloppy fit in the bores, excessive amounts of fuel will be allowed to enter the carburetor and flooding will occur.
31 After cleaning the jets in solvent, check them for deposits in their bores. Use compressed air to blow them out. *Never use a piece of wire or a drill bit to clean the jets, as they could enlarge the bores, upsetting the fuel and air metering rate.*

Choke valve inspection
32 Carefully inspect the tip of the choke valve and its seat in the body for any nicks, scoring or other damage that would allow fuel to leak through. Also, check the condition of the rubber seal around the valve tip for deterioration or damage (photo).
33 If any defects are found, not only should this valve and pos-

sibly the carburetor body itself be replaced, but the carburetors should be separated and the remaining choke valves inspected.

Float level adjustment and float chamber reassembly
34 **Note:** *During reassembly, be sure to use the new parts supplied with the rebuild kit.* Position the float valve seat filter and a new O-ring on the float valve seat and reinstall it in the carburetor body.
35 Reinstall the starter jet, main jet and needle jet in the carburetor body. Do not overtighten them. Be sure the slot in the bottom of the needle jet aligns with the tab in its bore.
36 Place the float needle in its seat. Hold the float in position on the carburetor and slip the pivot into place.
37 Check the float level with calipers. Hold the carburetor in an inverted position so the float tang is just resting against the float valve. Do not apply any force to the float. If the level is not within the specified range, carefully bend the tab that contacts the float valve until the level is as specified. Always remove the float to bend the tab so the inlet needle will not be damaged.
38 Reinstall the float chamber and mounting screws, tightening them evenly and securely.

Vacuum chamber reassembly
39 If the needle has been removed from the slide, be sure the needle spring, washer, E-ring and clip are properly positioned and insert the assembly into the slide. Install the guide holder and snap-ring. Be sure the snap-ring is properly seated in its groove.
40 Insert the slide assembly into the carburetor bore, making sure the diaphragm tongue is properly aligned with the indentation in the body.
41 Install the slide spring into the slide and attach the vacuum chamber cover to the carburetor. Again, tighten the cover screws evenly and securely.
42 Reinstall the throttle cable bracket, if removed.

Choke valve installation
43 Assemble the valve, spring, nut and starter lever as an assembly and insert it into the carburetor body. Be sure the starter lever is over the starter shaft. Tighten the valve nut securely, then tighten the starter lever screw.

Constant velocity carburetors — separation and reconnection
44 Although the carburetors do not need to be separated for inspection and servicing of the vacuum chamber components and float chamber components (described in the previous subsection), they should be separated for a complete carburetor overhaul.
45 Remove the fuel pipes from the carburetor assembly.

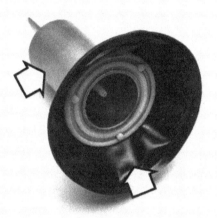

5.28 The surface of the slide should be inspected for scoring or roughness and the diaphragm checked for tears and other damage

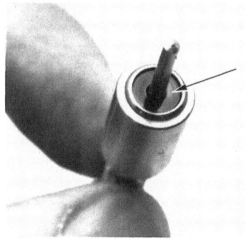

5.32 The tip of the choke valve should be inspected for nicks or scoring and the rubber seal (arrow) checked for deterioration

5.46 The starter lever screws (arrows) must be loosened to remove the starter shaft

46 Loosen the starter lever screws so the starter shaft can be withdrawn (photo) along with the starter levers. Also remove the starter bracket.

47 Separate the carburetors by removing the two mounting plates (photo). Note the positioning of all fuel pipes and springs for reassembly (photo).

48 Remove the nut that retains the adjusting lever to the number three carburetor and lift off the lever. Then remove the three screws and lift off the adjuster bracket.

49 With the carburetors separated, the choke valves can be removed and inspected. For this information, refer to the previous subsection.

50 If a carburetor body is to be replaced, refer to the previous subsection for disassembly of the vacuum chamber and float chamber components.

51 Prior to reconnection of the carburetors, inspect the fuel pipes for cracks, blockage or damage and clean them thoroughly with solvent.

52 Reconnection is basically the reverse of the separation procedure with the following notes:

a) Connect the carburetors one at a time to the mounting plates, making sure the fuel pipes and all springs are properly installed before mounting the next carburetor.

b) Apply a thread sealing agent to all mounting screws prior

to installing them.

53 After reconnection is complete, a bench synchronization procedure should be carried out as follows:

a) Turn the throttle valve stop screw to position the throttle valve of the number three carburetor so the top end of the valve just meets the foremost by-pass, or until no light can be seen between the valve and the bore when looking through the venturi.

b) Set each of the other three carburetor throttle valves to match the number three valve. These are adjusted by loosening the locknuts and turning the balance screws (photo). Set the number two carburetor first, followed by the number one and four carburetors.

54 Open the throttle slightly by pressing on the throttle linkage, then release it and make sure it returns smoothly with no drag or binding. Also check the starter shaft and linkage for smooth operation.

55 Any time the carburetors have been separated, or even loosened on their mounting plates, they must be synchronized after installation on the motorcycle. For this procedure refer to the following subsection.

Constant velocity carburetors — synchronization

56 Carburetor synchronization is simply the process of adjusting the carburetors so they pass the same amount of fuel/air mixture to each cylinder. This is done by measuring the vacuum produced in each cylinder. Carburetors that are out of synchronization will result in decreased fuel mileage, increased engine temperature, less than ideal throttle response and higher vibration levels.

57 Note that while carburetor synchronization is basically a simple task it requires the use of an expensive vacuum gauge assembly and of some skill on the owner's part. Furthermore it is complicated by the need to set the outer two carburetors at a higher level than the inner two to compensate for the different lengths of the inlet tracts between the inner and outer carburetors and the air filter element. For this reason it is recommended that the machine be taken to a Suzuki Service Agent for the work to be carried out by an expert using the correct equipment. Those owners who wish to carry out the work themselves should proceed as follows.

58 The most accurate type of vacuum gauge is the mercury manometer, but because these are extremely sensitive they require a great deal of skill to use effectively; since they also require the presence of mercury, which is an extremely toxic and dangerous liquid, their use is not recommended. The best alternative is the Suzuki service tool 09913-13121 which consists of steel balls floating in four calibrated tubes; this is almost as sensitive as the mercury manometer type, but much

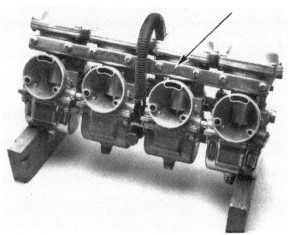

5.47a   The carburetors are attached by two mounting plates, one on each side

5.47b   While separating the carburetors, take note of the location of the springs (arrows) and how they are installed

5.53   The balancing screws are used to synchronize the carburetors

easier and safer for the average owner to use. The last alternative is to use dial-type vacuum gauges which are widely available and relatively easy to use; **it is essential** however, that the accuracy of such gauges is checked first by connecting each gauge in turn to any one cylinder. If any gauge does not give exactly the same reading as its counterparts, or if any is inconsistent, then the complete set cannot be used. Only the best quality, glycerine-damped, dial type gauges are accurate enough for this task. Once the equipment has been selected proceed according to the relevant paragraphs below.

59 **With both types of balancing equipment** the engine must first be checked thoroughly to ensure that it is in good condition, ie that the air filter element is clean and lightly oiled, that there are no leaks in the filter assembly or hoses, that the carburetor fuel levels and (where applicable) the pilot screw settings are correct, that the carburetors are clean and securely fastened and that the ignition timing and spark plugs are correctly adjusted. Check also the valve clearances and engine compression pressures to ensure that the engine is mechanically sound and ensure that the exhaust system is in good condition and is securely fastened, with no leaks. Start the engine and warm it up to normal operating temperature then set the idle speed to the specified amount.

60 Note that if the rear of the tank is raised or if it is removed completely to improve access to the balancing screws, either an alternative fuel supply must be arranged or the fuel and vacuum hoses must be temporarily extended. If the vacuum hose is disconnected it must be plugged securely to allow the engine to run and to ensure that the gauge readings are correct.

61 Remove the blanking Allen screw from each inlet port and substitute the gauge adaptors, then connect the gauge hoses to the adaptors. Check the gauges and readings obtained as described below. If adjustment is necessary a specific sequence must be followed; note that the cylinders are numbered 1, 2, 3 and 4 in sequence from left to right and that all are balanced against No. 3 cylinder. Use the centre screw first to match No. 2 cylinder with No. 3, then the left-hand screw to set No. 1 cylinder. Finally use the right-hand screw to set No. 4 cylinder. Do not press down on the screws when making adjustments and ensure that the setting does not alter when the locknuts are tightened. After each adjustment open and close the throttle quickly to settle the linkage, wait for the gauge reading to stabilise and note the effect of the adjustment before proceeding; the idle speed and vacuum reading may vary noticeably.

62 During the course of adjustment do not allow the engine to overheat; stop it and wait for it to cool down if necessary. When the carburetors are correctly synchronised stop the engine, disconnect the gauges and refit the fuel tank and blanking plugs. Check the idle speed and throttle cable free play, resetting each if necessary.

63 **When using the Suzuki service tool,** it must first be calibrated by connecting each gauge in turn to any one cylinder and using the damper screw to ensure that the steel ball is aligned with the tube's centre line. When all four gauges have been calibrated to the same cylinder connect them all to their respective cylinders and start the engine.

64 With the engine idling, the steel balls of the gauges for the two inner cylinders (Nos 2 and 3) should be aligned with their top edges just touching the gauge centre lines, while those for the gauges of the two outer cylinders should be aligned so that they are bisected by the centre line, ie the two inner cylinders should show half of a ball diameter less vacuum than the outer two.

65 If adjustment is necessary, proceed as described in paragraphs 61 and 62 above.

66 **When using dial-type gauges,** first check that they are sufficiently accurate by checking that each produces the same reading on any one cylinder as described above. If the damping is adjustable, set it so that needle flutter is just eliminated, but so that the gauge can record the slightest change in pressure.

67 When the gauges are known to be accurate, connect each to its respective cylinder. Since Suzuki do not give the necessary information the difference in pressure between the inner and outer cylinder can only be approximated; the actual figure will vary greatly depending on the quality of the gauges used.

68 Since this difference in pressure is due to the presence of the air filter element, a reasonably accurate setting can be achieved by temporarily removing the element for the duration of the adjustment and then balancing all four cylinders to exactly the **same** level; if the element is then refitted the difference in pressure can be noted for future reference.

69 With the gauges connected and the element removed, therefore, check that all cylinders give the same reading and make the necessary adjustments as described in paragraphs 61 and 62 above. Do not forget to refit the filter element once adjustment is complete. **Note:** *this operation is described only as an alternative for those owners who have access to a set of dial-type gauges but not to the Suzuki service tool. The results obtained can only approximate the correct setting and will depend on the accuracy of the gauges used and the skill of the owner. If there is any doubt about the results, the machine must be taken to a Suzuki Service Agent for the carburetor synchronization to be checked using the correct tool.*

70 **With both types of gauge,** it should be noted that if aftermarket accessory filters have been substituted for the standard filter assembly and plenum chamber, some experimentation may be necessary to achieve the correct setting. Since the difference in inlet tract lengths will no longer exist, it is possible that the best results will be obtained with all cylinders set to the same level.

Choke adjustment (cable operated choke)

71 The choke cable is adjusted at the carburetors. When fully released, the cable free play should be 0.5 to 1.0 mm (0.02 to 0.04 in). If adjustment is needed, loosen the locknut and turn the adjusting nut until the correct free play is obtained.

72 On steering stem mounted chokes, the stiffness of the choke knob can also be adjusted by raising the rubber cover and turning the knurled adjusting wheel to either loosen or tighten the knob.

Choke cable (steering stem mounted choke) — removal and installation

73 At the carburetors, locate the choke lever which the end of the choke cable is attached to. Lift up the lever and disengage the cable end from it. Pull the cable out of the adjuster.

74 Lift the rubber cover of the choke knob and loosen the knurled locknut until the knob and cable can be removed.

75 Installation is the reverse of the removal procedure. Do not overtighten the choke knob locknut. Following installation, adjust the cable free play as previously described.

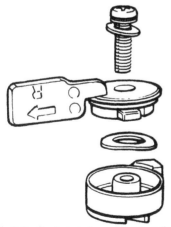

Fig.7.2 Exploded view of the handlebar-mounted choke assembly (1982 models) (Sec 5)

Choke cable (1982) — removal and installation

76 On 1982 models, the choke lever is positioned on the left side of the handlebars, below the switch assembly.

77 Disconnect the choke cable from the carburetors in the same manner as described in the above subsection.

78 Remove the single choke lever mounting screw.

79 Carefully lower the lever and disconnect the cable end from it. If the wave washer drops out, do not lose it.

80 The cable end can be withdrawn from the lever housing and the cable removed from the motorcycle.

81 Installation is the reverse of the removal procedure. **Note:** *Apply a thin coat of grease to the wave washer during installation.*

---

6 Ignition system

Transistorized ignition system—general information

1   The transistorized ignition system was introduced on the 1980 USA and Canada models and introduced in the UK with the 1981 models. With the transistorized system, the need for mechanical contact breaker points, along with the necessary maintenance, is eliminated. In addition, this system maintains the proper ignition timing at all engine speeds, automatically advancing it at the proper rpm.

2   A signal generator is mounted on the right side of the engine where the contact breaker points were previously located. The generator uses a magnet embedded rotor and two pick-up coils to produce AC current. This current is transmitted to the transistor unit which, through the ignition coils, fires the spark plugs at the right moment.

3   The ignition coils are conventional in design, transforming the low primary voltage from the transistor unit into a much higher secondary voltage used to jump the spark plug gap. One ignition coil fires the number 1 and 4 plugs, while the other fires the number 2 and 3 plugs.

4   If the spark plugs in either the number 1 and 4 or the 2 and 3 cylinders are not firing, the problem can either be in the ignition coils, the transistor unit or the signal generator. The ignition coils can be checked by simply switching the two and again checking the spark at the spark plugs. Now, if the other pair of plugs is not firing, then it's clear the ignition coil is at fault. If the original plugs are still not firing, the coil is not the problem.

5   The remainder of the system should be checked out by a Suzuki dealer or other qualified repair shop.

---

7 Frame and forks

Fork oil measurement (1979 through 1982)

1   Beginning with 1979 models, whenever oil is being added to

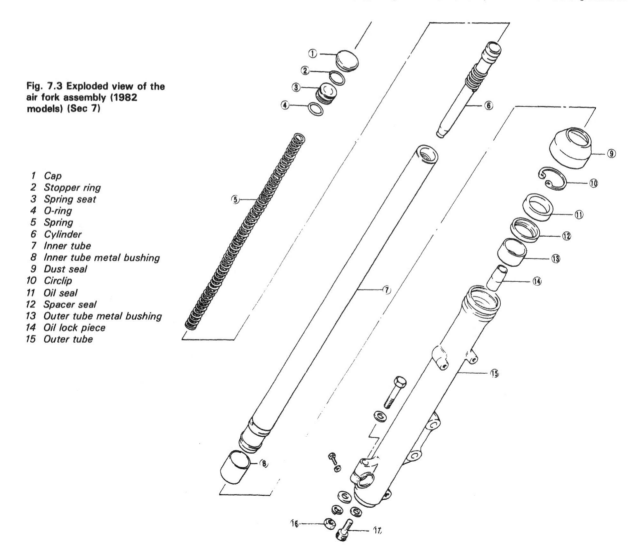

Fig. 7.3 Exploded view of the air fork assembly (1982 models) (Sec 7)

1 Cap
2 Stopper ring
3 Spring seat
4 O-ring
5 Spring
6 Cylinder
7 Inner tube
8 Inner tube metal bushing
9 Dust seal
10 Circlip
11 Oil seal
12 Spacer seal
13 Outer tube metal bushing
14 Oil lock piece
15 Outer tube

the forks, the oil level must be measured to be sure that exactly the same amount is in each fork. The following procedure is the recommended method.

2 The fork tube must be secured in a vertical position, so it is recommended that this be done after it is removed from the motorcycle.

3 With the fork cap off and the spring(s) removed, compress the inner fork tube completely into the slider. Using a graduated bottle to maintain accuracy, pour slightly less than the specified amount of oil into the fork. **Note:** *Pour the oil in slowly so it has time to settle.*

4 Measuring from the top of the tube, use a ruler, or pre-measured rod, to check that the oil is not yet up to the specified level (see the Specifications).

5 Slowly pour in the rest of the oil, a little at a time, until the oil level is as specified in both forks. The difference between the forks should not be more than one millimeter.

6 Commercially available measuring devices can also be used by following the directions supplied with the product.

7 Withdraw the inner tube from the slider and install the spring(s) and fork cap in the normal fashion.

Forks (air assisted only) — disassembly and reassembly

8 In 1982, air forks were introduced on several models. While the basic disassembly and reassembly procedures are the same as described in Chapter 4, certain exceptions should be noted.

9 Prior to removing the fork cap, always relieve the air pressure first by depressing the valve stem.

10 Once the fork cap is removed, push down on the spring seat in order to remove the stopper ring, then lift out the spring seat and spring. Always replace the stopper ring with a new one.

11 Only one spring is used on these models, instead of the two springs used in previous models.

12 After the forks are reassembled, use a hand-operated air pump to fill the tubes to the specified air pressure level. **Note:** *Do not use compressed air to fill the fork tubes, as excessive pressures can damage the internal fork components. The pressure in both forks should be as close as possible.*

Steering stem (1980 through 1982)—disassembly and reassembly

13 In 1980 the steering stem bearing was changed from the

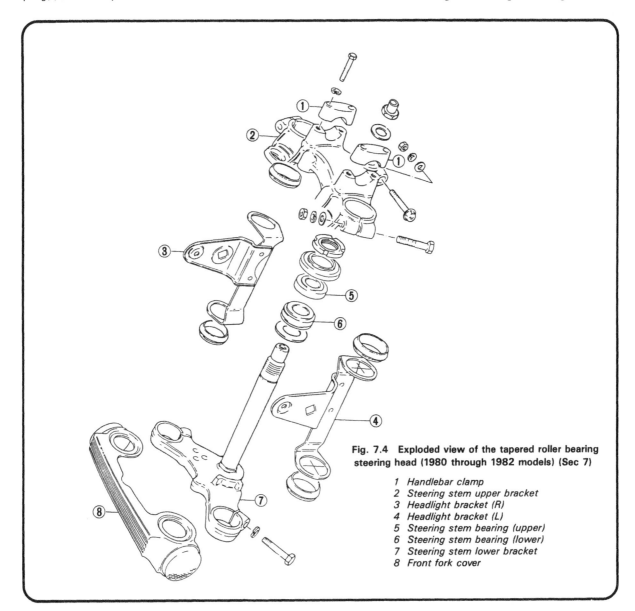

Fig. 7.4 Exploded view of the tapered roller bearing steering head (1980 through 1982 models) (Sec 7)

1 Handlebar clamp
2 Steering stem upper bracket
3 Headlight bracket (R)
4 Headlight bracket (L)
5 Steering stem bearing (upper)
6 Steering stem bearing (lower)
7 Steering stem lower bracket
8 Front fork cover

steel ball type used previously to a tapered roller bearing type, affecting certain aspects of the disassembly and reassembly procedures.

14   Remove the front wheel, forks, instrument cluster, handlebars and front brake components as described in Chapter 4, Section 2.

15   Remove the choke cable as described in Section 5.

16   Loosen the steering stem pinch bolt and remove the steering stem head nut.

17   Lift off the steering stem upper bracket.

18   While holding the lower bracket, use an appropriate wrench to remove the steering stem nut. With the nut removed, carefully lower the bracket from the frame while simultaneously lifting out the upper bearing and dust cap.

19   Inspect the bearings and races for pitting, cracking, rough spots or damaged rollers or cages. To remove a damaged or worn lower bearing. It can usually be pried off with two large screwdrivers. In some cases, though, a bearing puller or press must be used. If this lower bearing is removed, always replace the dust seal below it.

20   Before installing a new bearing in the frame, pack it with grease. To install the bearing on the stem, fit a new dust seal, then position the bearing squarely on the edge of the press fit area. Using a piece of pipe with an inside diameter slightly larger than the shaft but no larger than the width of the inner bearing race, drive the bearing down snug with a hammer. Do not strike the cage or rollers.

21   Damaged or worn outer races can be removed from the frame head with a hammer and long punch. Check for ovalling of the frame head, especially if the motorcycle has been crashed.

22   To install the outer races in the head, care must be taken to drive them in squarely while avoiding marring or striking the bearing surface. The old race can be used to start the new one in the bore, then a large socket or pipe section that fits the outer race flange should be used to seat it.

23   Pack the bearings with lithium-based grease by forcing it past the rollers. This is done by pressing the bearing against some fresh grease in the palm of the hand. In a scooping-type motion, continue to press the grease into the bearing until it comes out uniformly around the rollers and cage. Coat the outer races with grease.

24   Install the stem and bearings in the reverse order of disassembly. tighten the slotted steering stem nut to the specified torque. Turn the steering arm lock-to-lock five times to seat the bearings, then loosen the nut about 1/4 to 1/2 turn.

25   Reinstall the upper bracket into position and install the steering stem head nut loosely.

26   The remainder of the installation procedure is the reverse of the removal procedure, with the following notes:

   a)   Do not tighten the steering stem nut until after the fork tubes have been inserted through both steering stem brackets. This will ensure that they are properly aligned.

   b)   Be sure to reroute all cables and wiring harnesses in their original positions.

   c)   Following installation of the forks, grasp them with a hand on each fork slider and attempt to rock them backward and forward, checking for play. If any play exists, the steering stem nut must be tightened more.

   d)   Also, with the front wheel installed, the bars should turn easily and smoothly from left to right. Again, if there is too much resistance, the steering stem nut is too tight.

8   Wheels, brakes and tires

Cast wheels — inspection

1   Although cast wheels require less maintenance than spoked wheels, periodically they should be visually inspected for cracks, flat spots on the rim and other damage. Look very closely for dents in the area where the tire bead contacts the rim. Dents in this area may prevent complete sealing of the tire against the rim, which leads to deflation of the tire over a period

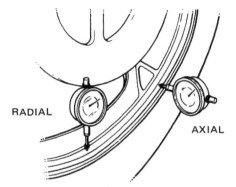

Fig. 7.5   Proper positioning of the dial gauge when measuring axial and radial runout of the cast wheel (Sec 8)

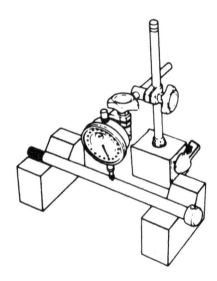

Fig. 7.6   Proper set-up for measuring runout of the axle (Sec 8)

8.11   Location of the front brake caliper-to-bracket bolts

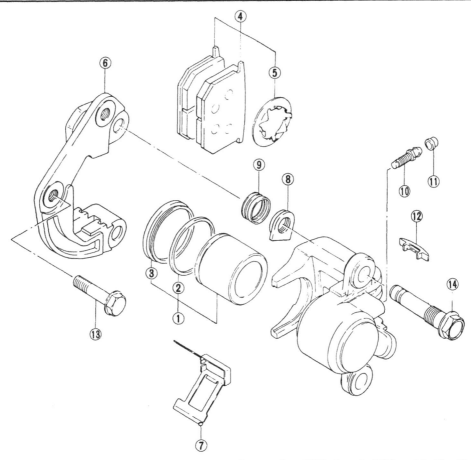

Fig. 7.7   Exploded view of the front brake caliper used on 1980 through 1982 models (Sec 8)

1 Piston set	5 Pad shim	8 Nut	11 Bleeder cap
2 Piston seal	6 Caliper holder	9 Boot	12 Cover
3 Piston boot	7 Spring	10 Bleeder	13 Bolt
4 Pad set			14 Bolt

of time. Also, check the axial and radial runout as described below.

2   Place the motorcycle on the centerstand with the wheel in the air. Position a dial indicator so the stem is against the side of the rim. Spin the wheel slowly and check the side-to-side (axial) runout of the rim. In order to accurately check radial runout with the dial indicator, position it so it is just touching the underside of the wheel rim. Again spin the wheel slowly to measure the runout.

3   An easier, though slightly less accurate method is to attach a stiff wire pointer to the fork slider and position the end a fraction of an inch from the wheel (where the wheel and tire join). If the wheel is true, the distance from the pointer to the rim will be constant as the wheel is rotated.

4   If damage is evident, or if runout in either direction is excessive, the wheel will have to be replaced with a new one. Never attempt to repair a damaged cast wheel.

5   A more thorough inspection involves removing the wheel from the motorcycle. Refer to Chapter 5.

6   With the wheel removed, place the axle on V-blocks and set up a dial indicator to measure the runout. The indicator should just touch the axle so when the axle is rotated any runout will be indicated. The runout measurement should be done in three places; once in the center and then half-way between the center and either end.

7   While the rear wheel is removed, also check the condition of the cushion drive as described in Chapter 5.

8   A final check for the front wheel is for leakage around the grease seals. If any is noticed, the seals must be replaced with new ones.

Brake system bleeding (dual front disc brakes)

9   The procedure for bleeding the brake system (dual front disc models) is the same as described in Chapter 5, except that each caliper should be bled separately, bleeding the left caliper first and then the right one.

Front disc brake (1980 through 1982) — pad replacement

10   Always replace the brake pads in pairs to ensure even pressure on the disc.

11   Remove the two bolts that retain the brake caliper to the caliper holder (photo) and lift the caliper off. It is not necessary to disconnect the brake hose from the caliper. **Note:** *Do not operate the brake lever after the caliper has been removed.*

12   Pull the brake pads to the rear to remove them from the caliper holder.

13   Prior to installing the new pads, depress the caliper piston into the caliper body so it is flush with the inner surface of the caliper. This will provide enough clearance for the new pads.

14   Do not apply grease to the new pads and avoid touching the lining surfaces with your fingers. Slip the pads into place and then reinstall the caliper.

15   Install the two caliper mounting bolts and tighten them to

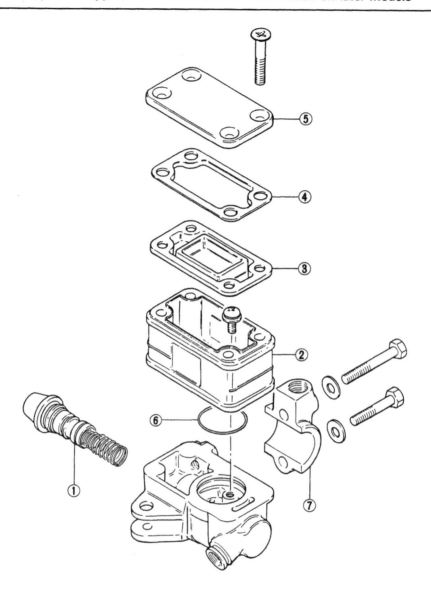

Fig. 7.8 Exploded view of the front brake master cylinder components (1980 and 1981 models) (Sec 8)

1 Piston cap set
2 Reservoir
3 Diaphragm
4 Plate

5 Cap
6 O-ring
7 Holder

their specified torque.

16   Check the brake fluid level in the master cylinder. After installing new brake pads, the level may be too high. If so, remove the cover and carefully siphon off the excess fluid.

Rear disc brake (GS550) — general information

17   The service procedures for the rear disc brake used on some GS550 models are essentially the same as those described in Chapter 5 for the GS750.

18   One exception is that shims are used between the pads and the caliper pistons to reduce friction and noise. When installing the pads in the caliper, be sure these shims are installed so that the triangular holes stamped into them are facing toward the front of the motorcycle.

Rear drum brake (1982 GS550L) — general information

19   In 1982, rear drum brakes are used on GS550L models in place of the disc brakes used in the several years prior. Refer to the appropriate information on Drum brakes in Chapter 5 for all servicing procedures.

Front brake master cylinder (1980 and 1981) — disassembly and reassembly

20   With the 1980 models, the front brake master cylinder was redesigned to use a rectangular reservoir and a cover that is retained by four screws.

21   The disassembly and reassembly procedures are basically the same as those described in Chapter 5, except for the infor-

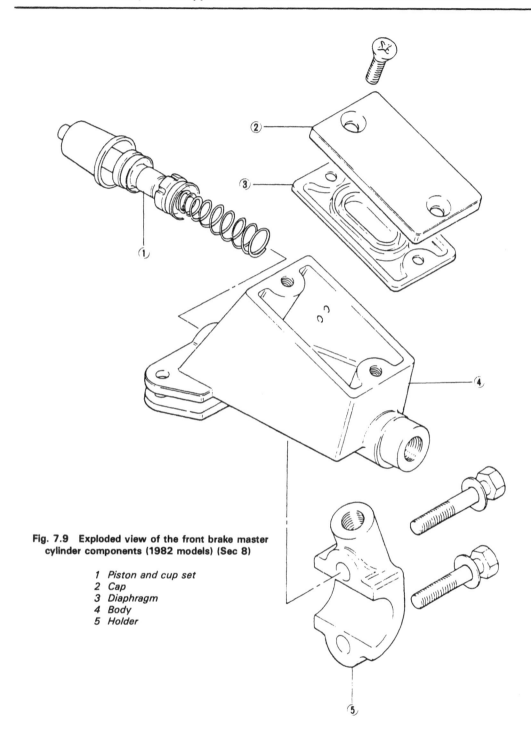

Fig. 7.9 Exploded view of the front brake master cylinder components (1982 models) (Sec 8)

1 Piston and cup set
2 Cap
3 Diaphragm
4 Body
5 Holder

mation pertaining to the cover and reservoir.

22 The cover is removed by removing the four mounting screws. With the cover removed, the plate and diaphragm can be lifted off.

23 The reservoir is held to the cylinder body by two screws which are removed from inside the reservoir.

24 An O-ring is used between the reservoir and the cylinder body; it's a good idea to replace it whenever the two are separated.

Front brake master cylinder (1982) — disassembly and reassembly

25 On 1982 models, the brake master cylinder was redesigned so the fluid reservoir is integral with the cylinder body. A window in the rear of the body allows for easy checking of the fluid level. In addition, the cover is held on by two screws and a diaphragm is located under the cover.

26 Other than these changes, the disassembly, inspection and reassembly procedures described in Chapter 5 still apply.

Rear brake master cylinder (remote reservoir) — general information

27 GS750L models, as well as later model GS550s equipped with a rear disc brake, use a rear master cylinder connected to a remote fluid reservoir. This is in contrast to the integral reservoir used on earlier models.

28 The remote reservoir is mounted behind the right frame cover and is attached to the frame by a single mounting bolt.

29 The service procedures described in Chapter 5 also apply to this new master cylinder.

Tire changing (cast wheels)

30 Changing a tire mounted on a cast wheel is very similar to the procedure given in Chapter 5 for spoked wheels except for the following.

31 Prior to removing the tire from the wheel, mark the position of the valve stem with chalk and the rotational direction of the tire on the wheel. This will allow the tire to be mounted in the same position it was originally in.

32 Suzuki recommends that rim protectors be used between the wheel rim and the tire iron to prevent the rim from being damaged. Excessive dents or indentations in the rim is cause for wheel replacement. Plastic rim protectors that fit over the edge of the rim are available from Suzuki dealers.

33 When mounting the rear tire, note that the embossed arrow mark on the side of the tire should face in the rotational direction of the wheel.

---

9 Electrical system

Fuses (1979 through 1982)

1   In 1979, a fuse box located behind the side cover is used in addition to the single main fuse used in previous years. The fuse box contains four fuses, each controlling a specific individual electrical circuit. Refer to the fuse box or wiring diagrams for identification of the fuses.

Charging system inspection (1979 L and all 1980 through 1982 models)

2   The charging system on these models has been modified so that the regulator and rectifier are contained in one unit.

3   If the system is suspected of malfunctioning, first check all appropriate wires and connectors to be sure they are tight, clean and in good condition.

AC generator test

4   Disconnect the yellow, white/green and white/blue wires from the AC generator.

5   Start the engine and keep it running at 5000 rpm. Use a voltmeter to measure the voltage between each pair of the three wires. A reading of 75V (for 1979 GS750 models) 70V (for 1979 GS550 models) or 80V (for 1980 through 1982 models) or more should be obtained in each case.

6   If the reading is under the correct amount, the AC generator is defective.

7   If the AC generator is indicated to be faulty, use a continuity tester to check for continuity between each of the three lead wires. Continuity should exist between all three wires.

8   Also check for continuity between the stator core and all three wires. In this case no continuity should be present or else the stator core insulation is defective.

9   If either of the above tests does not produce the desired results, the stator should be replaced with a new one.

10 If the stator is in good condition, but the AC generator is shown to be defective, replace the rotor with a new one.

Regulator/rectifier test

11 With the engine stopped, reconnect the wires disconnected for the last test.

12 Prior to checking the regulator/rectifier, be sure the battery is fully charged. This is accurately checked by measuring the

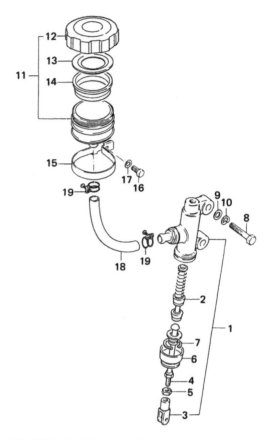

Fig. 7.10 Exploded view of the rear brake master cylinder with remote reservoir (Sec 8)

1 Rear master cylinder assembly	10 Lock washer
2 Piston and cup set	11 Reservoir tank assembly
3 Yoke	12 Cap
4 Push rod	13 Diaphragm plate
5 Nut	14 Diaphragm
6 Boot	15 Clamp
7 Circlip	16 Bolt
8 Bolt	17 Lock washer
9 Washer	18 Hose
	19 Clamp

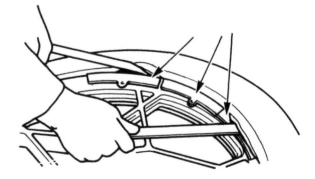

Fig. 7.11 To prevent damage to the cast wheel, rim protectors (arrows) should be used under the tire irons when changing a tire (Sec 9)

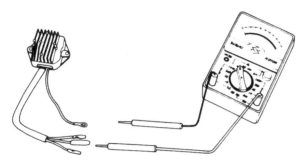

Fig. 7.12   Using an ohmmeter to check for continuity in the regulator/rectifier (Sec 11)

specific gravity of the battery electrolyte. If it is not fully charged, charge it with a battery charger.

13   On 1979 models, the headlight must be off for this test. If it cannot be turned off with a switch, remove the appropriate (10A) fuses from the fuse box. On 1980 and later models, the light should be On in the High beam position.

14   Connect the voltmeter directly to the battery (be sure the positive lead is on the positive terminal). Start the engine and with the engine speed at 5000 rpm, measure the voltage. The reading should be 14 to 15.5V. If it is either under or over this amount, the regulator/rectifier is suspect. Again, make sure that all wires and connections are in good condition. Repeat the test if in doubt.

15   A final check of the regulator/rectifier is to disconnect all the wires leading to it and check for continuity between the wires listed below. Be sure the probes are hooked up in the proper manner. Continuity should be shown *only* when the probes are hooked up in the manner described.

Positive voltmeter probe	Negative voltmeter probe
GS750 models only	
Black/white	Yellow
GS750 and 1980 through 1982 GS 550 models	
Red	Yellow
Red	White/blue
Red	White/red
Red	Black/white
Yellow	Black/white
White/blue	Black/white
White/red	Black/white
1979 GS550 models	
Red	White/red
Red	Yellow
Red	White/blue
Red	Black/white
White/blue	White/red
White/blue	Yellow
White/blue	Red
White/blue	Black/white
White/red	Black/white
Yellow	Black/white

16   If continuity is not shown at each of these connections, the regulator/rectifier should be replaced with a new unit.

17   Also, make the same connections, reversing the probes, and

again check for continuity. In this case, no continuity should be shown (with the exception of the connection made in both directions in the above test). If continuity is shown the regulator/rectifier is defective.

Gear indicator — testing

18   If the gear indicator or neutral indicator fails to light, the problem is either in the bulbs, the indicator itself, the gear shifting switch or in the wiring of the circuit.

19   First, make sure that the light bulbs are not burned out. Then check all wiring and connections to be sure they are clean, tight and in good condition.

20   the wires running from the gear indicator lead to one five-prong connector and one single-prong connector. Use the wiring diagrams at the rear of this Chapter to locate and identify these connectors, then disconnect them.

21   Use a continuity tester to check for continuity between the orange and blue wires, with the negative probe connected to the orange wire. Also, check for continuity between the orange wire and each of the terminals in the five-prong connector (again with the negative probe connected to the orange wire). Continuity should exist between all connections. If not, the indicator is defective.

22   If no problems are revealed in the gear indicator, remove the shifter and left crankcase cover to expose the countershaft sprocket. Mounted below and in front of the sprocket is the gear shifting switch, which should also be removed from the crankcase.

23   Turn the ignition switch On.

24   Ground one end of a jumper wire to the engine and touch the other end to each of the switch contacts, one at a time. If the neutral and gear indicator bulbs light in the indicator, the switch is working properly. If not, the switch needs to be replaced with a new one.

Fuel gauge — testing

25   Accurate troubleshooting and testing of the fuel gauge is complicated and best left to a dealer or other qualified repair shop.

26   However, if the fuel gauge is giving inaccurate readings, one easy test is to measure the resistance of the gauge sending unit inside the fuel tank. This is a conventional-type sending unit which uses a float to sense the level of the fuel. the float is connected to the sending unit by a thin rod and pivots up and down inside the tank. The higher the float sits, the less resistance is in the sending unit and the further across the gauge face the needle can swing.

27   With the fuel tank nearly empty, locate and disconnect the wiring connector leading to the fuel level sending unit, mounted to the underside of the tank.

28   Connect an ohmmeter to the wiring connector terminals and, with the ignition switch On, measure the resistance. Following this, add fuel in the amounts shown below and after each addition, again measure the resistance. Also, check the position of the fuel gauge needle.

Total amount of fuel	Resistance	Gauge needle position
1.5 liters (1.6 qts)	110 ohms	Below E
1.9 liters (2 qts)	95 ohms	E
3.6 liters (3.8 qts)	50 ophms	Red zone edge
4.8 liters (1.3 gal)	32.5 ohms	1/2
8.2 liters (2.2 gal)	7 ohms	F
9.1 liters (2.4 gal)	3 ohms	Above F

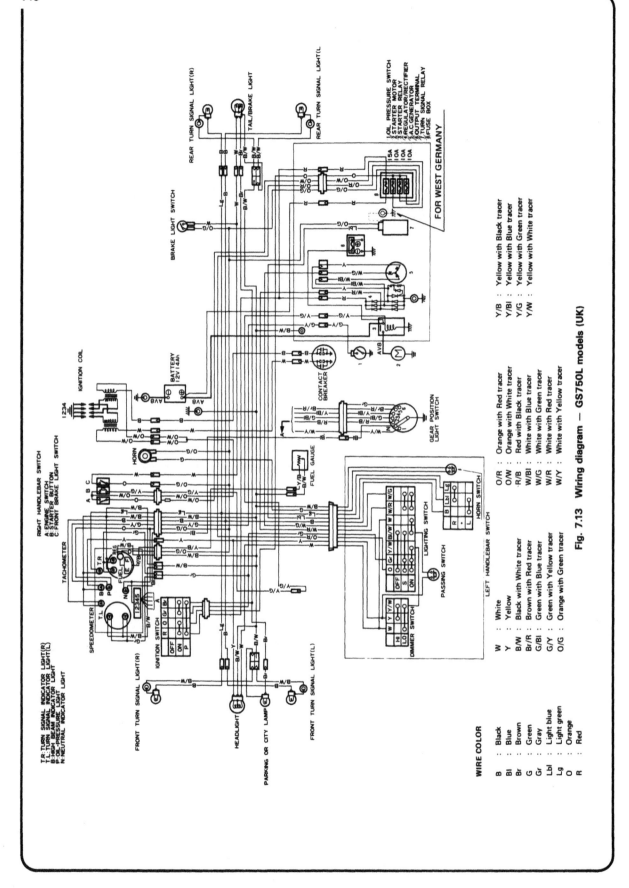

Fig. 7.13 Wiring diagram — GS750L models (UK)

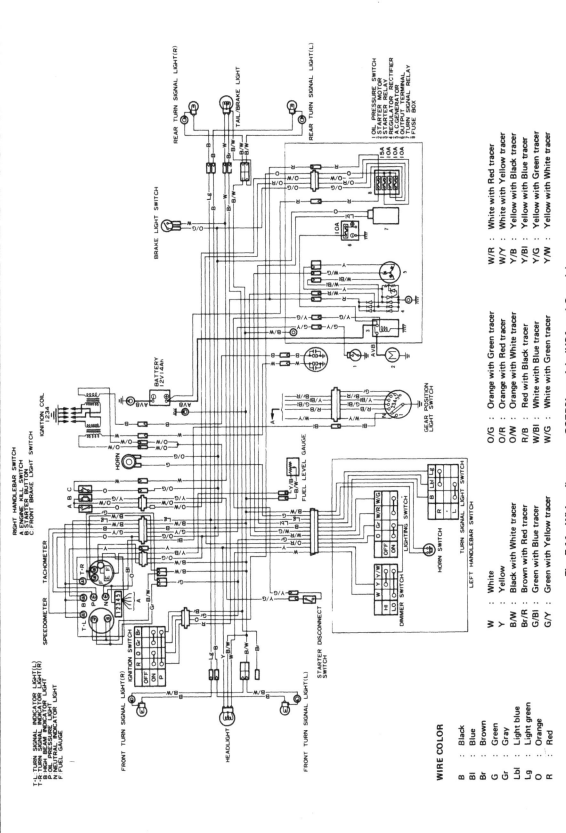

Fig. 7.14 Wiring diagram — GS750L models (USA and Canada)

WIRE COLOR

B : Black
Bl : Blue
Br : Brown
G : Green
Gr : Gray
Lbl : Light blue
Lg : Light green
O : Orange
R : Red

W : White
Y : Yellow
B/W : Black with White tracer
Br/R : Brown with Red tracer
G/Bl : Green with Blue tracer
G/Y : Green with Yellow tracer

O/G : Orange with Green tracer
O/R : Orange with Red tracer
O/W : Orange with White tracer
R/B : Red with Black tracer
W/Bl : White with Blue tracer
W/G : White with Green tracer

W/R : White with Red tracer
W/Y : White with Yellow tracer
Y/B : Yellow with Black tracer
Y/Bl : Yellow with Blue tracer
Y/G : Yellow with Green tracer
Y/W : Yellow with White tracer

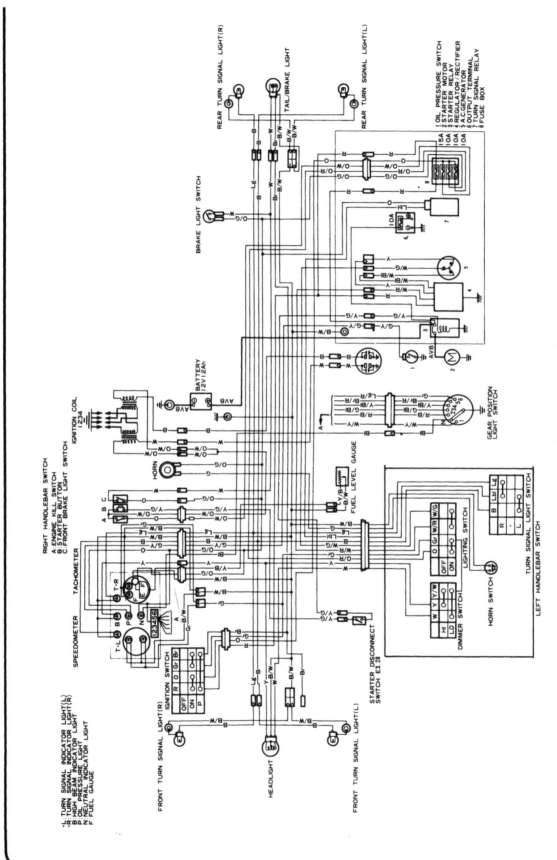

Fig. 7.15 **Wiring diagram — 1979 GS550L models (USA and Canada)**

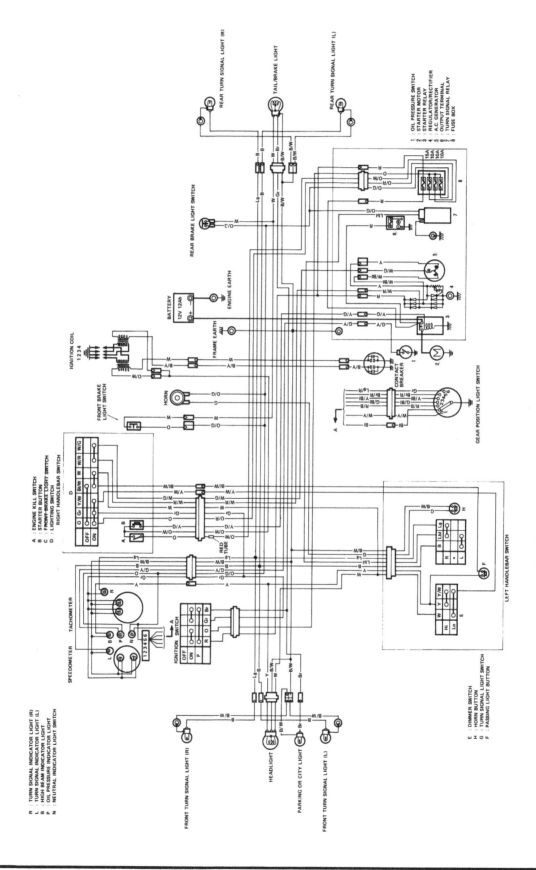

Fig. 7.16 Wiring diagram — 1980 GS550E models (UK)

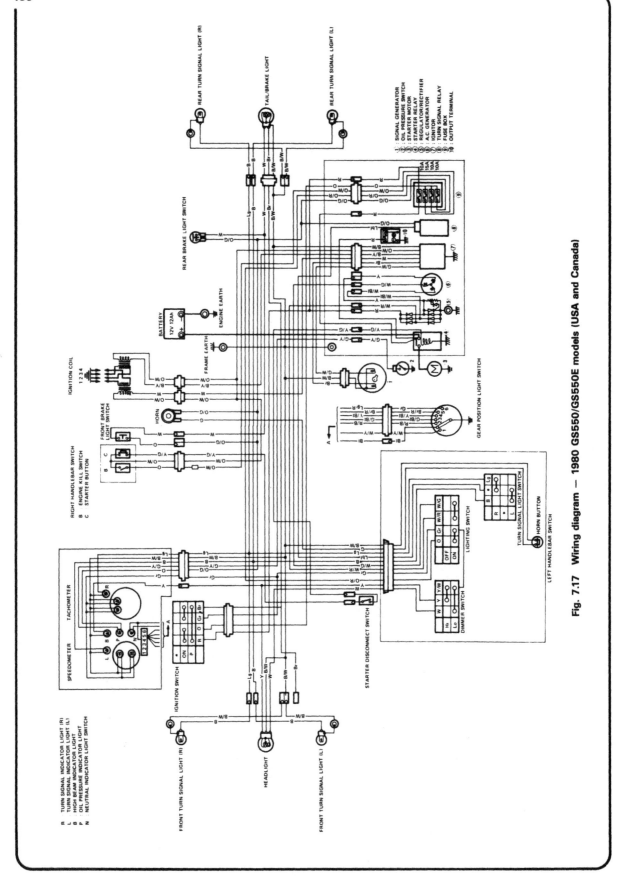

Fig. 7.17 Wiring diagram — 1980 GS550/GS550E models (USA and Canada)

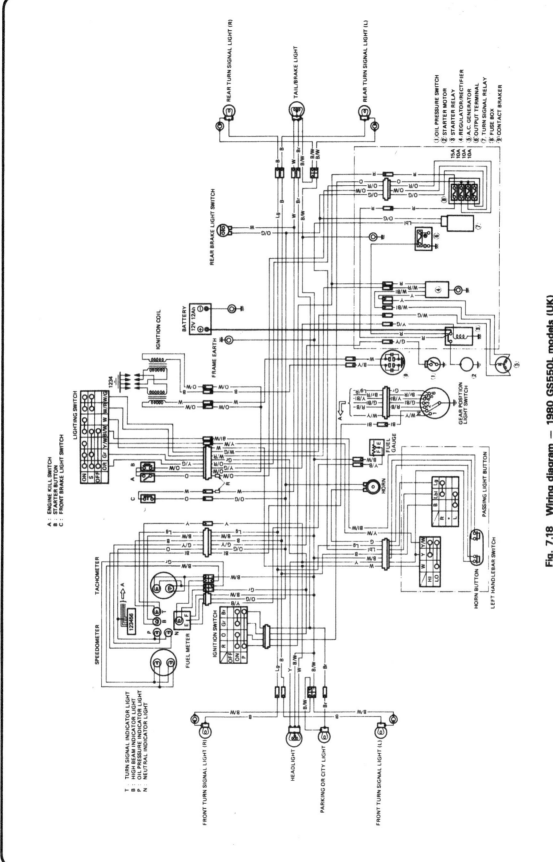

Fig. 7.18 Wiring diagram — 1980 GS550L models (UK)

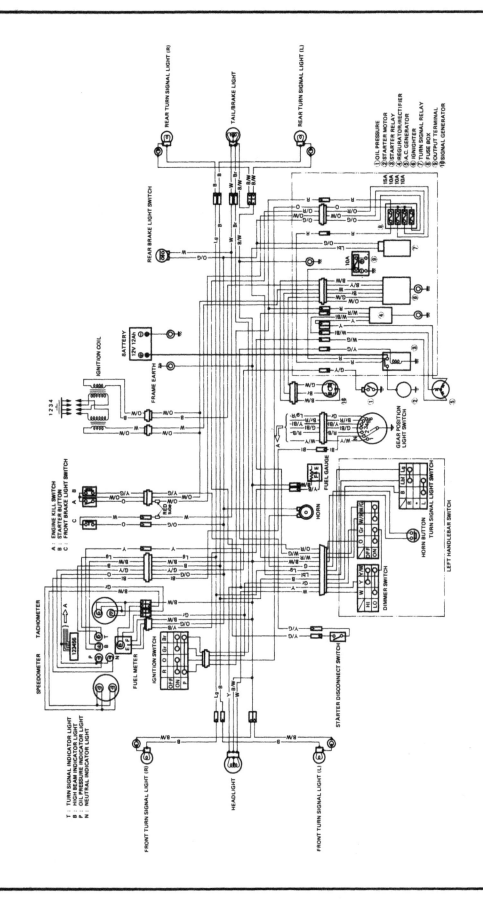

Fig. 7.19 Wiring diagram — 1980 GS550L models (USA and Canada)

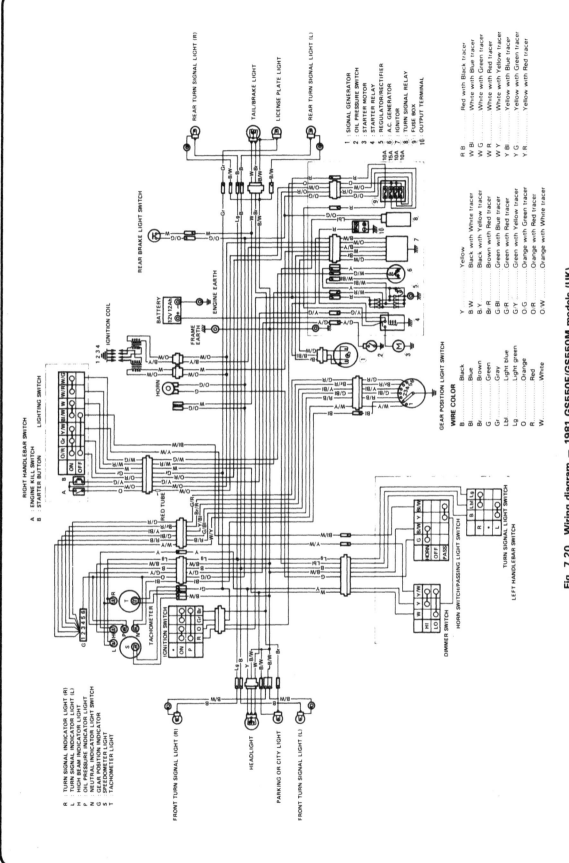

Fig. 7.20 Wiring diagram — 1981 GS550E/GS550M models (UK)

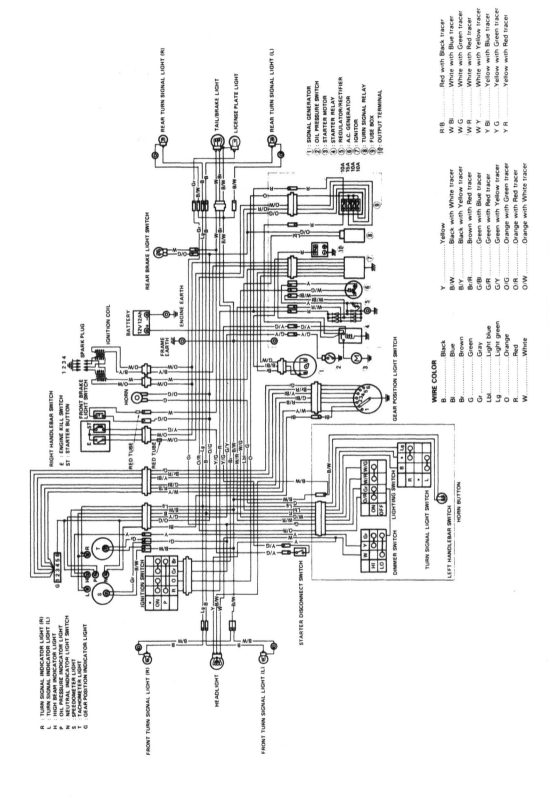

Fig. 7.21 Wiring diagram — 1981 GS550E models (Canada)

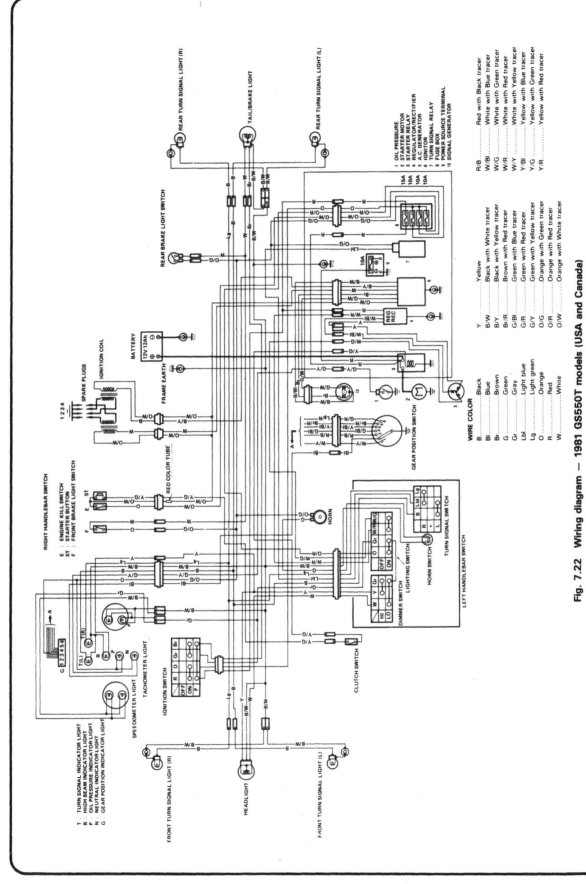

Fig. 7.22 Wiring diagram — 1981 GS550T models (USA and Canada)

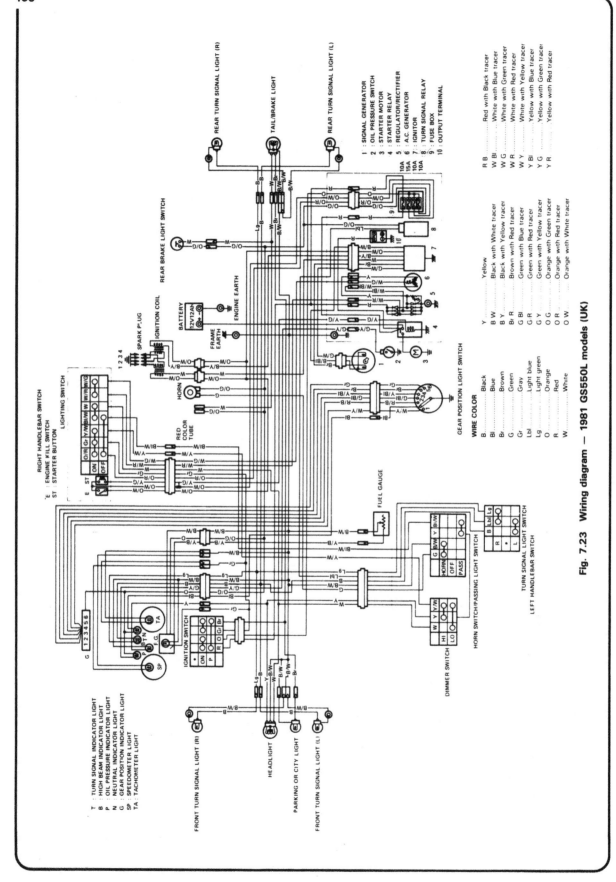

Fig. 7.23 Wiring diagram — 1981 GS550L models (UK)

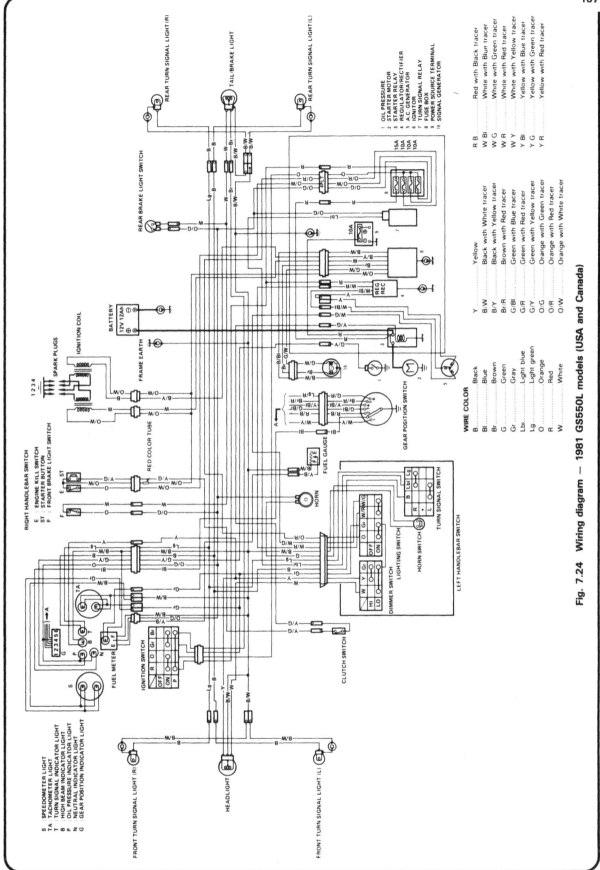

Fig. 7.24 Wiring diagram — 1981 GS550L models (USA and Canada)

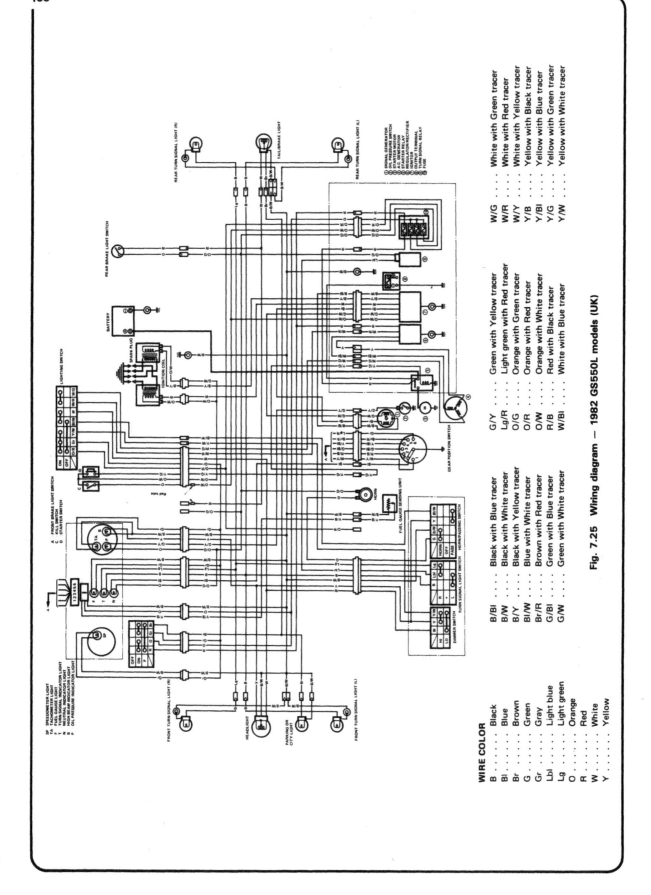

Fig. 7.25 Wiring diagram — 1982 GS550L models (UK)

WIRE COLOR

B	. . . . .	Black
Bl	. . . . .	Blue
Br	. . . . .	Brown
G	. . . . .	Green
Gr	. . . . .	Gray
Lbl	. . . . .	Light blue
Lg	. . . . .	Light green
O	. . . . .	Orange
R	. . . . .	Red
W	. . . . .	White
Y	. . . . .	Yellow

B/Bl	. . . . .	Black with Blue tracer
B/W	. . . . .	Black with White tracer
B/Y	. . . . .	Black with Yellow tracer
Bl/W	. . . . .	Blue with White tracer
Br/R	. . . . .	Brown with Red tracer
G/Bl	. . . . .	Green with Blue tracer
G/W	. . . . .	Green with White tracer

G/Y	. . . . .	Green with Yellow tracer
Lg/R	. . . . .	Light green with Red tracer
O/G	. . . . .	Orange with Green tracer
O/R	. . . . .	Orange with Red tracer
O/W	. . . . .	Orange with White tracer
R/B	. . . . .	Red with Black tracer
W/Bl	. . . . .	White with Blue tracer

W/G	. . . . .	White with Green tracer
W/R	. . . . .	White with Red tracer
W/Y	. . . . .	White with Yellow tracer
Y/B	. . . . .	Yellow with Black tracer
Y/Bl	. . . . .	Yellow with Blue tracer
Y/G	. . . . .	Yellow with Green tracer
Y/W	. . . . .	Yellow with White tracer

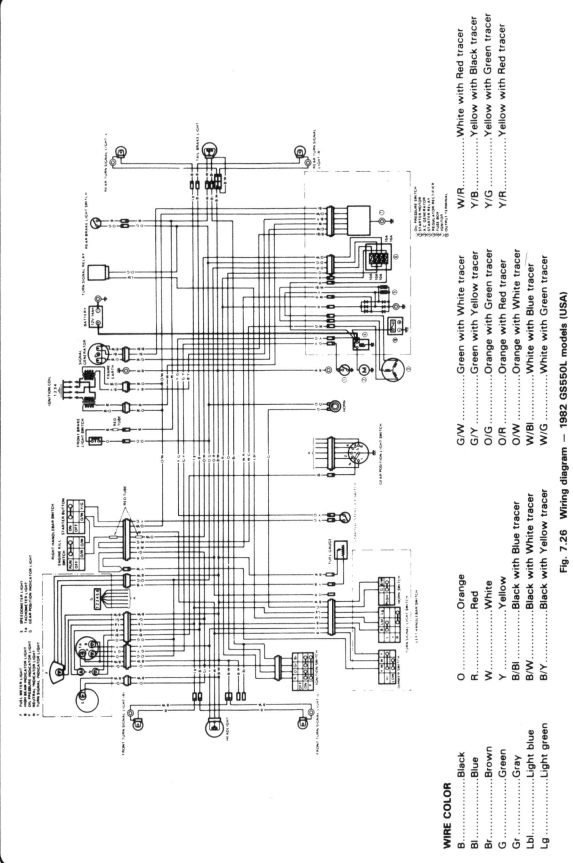

Fig. 7.26 Wiring diagram — 1982 GS550L models (USA)

WIRE COLOR

B .... Black
Bl .... Blue
Br .... Brown
G .... Green
Gr .... Gray
Lbl .... Light blue
Lg .... Light green

O .... Orange
R .... Red
W .... White
Y .... Yellow
B/Bl .... Black with Blue tracer
B/W .... Black with White tracer
B/Y .... Black with Yellow tracer

G/W .... Green with White tracer
G/Y .... Green with Yellow tracer
O/G .... Orange with Green tracer
O/R .... Orange with Red tracer
O/W .... Orange with White tracer
W/Bl .... White with Blue tracer
W/G .... White with Green tracer

W/R .... White with Red tracer
Y/B .... Yellow with Black tracer
Y/G .... Yellow with Green tracer
Y/R .... Yellow with Red tracer

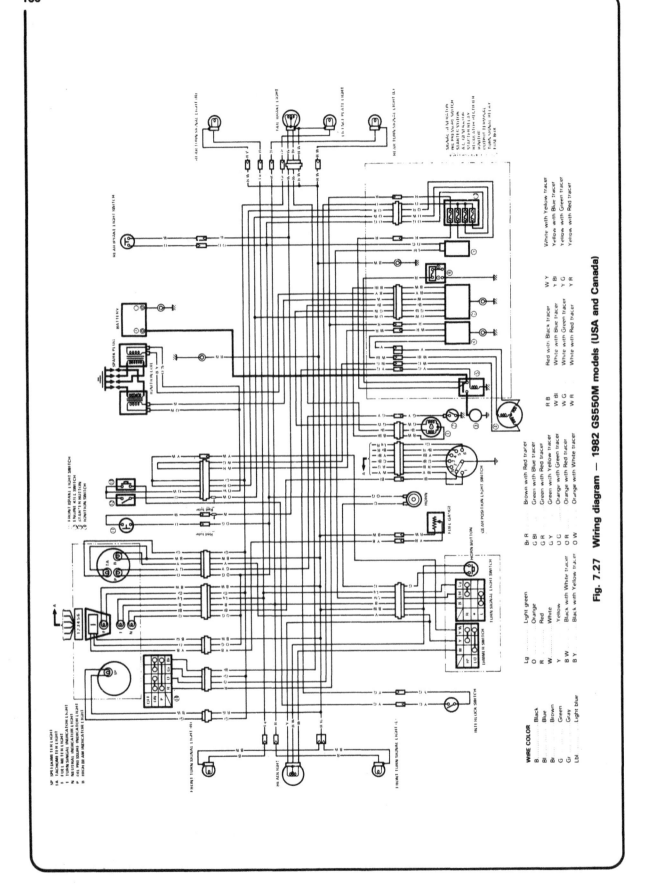

Fig. 7.27 Wiring diagram — 1982 GS550M models (USA and Canada)

WIRE COLOR

B	Black
Bl	Blue
Br	Brown
G	Green
Gr	Gray
Lbl	Light blue
Lg	Light green
O	Orange
R	Red
W	White
Y	Yellow
B/W	Black with White tracer
B/Y	Black with Yellow tracer

Br/R	Brown with Red tracer
G/Bl	Green with Blue tracer
G/R	Green with Red tracer
G/Y	Green with Yellow tracer
O/G	Orange with Green tracer
O/R	Orange with Red tracer
O/W	Orange with White tracer

R/B	Red with Black tracer
W/Bl	White with Blue tracer
W/G	White with Green tracer
W/R	White with Red tracer

W/Y	White with Yellow tracer
Y/Bl	Yellow with Blue tracer
Y/G	Yellow with Green tracer
Y/R	Yellow with Red tracer

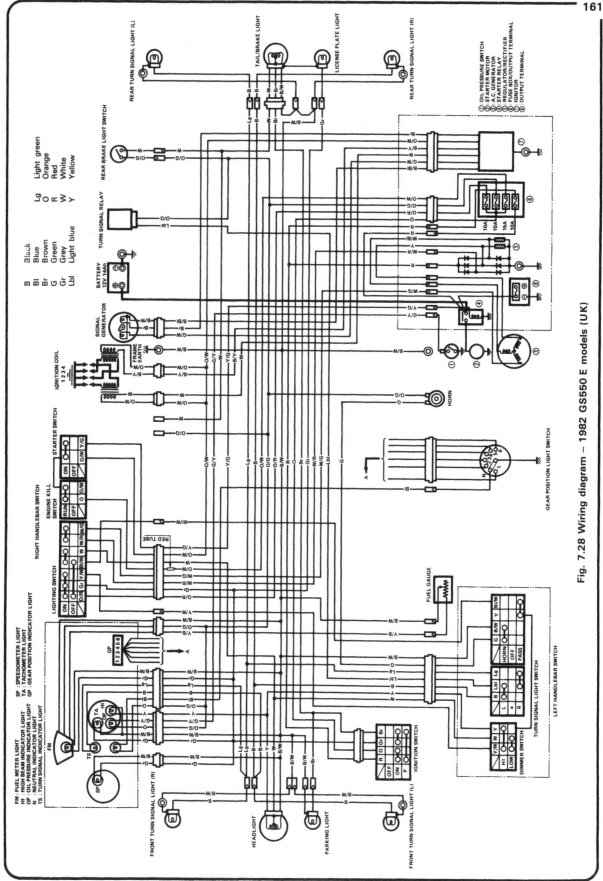

Fig. 7.28 Wiring diagram – 1982 GS550 E models (UK)

Conversion factors

Length (distance)

Inches (in)	X	25.4	= Millimetres (mm)	X 0.0394	= Inches (in)
Feet (ft)	X	0.305	= Metres (m)	X 3.281	= Feet (ft)
Miles	X	1.609	= Kilometres (km)	X 0.621	= Miles

Volume (capacity)

Cubic inches (cu in; in³)	X	16.387	= Cubic centimetres (cc; cm³)	X 0.061	= Cubic inches (cu in; in³)
Imperial pints (Imp pt)	X	0.568	= Litres (l)	X 1.76	= Imperial pints (Imp pt)
Imperial quarts (Imp qt)	X	1.137	= Litres (l)	X 0.88	= Imperial quarts (Imp qt)
Imperial quarts (Imp qt)	X	1.201	= US quarts (US qt)	X 0.833	= Imperial quarts (Imp qt)
US quarts (US qt)	X	0.946	= Litres (l)	X 1.057	= US quarts (US qt)
Imperial gallons (Imp gal)	X	4.546	= Litres (l)	X 0.22	= Imperial gallons (Imp gal)
Imperial gallons (Imp gal)	X	1.201	= US gallons (US gal)	X 0.833	= Imperial gallons (Imp gal)
US gallons (US gal)	X	3.785	= Litres (l)	X 0.264	= US gallons (US gal)

Mass (weight)

Ounces (oz)	X	28.35	= Grams (g)	X 0.035	= Ounces (oz)
Pounds (lb)	X	0.454	= Kilograms (kg)	X 2.205	= Pounds (lb)

Force

Ounces-force (ozf; oz)	X	0.278	= Newtons (N)	X 3.6	= Ounces-force (ozf; oz)
Pounds-force (lbf; lb)	X	4.448	= Newtons (N)	X 0.225	= Pounds-force (lbf; lb)
Newtons (N)	X	0.1	= Kilograms-force (kgf; kg)	X 9.81	= Newtons (N)

Pressure

Pounds-force per square inch (psi; lbf/in²; lb/in²)	X	0.070	= Kilograms-force per square centimetre (kgf/cm²; kg/cm²)	X 14.223	= Pounds-force per square inch (psi; lbf/in²; lb/in²)
Pounds-force per square inch (psi; lbf/in²; lb/in²)	X	0.068	= Atmospheres (atm)	X 14.696	= Pounds-force per square inch (psi; lbf/in²; lb/in²)
Pounds-force per square inch (psi; lbf/in²; lb/in²)	X	0.069	= Bars	X 14.5	= Pounds-force per square inch (psi; lbf/in²; lb/in²)
Pounds-force per square inch (psi; lbf/in²; lb/in²)	X	6.895	= Kilopascals (kPa)	X 0.145	= Pounds-force per square inch (psi; lbf/in²; lb/in²)
Kilopascals (kPa)	X	0.01	= Kilograms-force per square centimetre (kgf/cm²; kg/cm²)	X 98.1	= Kilopascals (kPa)
Millibar (mbar)	X	100	= Pascals (Pa)	X 0.01	= Millibar (mbar)
Millibar (mbar)	X	0.0145	= Pounds-force per square inch (psi; lbf/in²; lb/in²)	X 68.947	= Millibar (mbar)
Millibar (mbar)	X	0.75	= Millimetres of mercury (mmHg)	X 1.333	= Millibar (mbar)
Millibar (mbar)	X	0.401	= Inches of water (inH₂O)	X 2.491	= Millibar (mbar)
Millimetres of mercury (mmHg)	X	0.535	= Inches of water (inH₂O)	X 1.868	= Millimetres of mercury (mmHg)
Inches of water (inH₂O)	X	0.036	= Pounds-force per square inch (psi; lbf/in²; lb/in²)	X 27.68	= Inches of water (inH₂O)

Torque (moment of force)

Pounds-force inches (lbf in; lb in)	X	1.152	= Kilograms-force centimetre (kgf cm; kg cm)	X 0.868	= Pounds-force inches (lbf in; lb in)
Pounds-force inches (lbf in; lb in)	X	0.113	= Newton metres (Nm)	X 8.85	= Pounds-force inches (lbf in; lb in)
Pounds-force inches (lbf in; lb in)	X	0.083	= Pounds-force feet (lbf ft; lb ft)	X 12	= Pounds-force inches (lbf in; lb in)
Pounds-force feet (lbf ft; lb ft)	X	0.138	= Kilograms-force metres (kgf m; kg m)	X 7.233	= Pounds-force feet (lbf ft; lb ft)
Pounds-force feet (lbf ft; lb ft)	X	1.356	= Newton metres (Nm)	X 0.738	= Pounds-force feet (lbf ft; lb ft)
Newton metres (Nm)	X	0.102	= Kilograms-force metres (kgf m; kg m)	X 9.804	= Newton metres (Nm)

Power

Horsepower (hp)	X	745.7	= Watts (W)	X 0.0013	= Horsepower (hp)

Velocity (speed)

Miles per hour (miles/hr; mph)	X	1.609	= Kilometres per hour (km/hr; kph)	X 0.621	= Miles per hour (miles/hr; mph)

Fuel consumption*

Miles per gallon, Imperial (mpg)	X	0.354	= Kilometres per litre (km/l)	X 2.825	= Miles per gallon, Imperial (mpg)
Miles per gallon, US (mpg)	X	0.425	= Kilometres per litre (km/l)	X 2.352	= Miles per gallon, US (mpg)

Temperature

Degrees Fahrenheit = ($°C$ x 1.8) + 32   Degrees Celsius (Degrees Centigrade; $°C$) = ($°F$ - 32) x 0.56

*It is common practice to convert from miles per gallon (mpg) to litres/100 kilometres (l/100km), where mpg (Imperial) x l/100 km = 282 and mpg (US) x l/100 km = 235

English/American terminology

Because this book has been written in England, British English component names, phrases and spellings have been used throughout. American English usage is quite often different and whereas normally no confusion should occur, a list of equivalent terminology is given below.

English	American	English	American
Air filter	Air cleaner	Number plate	License plate
Alignment (headlamp)	Aim	Output or layshaft	Countershaft
Allen screw/key	Socket screw/wrench	Panniers	Side cases
Anticlockwise	Counterclockwise	Paraffin	Kerosene
Bottom/top gear	Low/high gear	Petrol	Gasoline
Bottom/top yoke	Bottom/top triple clamp	Petrol/fuel tank	Gas tank
Bush	Bushing	Pinking	Pinging
Carburettor	Carburetor	Rear suspension unit	Rear shock absorber
Catch	Latch	Rocker cover	Valve cover
Circlip	Snap ring	Selector	Shifter
Clutch drum	Clutch housing	Self-locking pliers	Vise-grips
Dip switch	Dimmer switch	Side or parking lamp	Parking or auxiliary light
Disulphide	Disulfide	Side or prop stand	Kick stand
Dynamo	DC generator	Silencer	Muffler
Earth	Ground	Spanner	Wrench
End float	End play	Split pin	Cotter pin
Engineer's blue	Machinist's dye	Stanchion	Tube
Exhaust pipe	Header	Sulphuric	Sulfuric
Fault diagnosis	Trouble shooting	Sump	Oil pan
Float chamber	Float bowl	Swinging arm	Swingarm
Footrest	Footpeg	Tab washer	Lock washer
Fuel/petrol tap	Petcock	Top box	Trunk
Gaiter	Boot	Torch	Flashlight
Gearbox	Transmission	Two/four stroke	Two/four cycle
Gearchange	Shift	Tyre	Tire
Gudgeon pin	Wrist/piston pin	Valve collar	Valve retainer
Indicator	Turn signal	Valve collets	Valve cotters
Inlet	Intake	Vice	Vise
Input shaft or mainshaft	Mainshaft	Wheel spindle	Axle
Kickstart	Kickstarter	White spirit	Stoddard solvent
Lower leg	Slider	Windscreen	Windshield
Mudguard	Fender		

Index